With the support of extensive and highly original multi-archival and multi-source research, authors of Beyond the Kremlin's Reach convincingly demonstrate that the Cold War was a phenomenon much broader and more complicated than the confrontation between the two superpowers and the two blocs that they headed. This volume is a valuable contribution to deepening our understanding of the history of the Global Cold War.

Chen Jian, Author of *Mao's China and the Cold War*

For those still clinging to an NSC 68-like view of the Cold War-era communist world as a Kremlin-led "monolith," this book usefully and vividly illuminates some of the nuances and subtleties that characterized interactions between the People's Republic of China (during and after the Mao Zedong era) and various Soviet "satellites" in East-Central Europe, even when those Warsaw Pact nations knew they had to stay, generally speaking, on the USSR's side of the Sino-Soviet split. Rather than simply parroting a script penned in Moscow, however, the authors show vividly how, in areas ranging from ideology and economic theory to agriculture, "journalism" (or at least news coverage and propaganda) to the performing arts, and more, the interactions between Beijing and Moscow's socialist allies often concealed divergent, interesting motivations and agendas on one or both sides. Using a wide array of Chinese and recently opened European communist archives, the authors contribute fresh stories and insights to our knowledge of these relationships and raise questions for further investigation.

James G. Hershberg, Professor of History and International Affairs, Elliott School of International Affairs, The George Washington University

During the Cold War, especially in the 1950s, the People's Republic of China (PRC) and the East European member-states of the Soviet-sponsored Council for Mutual Economic Cooperation had significant interactions with each other. The split that emerged between the Soviet Union and the PRC at the end of the 1950s caused major changes in the nature and extent of China's interactions with East European countries. Scholars at the time tried to keep track of the PRC's evolving relations with East European countries, but they often lacked sufficient evidence to trace precisely what was going on. Fortunately, the end of the Cold War has been a huge boon for scholarship on the topic. Archival documents that have been declassified over the past three decades have shed a great deal of light on the various interactions between China and individual East European countries throughout the Cold War. This book brings together valuable scholarship on the topic by leading experts who collectively address the important themes and questions raised by the editors.

Mark Kramer, Director of Cold War Studies, Harvard University

Pushing the boundaries of Cold War history, Beyond the Kremlin's Reach? Eastern Europe and China in the Cold War Era reveals the surprisingly great diversity of relations between the PRC and Eastern European socialist states outside of direct Soviet control during the Cold War. Bringing together seven deeply researched chapters, this remarkable volume places mutual interactions in the parallel arenas of national self-promotion, competing ideological agendas, internal political debates, and long-standing cultural biases about the other. A very important contribution to Cold War historiography!

Lorenz Lüthi, Professor of the History of International Relations, McGill University

This important collection of essays shows the complexity of interactions between China and Eastern Europe during the Cold War. Broaching political, economic, cultural, and social dimensions of the complicated relationship, the book highlights the limits of Soviet leverage over their Eastern European allies and paints a nuanced picture of the Chinese policy of "differentiation" between Moscow and Eastern Europe. An essential read for historians of Communist foreign relations.

Sergey Radchenko, Wilson E. Schmidt Distinguished Professor at the Johns Hopkins School of Advanced International Studies

Beyond the Kremlin's Reach?

This volume examines relations between the People's Republic of China (PRC) and socialist Eastern European states during the Cold War. The chapters take previous findings on government policy and China's role as a global player in the Cold War game as a starting point to locate the PRC in the socialist world and assess levels of interaction beyond diplomatic and governmental relations. By focusing on transfers and interconnections and the social dimension of governmental interactions, the primary goal of this book is to explore structures, institutions, and spaces of interaction between China and Eastern Europe and their potential autonomy from political conjunctures.

The guiding question that the edited volume raises is: To what extent did Chinese and Eastern European players, outside the range of the power centres, have room to manoeuvre beyond the agendas of the Kremlin, national governments, or party leaderships? The question of the relative autonomy becomes especially vibrant against the backdrop of the development of Sino-Soviet relations through the Cold War era, from alliance to split to reconciliation.

This book contributes to the growing scholarship on East-South and intra-bloc relations from the perspective of global and transnational history and will be of interest to researchers, students, and policy makers in the fields of History, East European and Russian studies, International Relations, and Politics.

Jan Zofka is a Research Fellow at the Leibniz-Institute for the History and Culture of Eastern Europe (GWZO), Leipzig, Germany. He specializes in the transnational history of Cold War socialist economies and is the author of the articles "Chairman Cotton: Socialist Bulgaria's cotton trade with African countries during the early Cold War (1946–70)," *Journal of Global History* (2022); "The Economy of the Sino-Soviet Alliance: Trade and transfers between Eastern Europe and China during the early Cold War" (together with Tao Chen), *Jahrbuch für Wirtschaftsgeschichte* (2022); "Technokratischer Internationalismus. Kohle-Experten der DDR der 1950er Jahre in globalgeschichtlicher Perspektive", *Geschichte und Gesellschaft* (2022); and the monograph *Postsowjetischer Separatismus: Die pro-russländischen Bewegungen im Dnjestr-Tal und auf der Krim (1989–1995)* (2015).

Péter Vámos is a Research Professor at the Institute of History of the Research Centre for the Humanities and Associate Professor of Chinese at Károli Gáspár University of the Reformed Church in Hungary, Budapest. His research focuses on the modern history and international relations of China, the relations between the Soviet bloc and China, and the history of Christianity in China. His publications include *Magyar jezsuita misszió Kínában* [Hungarian Jesuit Mission in China] (Budapest: 2003); *Kína mellettünk? Kínai külügyi iratok*

Magyarországról, 1956 [Is China with Us? Chinese Diplomatic Records on Hungary, 1956] (2008); and *Magyar–kínai kapcsolatok, 1949–1989.* [Hungarian-Chinese Relations, 1949-1989] (2020).

Sören Urbansky is a Research Fellow and the Head of the Pacific Office of the German Historical Institute Washington at UC Berkeley, USA. He is a historian of late Imperial Russian and Soviet history, interested in Russia's place in Asia, and the intersection of its history with that of race, diaspora, and borders. Sören is the author of three monographs, including *Beyond the Steppe Frontier: A History of the Sino-Russian Border* (2020) and *An den Ufern des Amur: Die vergessene Welt zwischen China und Russland* [On the River Amur: The Forgotten Land between China and Russia] (2021).

Beyond the Kremlin's Reach?
Eastern Europe and China in the Cold War Era

Edited by
Jan Zofka, Péter Vámos and Sören Urbansky

LONDON AND NEW YORK

First published 2023
by Routledge
4 Park Square, Milton Park, Abingdon, Oxon, OX14 4RN

and by Routledge
605 Third Avenue, New York, NY 10158

Routledge is an imprint of the Taylor & Francis Group, an informa business

Introduction, Chapters 1–7 © 2023 Taylor & Francis

All rights reserved. No part of this book may be reprinted or reproduced or utilised in any form or by any electronic, mechanical, or other means, now known or hereafter invented, including photocopying and recording, or in any information storage or retrieval system, without permission in writing from the publishers.

Trademark notice: Product or corporate names may be trademarks or registered trademarks, and are used only for identification and explanation without intent to infringe.

British Library Cataloguing-in-Publication Data
A catalogue record for this book is available from the British Library

ISBN13: 978-1-032-47053-5 (hbk)
ISBN13: 978-1-032-47055-9 (pbk)
ISBN13: 978-1-003-38441-0 (ebk)

DOI: 10.4324/9781003384410

Typeset in Minion Pro
by codeMantra

Publisher's Note
The publisher accepts responsibility for any inconsistencies that may have arisen during the conversion of this book from journal articles to book chapters, namely the inclusion of journal terminology.

Disclaimer
Every effort has been made to contact copyright holders for their permission to reprint material in this book. The publishers would be grateful to hear from any copyright holder who is not here acknowledged and will undertake to rectify any errors or omissions in future editions of this book.

Contents

Citation information		viii
Notes on contributors		x
Acknowledgment		xii
	Introduction: Beyond the Kremlin's reach? Eastern Europe and China in the Cold War era *Jan Zofka, Péter Vámos and Sören Urbansky*	1
1	Performing socialist Hungary in China: 'modern, Magyar, European' *József Böröcz*	7
2	Socialist exhibits and Sino-Soviet relations, 1950–60 *Austin Jersild*	25
3	Sino-Czechoslovak cooperation on agricultural cooperatives: the twinning project *Daniela Kolenovska*	40
4	Kremlinology revisited: the nuances of reporting on China in the Eastern bloc press *Sören Urbansky and Max Trecker*	56
5	China as a role model? The 'Economic Leap' campaign in Bulgaria (1958–1960) *Jan Zofka*	73
6	Promoting the 'China Way' of communism in Poland and beyond during the Sino-Soviet Split: the case of Kazimierz Mijal *Margaret K. Gnoinska*	90
7	A Hungarian model for China? Sino-Hungarian relations in the era of economic reforms, 1979–89 *Péter Vámos*	107
	Index	125

Citation Information

The chapters in this book were originally published in the journal *Cold War History*, volume 18, issue 3 (2018). When citing this material, please use the original page numbering for each article, as follows:

Introduction
Beyond the Kremlin's reach? Eastern Europe and China in the Cold War era
Jan Zofka, Péter Vámos and Sören Urbansky
Cold War History, volume 18, issue 3 (2018) pp. 251–256

Chapter 1
Performing socialist Hungary in China: 'modern, Magyar, European'
József Böröcz
Cold War History, volume 18, issue 3 (2018) pp. 257–274

Chapter 2
Socialist exhibits and Sino-Soviet relations, 1950–60
Austin Jersild
Cold War History, volume 18, issue 3 (2018) pp. 275–289

Chapter 3
Sino-Czechoslovak cooperation on agricultural cooperatives: the twinning project
Daniela Kolenovska
Cold War History, volume 18, issue 3 (2018) pp. 291–306

Chapter 4
Kremlinology revisited: the nuances of reporting on China in the Eastern bloc press
Sören Urbansky and Max Trecker
Cold War History, volume 18, issue 3 (2018) pp. 307–324

Chapter 5
China as a role model? The 'Economic Leap' campaign in Bulgaria (1958–1960)
Jan Zofka
Cold War History, volume 18, issue 3 (2018) pp. 325–342

CITATION INFORMATION

Chapter 6
Promoting the 'China Way' of communism in Poland and beyond during the Sino-Soviet Split: the case of Kazimierz Mijal
Margaret K. Gnoinska
Cold War History, volume 18, issue 3 (2018) pp. 343–359

Chapter 7
A Hungarian model for China? Sino-Hungarian relations in the era of economic reforms, 1979–89
Péter Vámos
Cold War History, volume 18, issue 3 (2018) pp. 361–378

For any permission-related enquiries please visit:
http://www.tandfonline.com/page/help/permissions

Notes on Contributors

József Böröcz is a Professor of Sociology at Rutgers, The State University of New Jersey, USA. He is the author *The European Union and Global Social Change: A Critical Geopolitical-Economic Analysis* (2009) and *Hasított fa: A világrendszer-elmélettől a globális struktúraváltásokig* (2017). His current interests include narrative and visual sociologies of historical experiences; politics and performing arts; knowledge and otherness; large-scale (indeed global) transformations; and intersections of political economy, geopolitics, coloniality, ethics, aesthetics, and power.

Margaret K. Gnoinska is an Associate Professor of History at Troy University, USA. She is a Fulbright Scholar and Boren NSEP Fellow. Her research focuses on the effects of the Sino-Soviet split on the relations between Eastern Europe and East Asia during the Cold War and international peacekeeping on the Korean Peninsula and in Indochina.

Austin Jersild is a Professor of History at Old Dominion University, Norfolk, USA, and the Chair of the Department of History. He is the author of *Orientalism and Empire: North Caucasus Mountain Peoples and the Georgian Frontier, 1845-1917* (2002) and *The Sino-Soviet Alliance: An International History* (2014). In 2016, he was a Research Fellow at the Berlin Center for Cold War Studies.

Daniela Kolenovská is an Assistant Professor of Contemporary Russian History at Charles University, Prague, Czech Republic. Her areas of specialization are the history of Russian historiography and the Soviet (Russian) history with special regard to its influence on the Czechoslovak (Czech) foreign policy during the Cold War.

Max Trecker studied history and economics at LMU Munich and CEU Budapest. His dissertation deals with the coordination of East-South economic relations in the Council for Mutual Economic Assistance (CMEA). He is a Postdoctoral Researcher at the Institute for Contemporary History Munich-Berlin and pursues a research project on the privatization of the East German economy after reunification.

Sören Urbansky is a Research Fellow and the Head of the Pacific Office of the German Historical Institute Washington at UC Berkeley, USA. He is a historian of late Imperial Russian and Soviet history, interested in Russia's place in Asia, and the intersection of its history with that of race, diaspora, and borders. Sören is the author of three monographs, including *Beyond the Steppe Frontier: A History of the Sino-Russian Border* (2020) and *An den Ufern des Amur: Die vergessene Welt zwischen China und Russland* [On the River Amur: The Forgotten Land between China and Russia] (2021).

NOTES ON CONTRIBUTORS

Péter Vámos is a Research Professor at the Institute of History of the Research Centre for the Humanities and an Associate Professor of Chinese at Károli Gáspár University of the Reformed Church in Hungary, Budapest. His research focuses on the modern history and international relations of China, the relations between the Soviet bloc and China, and the history of Christianity in China. His publications include *Magyar jezsuita misszió Kínában* [Hungarian Jesuit Mission in China] (Budapest: 2003); *Kína mellettünk? Kínai külügyi iratok Magyarországról, 1956* [Is China with us? Chinese diplomatic records on Hungary, 1956] (2008); and *Magyar–kínai kapcsolatok, 1949–1989.* [Hungarian-Chinese Relations, 1949-1989] (2020).

Jan Zofka is a Research Fellow at the Leibniz-Institute for the History and Culture of Eastern Europe (GWZO), Leipzig, Germany. He specializes in the transnational history of Cold War socialist economies and is the author of the articles "Chairman Cotton: Socialist Bulgaria's cotton trade with African countries during the early Cold War (1946–70)," *Journal of Global History* (2022); "The Economy of the Sino-Soviet Alliance: Trade and transfers between Eastern Europe and China during the early Cold War" (together with Tao Chen), *Jahrbuch für Wirtschaftsgeschichte* (2022); "Technokratischer Internationalismus. Kohle-Experten der DDR der 1950er Jahre in globalgeschichtlicher Perspektive," *Geschichte und Gesellschaft* (2021); and the monograph *Postsowjetischer Separatismus: Die pro-russländischen Bewegungen im Dnjestr-Tal und auf der Krim (1989–1995)* (2015).

Acknowledgment

This volume is based on a special issue in *Cold War History* and a workshop at the Leibniz Institute for the History and Culture of Eastern Europe (GWZO) in 2015 – many people and organizations have helped us make it happen. We are grateful to Stefan Troebst, who organized the workshop with us and was the main driver behind initiating a China-related project at the GWZO. We thank all the participants at the workshop who gave comments and discussed our papers with us, not least the commentators Jordan Baev, Dennis Deletant, Beáta Hock, and Uwe Müller. Among these workshop participants, we especially thank our Chinese colleagues who accepted to come the long way to participate: the keynote speaker Shen Zhihua, Yu Weimin, Li Rui, Wu Wei, Gao Xiaochuan, Tai Yuri, Kong Fanjun, Liu Yong, Xiang Zuotao, and Ge Jun. For contributing to the organization and funding of the workshop, we have to thank the institutions behind: the GWZO and its Working Group Transnational Contemporary History of East Central Europe; the Institute of History, Research Centre for the Humanities at the Hungarian Academy of Sciences; the Graduate School for East and Southeast European Studies at the Ludwig Maximilian University of Munich; and the Centre for Cold War International History Studies at East China Normal University in Shanghai. We are very grateful to the German Association for East European Studies (DGO), the German Federal Ministry of Education and Research (BMBF), and the Konfuzius-Institut Leipzig for additional funding. We owe gratitude to the managing editor of *Cold War History*, Lindsay Aqui, for tireless efforts in editing the special issue.

Beyond the Kremlin's reach? Eastern Europe and China in the Cold War era

Jan Zofka, Péter Vámos and Sören Urbansky

ABSTRACT

This special issue examines relations between the People's Republic of China and socialist Eastern European states during the Cold War. By focusing on transfers and interconnections, and on the social dimension of governmental interactions, our main goal is to explore structures, institutions and spaces of interaction between China and Eastern Europe and their potential autonomy from political conjunctures. The guiding question we raise is: To what degree did Chinese and Eastern European players beyond the centres of power have room to manoeuvre outside the agendas of the Kremlin, national governments or party leadership?

This special issue examines relations between the People's Republic of China (PRC) and socialist Eastern European states during the Cold War. On the one hand, it might seem obvious to look at these ties and draw comparisons between socialist states of the era; on the other hand, there are heavy asymmetries between the small Eastern European Soviet bloc states and the most highly populated state in the world. Due to its sheer size and geostrategic location, the PRC played an important role in the Cold War. As Liu Xiaoyuan describes it, 'China was a calculative third force that kept changing partners in pursuance of its own agenda.'[1] In addition to Communist ideology, a 'Central Kingdom mentality' also drove PRC foreign policy. Achievement of 'modernity' (with the final aim of achieving communism) and restoration of centrality have been goals of primary importance for China's political elites throughout the past century. One of the variables in China's debate and split with the Soviet Union was its endeavour to reassert centrality in a geopolitical sense. In the summer of 1949, Mao Zedong announced that China would 'lean to one side': the side of socialism. Mao and his fellow leaders hoped that, after a century of imperialist humiliation, their country could regain its former greatness and a place at the heart of international affairs with the help of Soviet military and economic support. By the mid-1950s, however, the Beijing leadership made it increasingly clear that China was unwilling to be the subordinate member

---

[1] Liu Xiaoyuan's review of Yafeng Xia, 'The Study of Cold War International History in China: A Review of the Last Twenty Years,' *Journal of Cold War Studies* 10.1 (Winter 2008): 81–115.

of an alliance led by the USSR. At first, China's pursuit of an independent position on the world stage manifested itself in ideological debates, but by the mid-1960s became an open power struggle. The nature, methods and outcome of Sino-Soviet debates were determined by the fact that China was not willing to accept the status of a younger brother. As Mao's aim was to become the leading theoretician of the international communist movement, the PRC targeted not only East Asia, where China had occupied a central role until the 19th century, but also the socialist world in general with the Soviet Union at its helm. For China, assuming the leading role in the socialist camp entailed winning over the European socialist countries, and achieving modernity meant adopting all developments in science and technology, and the economic management system of these allegedly progressive nations.

Socialist Eastern Europe, for its part, had been part of the Soviet sphere of influence, and as such cut off from the mainstream developments of Western Europe. Soviet dominance in the political, economic, and cultural life of Eastern European socialist countries, between 1949–1989, meant that the particular political and economic interests of the 'satellites' had to be reconciled with the national interests of the Soviet Union. As a consequence, the socio-economic development of the Eastern European socialist countries was to a large extent determined by the generally accepted hierarchy – with the Soviet Union as the power centre. The Eastern European countries imported Soviet-style institutions and both formal and informal mechanisms of Soviet control existed throughout the whole period of the Cold War.

Due to this general picture of Soviet predominance, historians of post-war Eastern Europe have often considered the Soviet bloc countries' entanglements with other world regions as marginal.

However, after the collapse of the Soviet system, and with the opening of area studies to global, transnational and transregional history, there has been a clear tendency in the study of intra-bloc relations to consider the Eastern European states not only as satellites in Moscow's orbit, but also as entities with their own priorities and ambitions. In line with this shift, the guiding questions we raise in this special issue are as follows: to what extent did Chinese and Eastern European players beyond the centres of power have room to manoeuvre outside the agendas of the Kremlin, national governments and party leadership? In other words, to what degree could local political leaders act to represent national interests rather than merely executing Soviet policy, and what domestic and international factors defined where the limits of political foreign relations lay? To what extent did interactions between China and Eastern Europe – from the transfer of economic knowledge and models (Zofka, Vámos), pro-Chinese inner-party factions and their policing by national Party leadership (Gnoinska), the preservation of face-to-face-relationships, such as a friendship cooperative (Kolenovská), and the coining of images of the other and oneself through cultural programmes, trade fairs and in the press (Böröcz, Jersild, Urbansky/Trecker) – happen 'beyond the Kremlin's reach?' The question of the relative autonomy of these political players becomes especially vibrant against the backdrop of the development of Sino–Soviet relations from alliance to split to reconciliation through the Cold War era.

The articles in this special issue take previous findings on government policy and China's role as a global player in the Cold War game as a starting point to locate the PRC in the socialist world and assess levels of interaction beyond diplomatic and governmental relations. By focusing on transfers and interconnections, and on the social dimension of governmental interactions, our main goal is to explore structures, institutions and spaces of interaction between China and Eastern Europe and their potential autonomy from political conjunctures. This special issue is based on the contributions to a conference held in Leipzig in July 2015, which was organised through the cooperative efforts of the Centre for the History and Culture of East Central Europe (GWZO) Leipzig, the Research Centre for Humanities of the Hungarian Academy of Sciences and the Graduate School for East and Southeast European Studies at Ludwig Maximilian University Munich and the University of Regensburg.[2]

Eastern Europe in itself played a secondary role in Chinese foreign policy. The importance of the Eastern European region stems from the fact that it became part of the Soviet-dominated socialist world after 1948–49. In other words, Chinese foreign policy considered relations with individual states and with the whole region as a derivative of Sino-Soviet relations. Beijing's policies towards Eastern Europe can be understood only within this context. Nevertheless, as a result of their special relationship with the Soviet Union, China followed a differentiating and differentiated policy towards those countries. States closely cooperating with the USSR were not considered as fully independent by China, therefore Sino-Soviet debates had a direct effect on them as well. Starting in the 1960s, but especially in the 1970s and 1980s, China used those countries as a means to exert pressure on the Soviet Union, whom Beijing viewed as the most important national security threat. Moreover, both Beijing and Moscow used Eastern European satellites as intermediaries between the PRC and the USSR, and, as Vámos demonstrates, Beijing's interest in the Eastern European experiences of economic reform served China's need to affirm its socialist identity and legitimise the Party's new policies. Thus, we argue that small Eastern European states *did* matter to China's relations with the socialist camp.

The aim and the questions behind this special issue are part of a broader debate about a socialist world beyond the Soviet bloc and about relations between the socialist camp and the global south. In this debate, contributions to general global economic developments by the socialist camp as well as the creation of specific socialist forms of transnational political and economic interdependence based on peaceful coexistence, cooperation and solidarity are discussed as 'socialist globalisation'. The recently reawakened research field on East–South relations examines these entanglements from a new angle, going beyond the traditional assumption of bipolarity of Cold War studies.[3] Studies in this field put superpower omnipotence into doubt and explore the room to manoeuvre by players on the ground vis-à-vis Moscow or national party leadership and governments. Accordingly, these studies emphasise heavily Third World agency in these relations and interactions.

In Cold War studies China is often interpreted either as a great power in the US–USSR–PRC geopolitical triangle, or as the leader of the Third World, rather than as part of the

---

[2]The conference was made possible due to the generous support of the German Federal Ministry of Education and Research, the German Association for East European Studies (DGO), and the Centre for Cold War International History Studies at East China Normal University Shanghai.

[3]David C. Engerman, 'The Second World's Third World,' *Kritika: Explorations in Russian and Eurasian History* 12, no. 1 (2011): 183–211; Oscar Sanchez-Sibony, *Red Globalisation. The Political Economy of the Soviet Cold War from Stalin to Khrushchev* (New York: Cambridge University Press, 2014).

socialist world – the angle from which this issue approaches China's relations with Eastern Europe.[4] It is not an easy task to categorise China in an East–South scheme, because of China's peculiar status between the Second and Third Worlds. China proclaimed itself to be part of the Third World (albeit as leader, with a special Third World definition): its economy in large parts was still based on agriculture and in the past it had been subjected to imperial policies of great powers. On the other hand, China was part of the socialist camp, it had an observer status in the Council for Mutual Economic Assistance (COMECON) until 1961, and in general was considered a state far too powerful to belong to the Third World. We argue that, regardless of whether China should be classified as a developed or developing country at this point in time, the PRC must be part of the debate about socialist globalisation. The industrialisation drive of the 1950s substantially supported by the Soviet Union and other COMECON states served as the basis for China's later rise – and it still shapes Chinese economic geography and thus the world as we know it today.

With the benefit of global and transnational historical perspectives, not only are East–South relations interpreted anew, but so also are East–East relations. Interest in 'socialist internationalism' within the socialist camp has grown significantly in recent years.[5] Instead of COMECON being perceived merely as a hollow hull, these studies highlight the systems of economic interaction and scientific-technical cooperation which caused people, ideas, technological knowledge and blueprints for machines and industrial facilities to cross borders. During the honeymoon period of COMECON, the PRC was part of these networks, signed treaties for scientific and technological cooperation with all Eastern European socialist states, and in this framework exchanged students, trainees, blueprints for technologies, and received engineers for politico-technical advisory bodies. The Soviet Union and its satellites greatly supported the industrialisation process. Industrial cooperation was important not only for China, but also for the Soviet bloc countries, which tried to use international trade with China as a basis for an export restructuring to develop complex industrial facilities. Even for the Soviet Union, the PRC became the most important trading partner and retained this position throughout the 1950s, as is pointed out in Zofka's contribution to this special issue. Very few studies focus on this aspect of Chinese participation and integration in the transnational web of the socialist camp. Among the exceptions are Shen Zhihua who has traced the presence of Soviet experts in the PRC, and Austin Jersild, who in his book on the

---

[4]On the strategic triangle see: Lowell Dittmer, *Sino-Soviet Normalisation and its International Implications, 1945–1990* (Seattle & London: University of Washington Press, 1992); Robert S. Ross, ed., *China, the United States, and the Soviet Union: Tripolarity and Policy Making in the Cold War* (Armonk: M. E. Sharpe, 1993); Michael M. Scheng, *Battling Western Imperialism: Mao, Stalin, and the United States* (Princeton: Princeton University, 1997). On China's relations with the Third World see: Chen Jian, 'Bridging Revolution and Decolonization: The "Bandung Discourse" in China's Early Cold War Experience', *Chinese Historical Review* 15, no. 2 (Fall 2008): 207–41; Jeremy Friedman, *Shadow Cold War: The Sino-Soviet Competition for the Third World* (Chapel Hill: The University of North Carolina Press, 2015); Lorenz M. Lüthi, 'The Sino-Soviet Split and its Consequences', in *The Routledge Handbook of the Cold War*, eds. Artemy M. Kalinovsky and Craig Daigle (London and New York: Routledge, 2014), 74–88; Chen Jian: 'China's Changing Policies Toward the Third World and the End of the Global Cold War', in *The End of the Cold War and the Third World*, eds. Artemy M. Kalinovsky and Sergey Radchenko (London and New York: Routledge, 2015), 101–21.

[5]Patryk Babiracki and Austin Jersild, eds., *Socialist Internationalism in the Cold War: Exploring the Second World* (London: Palgrave Macmillan, 2016); Rachel Applebaum, 'The Friendship Project: Socialist Internationalism in the Soviet Union and Czechoslovakia in the 1950s and 1960s', *Slavic Review* 74, no. 3 (2015): 484–507; Patryk Babiracki and Kenyon Zimmer, eds., *Cold War Crossings: International Travel and Exchange across the Soviet Bloc, 1940s–1960s* (College Station, TX: Texas A&M University Press, 2014); Michael David-Fox, 'The Implications of Transnationalism', *Kritika: Explorations in Russian and Eurasian History* 12, no. 4 (2011): 885–904; Anne E. Gorsuch and Diane P. Koenker, eds., *The Socialist Sixties. Crossing Borders in the Second World*, Bloomington: Indiana University Press, 2013; Austin Jersild, 'The Soviet State as Imperial Scavenger: "Catch Up and Surpass" in the Transnational Socialist Bloc, 1950–1960', *The American Historical Review* 116, no. 1 (2011): 109–34.

Sino-Soviet alliance describes postcolonial attitudes of Soviet leaders and reservations of technical experts as the cultural basis of the split, in contrast to earlier studies where these events were seen as a mere leadership quarrel.[6]

Building on these debates and perspectives, this special issue examines entanglements, connections and interactions in the socialist camp by focusing on the contributions of players on the ground outside of main leadership circles and official diplomatic relations. Undoubtedly, we recognise the immense significance of hierarchies, government decisions, and the influence that Moscow had on the actions, decisions and rationales of these players. Nonetheless, we identify them as protagonists with their own rationales, decisions and – even if to a limited extent – autonomous action. This approach also reflects a recent shift towards using hitherto neglected document repositories in researching postwar Chinese history.[7]

Some of the contributions focus on cultural representations of China in Eastern Europe (and vice versa) and discuss what part these images played in the Sino-Soviet split. József Böröcz follows the Performing Arts Ensemble of the Hungarian People's Army on a tour in the fateful year of 1956. Böröcz demonstrates clearly how the programme of the Ensemble's performances took on a national character, and how it played on the 'imagined, highly valued, deep cultural tie between the Chinese and Hungarian societies and cultures' and 'skipped' the Soviet Union that lies between, both geographically and in geopolitical terms. The determination of these protagonists, acting inside various hierarchical systems, is an astonishing example of the room to manoeuvre of individuals within these countries. 'High culture' and socialist attitudes towards it are also the crucial keyword in Austin Jersild's contribution on socialist trade fairs as a site of negotiation for power relations between the USSR and the PRC. With the Soviets looking west and failing to understand the need to revise their image of China as a disciple to be lectured, Jersild discovers the cultural fundament of the Sino-Soviet split. Sören Urbansky and Max Trecker study how the deterioration of reciprocal relations is mirrored in the main party newspapers of East Germany, Hungary and Poland and how the portrayal of China differed, at times significantly, in Moscow, Budapest, East Berlin and Warsaw. Their findings suggest that the uncertainty of future relations between China and the Soviet Union, combined with disagreements between Moscow and its satellites from 1956 onwards, forced leaderships in Eastern Europe to adapt to the new circumstances, while at the same time offering leeway for their own political agendas.

Other contributors study the nature and implications of transfers of ideas and knowledge between the PRC and Eastern European states, and the impact these exchanges had on the countries themselves. Péter Vámos examines the exchange of knowledge during the rapprochement in the 1980s in the context of reform policies in Eastern Europe and in China. The much more powerful Chinese state's economic planning bureaucracy was interested to 'learn' methods of reforming a centralised state economy from Hungarian

---

[6]Shen Zhihua, *Sulian zhuanjia zai Zhongguo (1948–1960) [Soviet Experts in China (1948–1960)]* (Beijing: Zhongguo guoji chubanshe, 2003); Austin Jersild, *The Sino-Soviet Alliance: An International History* (Chapel Hill: University of North Carolina Press, 2014). See also: Deborah Kaple, 'Agents of Change. Soviet Advisers and High Stalinist Management in China, 1949–1960,' *Journal of Cold War Studies* 18, no. 1 (Winter 2016): 5–30; William C. Kirby, 'China's Internationalisation in the Early People's Republic: Dreams of a Socialist World Economy,' *The China Quarterly* 188 (2006): 870–90; Baichun Zhang, Jiuchun Zhang & Fang Yao, 'Technology Transfer from the Soviet Union to the People's Republic of China 1949–1966,' *Comparative Technology Transfer and Society* 4, no. 2 (August 2006): 105–71.

[7]See, for example, the contributions in *China from Without: Doing PRC History in Foreign Archives,* eds. Arunabh Ghosh and Sören Urbansky, a special issue of *The PRC History Review* 2, no. 3 (June 2017).

economists, whom they considered to be more experienced in this area. Jan Zofka's contribution looks at a transfer in the other direction. The Bulgarian leadership in the late 1950s was highly fascinated by the Chinese Great Leap Forward campaign and proclaimed their own campaign for speeding up plan fulfilment, sending delegations to China to study the mobilisation of unpaid labour for big dam constructions and the structure of people's communes. Rather than being a geopolitical step of confrontation or bargaining with Moscow, Zofka interprets the interest in regulation methods and agricultural techniques as being enabled by the transnational web of the socialist world with repercussions on the daily life of Bulgarian villagers. These repercussions also are at the centre of Daniela Kolenovska's study on the 'friendship' between a Czechoslovak agricultural cooperative and its Chinese counterpart. Kolenovska shows how contacts during the 1950s influenced relations during the last decade of the Cold War and beyond. Margaret Gnoinska brings into focus the Polish intra-party opposition against Władysław Gomułka, which culminated in the forced resettlement to Albania of Kazimierz Mijal, the face of the 'pro-Chinese' Communist Party of Poland, and places it in the context of Mao's differentiation policy and the Sino-Soviet split. The cracks in the monolithic nature of the Soviet bloc become clearly visible through a closer examination of the lives and careers of individuals like Mijal, whose activities went beyond the control of the Kremlin.

Leaving the image of a Moscow-controlled monolith behind, the room to manoeuvre for players in socialist states beyond the centres of power has to be measured anew. This special issue aims to contribute to this task by providing new insights into the rationales behind foreign and economic policy behaviour of both China and Eastern Europe. From the PRC's perspective, the study of the experience of former European socialist countries is of vital importance even today. The lessons that the Chinese Communist Party (CCP) has learned from the collapse of Soviet bloc party-states contributed significantly to its survival as the reigning party. After the collapse of communist ruling parties in the Soviet Union and Eastern Europe, the CCP undertook systematic assessments of the causes of their failure to avoid a similar fate. The CCP not only reacted to the events in the USSR and Eastern European party-states, but it was also proactive in instituting reforms within itself and within China to strengthen the party's ruling capacity and remain in power as a one-party state. This, in turn, seems to have allowed the PRC to create a favourable international environment where Beijing is in the position to shape the rules. From the European perspective, the study of the history of relations with the PRC can also provide useful lessons for conducting relations with the China of today and tomorrow. With China now a global power that articulates its ambitions much more explicitly than in the Cold War era, the importance of maintaining relations with China is not be underestimated for the countries of Europe. After all, it was not until the 1995–2005 period that the EU and China really began to fashion their own relationship, free of the shadows of Cold War dynamics. Therefore it is in the greatest interests of the new EU member states from Eastern Europe to maintain 'correct handling' of their relations with China, if they are to build and maintain a place of influence on the global political stage.

Disclosure statement

No potential conflict of interest was reported by the authors.

Performing socialist Hungary in China: 'modern, Magyar, European'

József Böröcz

ABSTRACT

This paper reconstructs the ways in which the Hungarian People's Army Performing Arts Ensemble arranged its repertoire to perform socialist Hungary in the autumn of 1956, during the Ensemble's tour in the People's Republic of China. The paper performs a close reading of a single archival document, the program of the Ensemble's début performance before non-European socialist audiences that took place in Shenyang on September 21, 1956. The repertoire featured a simple chronological, quasi-historical overview of musical and dance traditions from Hungary. It offered a vague, highly stylized set of references to Hungary's military traditions. It attempted to realize the triple formula of a new, 'modern, Magyar, European,' art form, and foregrounded a plebian ('peasant-') progressive-patriotic theme with hints of ethnic nationalism. The program provided the absolute minimum of the standard Stalinist fare, resolutely avoided any reference to the USSR or Russia, and, most fascinating, closed with a self-ironical dance piece featuring a powerful allegorical story of socialism with a 'Hungarian face,' something that represented a resolute break with the Stalinist aesthetic canon and reinforced the group's political commitment to a socialism that is 'modern, Magyar and European.'

Introduction

On 7 September 1956, the Performing Arts Ensemble of the Hungarian People's Army left Budapest for a tour of the People's Republic of China. The tour involved 217 people, on a two-week journey through the Soviet Union. They travelled in a chartered train, tracing the route of the Trans-Siberia Railway. Once in China, they gave 104 performances in two and a half months and, then, took a two-week return trip to Hungary via the USSR, arriving in Budapest on Christmas Day 1956.

The Ensemble consisted of three groups, each with its soloists: a dance troupe of 40 performers with its own band; a 72-member men's choir along with a small group of opera singers; and a symphony orchestra. Accompanying the group were a number of political officers and a handful of Sinology students from Hungary serving as interpreters, along with stage hands, two journalists, a laryngologist, a Swiss-born ballet master (co-founder of, and widely admired professor at, the Budapest Ballet Institute), a graphic artist, a stage actor, and a two-member film crew, joined by local helpers and handlers organised by the PRC's Ministry of Defence, the People's Liberation Army – the official host of the tour – and the Central Song and Dance Company of the People's Liberation Army.

This paper reconstructs the aesthetic, social-historical, and political meanings and references embedded in the Ensemble's repertoire as it was assembled by its leading artists for the tour in China – a tour that began a mere six weeks before, and ended less than two months after, the suppression of the revolution of 23 October–4 November 1956, a truly consequential political event in Hungary's political history. That task requires, first, a brief look at the Ensemble's original charge as it was imagined eight years earlier.

The concept paper that justified the Ensemble's creation in 1948, entitled 'The question of the central Performing Arts Ensemble/choir, dance and music ensemble/ of the Army' blended two conventional, relatively low-ambition, 'adult education' aims – assistance in public education efforts within the Army and 'educative entertainment' of the members of the armed forces – with two considerably more ambitious goals.[1] The first of these goals was aesthetic – the 'creation of the [sic] new, progressive vocal, dance and music art style' – the other was political – suffusing all that activity with the increasing influence of the Communist Party.[2] The framers argued in favour of the establishment of the Ensemble by appealing to the revolutionary task of the newly emerging socialist state: transformation of society's consciousness through education and the arts. The framers of the Ensemble took a strong political stance in three interlinked ways:

(1) First, within the Party's own political universe, they worked to broaden the official view of the revolutionary transformation to include at least some segments, if not the entirety, of the peasantry under the concept of the 'working class' that could, in turn, be regarded as a class endowed with the historical agency to carry forward the task of transforming Hungarian society in a socialist direction;

(2) Second, they placed a clearly radical-left claim on the 'népi' ('populist') tradition in Hungarian intellectual life, rejecting '(petty) bourgeois' values and traditions.

(3) Third, they foregrounded the cultural sphere, and specifically the performing arts, as a set of tools effective in the social uplift of the peasantry and an important avenue for the socialist transformation overall.[3]

In sum, the framers invented the Ensemble as a creative centre that would produce a new, socialist *Gesamtkunstwerk* in the performing arts. In doing so, they linked a populist-plebeian-socialist reinvention of folk culture as a key component of cultural creativity, 'the peasant' as one – and the most powerful – among the (potentially) progressive working-class locations, and the idea of a plebian-'peasant' take on socialist realism as a form of revolutionary consciousness.

---

[1]'A honvédség központi müvészegyüttesének /ének-,tánc-és zeneegyüttes:/ kérdése,' N.d. Military History Institute, Military History Archive, Budapest, 272–7.

[2]Emphasis added.

[3]The 'népi-urbánus' opposition is arguably the most consequential political, social-historical, and aesthetic divide splitting Hungarian cultural and intellectual life at least since the interwar years. See, for example, Mihály Szegedy-Maszák, 'Szellemi élet. A polgári társadalom korának művelődése II. (1920–1948),' chapter 9 (428–59) in László Kósa, *Magyar művelődéstörténet* (Budapest: Osiris, 1998), especially 439–41. On its contemporary reverberations, see Éva Kovács, 'A nemzet einstandolása? Töprengések egy történészvita közben,' *CAFÉ BÁBEL* 20 (2013): 35–44.

Programming for China

The Ensemble's invitation to China came on the occasion of Chinese Defence Minister Zhu De's official state visit to Hungary in January 1956. The tour was a major departure from the past in its sheer magnitude. Cultural flows between the two countries had been marked by sporadic visits by small numbers of individual writers, visual artists or performers, sports teams, and a modest programme of student and academic exchanges.

Programming for the tour involved a set of unique challenges for the Ensemble. To start with, the programme had to be viable in terms of costumes and props, and sustainable in terms of human resources (so that it would not exhaust the Ensemble's members beyond reasonable limits).[4] This was an unprecedented, and monumental, task, to which should be added the issue of health concerns, the unpredictable effects of long confinement in railroad cars – after all, the trip through the USSR alone would take between 12 and 14 days – and the all-important task of maintaining the Ensemble's spirit through the long and exhausting trip.[5]

The prospect of the tour in China also produced some concerns about artistic quality, within the Ensemble as well as outside. Highly unusual in 'show business' – where rule number one is never to admit to problems, insufficiencies, difficulties, or mistakes – the same interview about the preparation of the dance group opens with an exchange in a rather (self-)critical tone:

> Th[e] question [of preparation] is all the more exciting since professional circles regarded with some trepidation the dance group's, by now, several years of uneven development, [concerns that] can be summed up [in stating] that artistic talent and stage execution may not have always been in complete sync.

> ... Let's start with the question of how the dance group prepared for the tour.

> Immediately upon return from [our tour in] Bulgaria, we began developing the final [shape of] our repertoire. We faced a double task: On the one hand, we polished up our best existing pieces, and we learnt the more important works in multiple casts. On the other, we have created three new compositions.

> We gave special priority to ballet training in our preparations. As a departure from the some-what liberal, and easygoing practices of the preceding few years, we set aside an hour and a half daily for [Ballet] Mistress [Marcella] Nádasi's ballet training [sessions]. All members of our dance troupe put in hard work, and that will no doubt benefit our work later.[6]

So, both journalist and interviewee hastened to acknowledge anxieties about both the scale of the tour and the quality of the productions. As part of the way to manage those apprehensions, the dance group's technical training – which was already widely considered superior to all other professional-stage folk ensembles in Hungary – was further enhanced for the Chinese tour.

A central concern was of course that the programme had to be comprehensible for Chinese audiences, not only in terms of communicating without a *lingua franca* between performers and audiences, but also, much more challenging, in terms of making sure that

---

[4] E.g. the dance troupe had to drop a very ambitious piece, developed specifically for this tour, from its repertoire simply because it would have produced too much of a logistical burden due to its costume design. See Cs. Gy [Csizmadia, György], 'A kínai út előtt. Beszélgetés Böröcz Józseffel,' *Táncművészet* VI, no. 9 (September 1956): 390–1 (390).

[5] Ibid., 390.

[6] Ibid., 390.

the programme offered something accessible to the Chinese audiences in spite of the vast, literally continent-scale, physical, cultural, and social-historical distance between the two countries.

It is an indication that the leadership anticipated this problem that the Ensemble had produced and shipped with it, along with the rest of the Ensemble's cargo, no fewer than 'twenty-five thousand copies of a leaflet printed in Russian, to which an appendix, in Mandarin, would be added in China'.[7] It seems that the Ensemble's leaders instrumentalised the hegemony of the USSR and the role of the Russian language as a *lingua franca* both inside the USSR and in official communication among the socialist-bloc states in making a gesture toward an intra-socialist 'people's diplomacy.'

A review of one of the Ensemble's last pre-tour performances, published in the Budapest paper *Magyar Nemzet*, captures the problem even in its title:

Chinese Eyes and Ears

— that is what the critic would have to have in order to be able to foretell what the Chinese audiences would like most about the People's Army's excellent Performing Arts Ensemble's program in the People's Republic of China. And that is almost impossible.[8]

The reviewer finds the Ensemble's China programme 'rich' and 'colourful,' he lists some of the biggest names among the composers and choreographers, and files a polite complaint about the absence of Franz Liszt from among them. He even volunteers suggestions as to which of Liszt's works he thinks would be appropriate for inclusion in the programme. The review repeats the mildly Orientalist thought that 'it is impossible to guess' what the Chinese audiences will like – and then proceeds to do just that, by criticising the programme, especially the second half, for reflecting too much 'music history' and 'music philology.' Finally, the critic also concedes the artistic material the Ensemble is bringing to China 'belongs in the best of our culture,' – i.e. he reverts, in the end, to an inside-Hungarian conversation.

The Ensemble gave a couple of dress rehearsals, followed by several gala performances, a few days before departure. Perhaps the most exulted of those was the men's choir's concert on the steps of the National Museum.[9] The location was chosen as a historical reference to the location where, according to apocryphal tradition, Sándor Petőfi, Hungary's leading romantic-nationalist poet, read his incendiary poem, 'National Song' on the day of the outbreak of the national uprising of 1848.[10]

Gyula Ortutay, a professor of ethnography, slated to become President of the Patriotic People's Front in the autumn of 1956, was the featured speaker of the concert on the steps

---

[7]György Csizmadia, 'ÚTRA KÉSZEN ...,' *Szabad Nép*, 31 August 1956: 4.

[8]Sándor Asztalos, 'A kínaiak szemével és fülével,' *Magyar Nemzet*, 24 August 1956.

[9]http://honismeret.hu/?modul=oldal&tartalom=1220168 (accessed 9 June 2015). To understand the symbolic power of the museum steps and the poem, it is important to remember that the 'National Song' is a standard, required part of elementary school curricula in Hungary, memorised by all students in their pre-teens. The opening line of the poem's refrain – 'On your feet now, Hungary calls you!' – is widely paraphrased in everyday speech. Arguably, 'National Song' is the single most widely known poem in Magyar. See also Lajos Rácz, 'Adalékok a magyar-kínai katinadiplomáciai kapcsolatok történetéhez,' *Hadtudomány* (2010): 1–21.

[10]The other venue was Károlyi Kert, a public park in downtown Budapest, a historically less symbolic, but no less central, outdoor location. The two performances attracted at least 15,000 spectators. See, e.g. Éva Bieliczkyné Buzás, *Nemzeti dal – bemutató*. http://fonix-sarok.hu/nemzeti-dal-bemutato/ (accessed 28 November 2017).

of the National Museum.[11] He went so far as to suggest that the entire 'motherland, the whole people was saying goodbye to its sons' [sic].[12] Imre Nagy – who was to become prime minister, an iconic hero, and one of the martyrs of the uprising of October 1956 – was in the audience, as was the old Kodály, along with a veritable who's who of the Budapest cultural elite.

The men's choir's concert on the museum steps featured, along with a number of other standards, a new piece by Kodály, dedicated to the very People's Army Men's Choir that gave its premiere. Kodály's work set to music none other than Petőfi's iconic poem, 'National Song.'[13] Major newspapers, the national radio, and the newsreel film service all covered the event.

The deluge of coverage of the Ensemble's last days before departure included a review in *Szabad Nép*, the central newspaper of the Communist Party at the time.[14] The reviewer, István Péterfi, was elated. He contended that Kodály's music was congenial with the poem: 'Kodály's music provides the "National Song" a place in musical history that matches its historical and literary significance.'[15] The article is filled with references to fire, light, flame, spark, and so on – metaphors that have been central to the rhetorical repertoire of left-revolutionary writing for centuries. The review takes care to point out that the enthusiastic crowd demanded an encore of the 'National Song' at both performances, and bid a passionate farewell to the Ensemble.

Clearly, in addition to the obvious exhilaration over the impending tour of the country's best performing arts ensemble in China, something else, something much more exciting was also 'in the air' in the last days of August and early September 1956. The political and emotional charge of the atmosphere 'before the storm' of the revolution was palpable. For his part, Kodály sent a brief, hand-written 'thank you' note to the Ensemble on the occasion of the premiere of his 'National Song' that echoes some of that excitement. Here it is in its entirety:

> The performance of "On your feet now" on the steps of the National Museum, on the sacred stones where it was first delivered 108 years ago, filled me with great pleasure. The Army Ensemble's exquisite performance and the audience response reinforce my belief that there still exist Hungarians who not only recite "On your feet now" but are ready act to help 'wash away the shame and dirt from our name. ZOLTÁN KODÁLY.[16]

The stakes in the Ensemble's work were thus elevated to a previously unseen level. At the point of their departure from Budapest, they found themselves at the centre – not only of concentrated media attention but also, more importantly, of a tremendous collective

---

[11]Ortutay's diary commemorates the event this way: 'By the way, the entire city is abuzz [with the news] that I will be the secretary general, or the executive vice president [of the National People's Front]. When I gave the speech in front of 5000 people on the steps of the National Museum, before the *Petőfi-Kodály* choir piece, the National People's Front sent me a car, and the driver already asked me to choose him [as my personal driver].' Gyula Ortutay, *Napló 2. 1955–1966* (Budapest: Alexandra, 2009), 120.

[12](rajki), 'ITT AZ IDŐ, MOST VAGY SOHA!', *Népszava*, 7 September 1956.

[13]I have not been able to locate an online video recording of the People's Army Men's Choir's performance of Kodály's 'National Song.' To give a sense of the music, the following link connects to a recent performance by another men's choir: https://www.youtube.com/watch?v=1XL0Yyl-a5 g (accessed 9 June 2015).

[14]István Péterfi, 'NEMZETI DAL. Kodály Zoltán új művének bemutatása', *Szabad Nép*, 8 September 1956: 4.

[15]Ibid.

[16]'On your feet now' is the first line of the refrain of the poem – the way in which popular conversation tended to refer to it. Kodály paraphrases another widely known line of the same poem, 'National Song.' The brilliance of the use of the 1848 revolutionary poem in the pre-revolutionary moment of September 1956 re-inscribes the references to the national 'shame and dirt' in the post-war, post-Holocaust, post-genocide context. Archive of the Army Ensemble.

emotional and political effervescence. As (rajki), a journalist who reviewed one of the Ensemble's last performances for *Népszava*, another national daily newspaper, suggested:

> It was almost as if not just the seventy excellent singers, but also the ... thousands of listeners sang together the lines that are so timely for our country and the rousing, beautiful melody, "Now is the moment, nothing stalls you."[17]

Major Lajos Vass, choir master and art director of the Ensemble's men's choir, took the issue one step further in a brief interview published a week before the Ensemble's departure for China. For, once the journalist mentioned that the men's choir learned two Chinese songs for the tour – 'one is an unison folk song, the other is an elaboration by a Chinese composer' – Major Vass volunteered the following anecdote about the choir's understandings and expectations of China and their own task as artists who bring Hungarian culture to Chinese audiences:

> It is interesting – Lajos Vass says – that it was easier for us to learn [the Chinese songs] than the Russian and Bulgarian texts earlier. For our premiere on August 18, we had planned to sing from sheet music but, by the time of the last rehearsal, it became clear that the choir knows [the songs] flawlessly without notes – so, when it came to the concert, nobody used the sheets.[18]

Major Vass articulates two related points. First, he asserts an imagined, highly valued, deep cultural tie between the Chinese and Hungarian societies and cultures. What the choir master is playing on is of course, the widely known (in Hungary) fact of the 'Asian' character of some aspects of Hungarian culture – the language, Magyar, is a member of the Finno-Ugric group, which is, in turn, part of a bigger central Asian context and, most relevant to men's choir art director Major Vass, the oldest layer of Hungarian folk music uses the pentatonic scale, something that is of course a mainstay in East Asian, including Chinese, classical and folk music.

In the context of the hot, late summer night performances before the Ensemble's departure for China, these words also carried an additional, directly political significance. Simply put, by insisting on the 'deep' cultural affinities between the Chinese and Hungarian 'folk' spirits, artistic or otherwise, Major Vass elegantly 'skipped' the vast entity that lies in between, both geographically and in terms of moral geopolitics, i.e. Soviet/Russian culture and society. Given what we know about the overall political atmosphere, this had to be perceptible in the late summer days of 1956 in Budapest – and especially so because, almost as if to remind everyone who might have missed his moral-geopolitical message, Major Vass not only constructed an imagined, direct link between the peoples of his country and faraway China, he also explicitly used not only the Bulgarian, but also, very significantly, the Russian (read, in the given political context: 'Soviet') example as negative counterpoints. Logically, excitement about the imagined Sino-Hungarian link did not strictly require counterpoints; by posing the putative distance to the two East European fellow-socialist cultures as contrasts to China's presumed moral, almost familial, proximity – 'it was easier for us to learn [the Chinese songs] than the Russian and Bulgarian texts earlier' – he asserts that there is a gap, an empty space, a non-familial territory between China and Hungary. It clearly signals the fatigue of official Soviet-Hungarian relations by late summer 1956 that the Party's central newspaper printed all this.

---

[17] This is how the article is signed. The author could not be identified. Emphasis in the original. (rajki), 'ITT AZ IDŐ ...'.
[18] Csizmadia, 'ÚTRA KÉSZEN ...', 4. Emphasis in the original. Csizmadia, 'ÚTRA KÉSZEN ...', 4.

Programming to represent

Having spent two months in preparation for the tour, and several weeks giving dress rehearsals and gala concerts of their material to the enthusiastic audiences in Budapest, the Ensemble gave its début performance in the northeastern city of Shenyang on 21 September 1956, i.e. exactly two weeks after their train rolled out of Nyugati Station in Budapest.

Figure 1 reproduces the programme of the Shenyang performance, as remembered and typed up by Lajos Mészáros, a long-time baritone singer, member, and soloist of the men's choir.[19] Table 1 presents the same programme list in English, annotated for authors and performers wherever it was possible to find out about the choreographers/composers omitted from the original list. In order to convey a sense of the materials, Table 1 also contains a set of endnotes that contain links to video recordings of the performances of 15 of the 20 pieces on the list.[20]

This programme signals a departure from the Ensemble's initial charge in two important ways: one of those is marked by its presence, the other by its absence.

Starting with a striking presence, the programme is marked by the predominance of a 'Hungarian', i.e. 'national', frame. The opening number, the 'Rákóczi March', was a popular, quasi-folkloric melody that came to be closely associated with the enlightened noblemen's uprising against Habsburg absolutism, led by Ferenc Rákóczi II between 1703 and 1711, a small war of anti-imperial independence that created a minor musical tradition of its own. The March has unclear origins.[21] It spread as quasi-folklore, and had served as the unofficial national quasi-anthem of Hungary before the inauguration today's national anthem in 1844.[22] Hector Berlioz inserted the Rákóczi March into his 1846 'dramatic legend', The Damnation of Faust. The second item opens with the men's choir's rendition of 'Meghalt a cselszövő', a very popular aria from Ferenc Erkel's romantic-nationalist historical opera *Hunyadi László*, and closes with two brief pieces from Kodály's 'song play' *Háry János*, an operatic piece based on a loosely connected set of anecdotal folk tales of a peasant boy recruited into the Habsburg Army, with intense comic effects due to the boy's proclivity to fibbing, through five 'adventures'. The fourth piece is a romantic-nationalist musical item par excellence, from the early nineteenth century. Item 8 includes three musical pieces, two of which – the 'Soldier Song' from Franz Liszt's Faust symphony and Kodály's score to the 'National Song' – are clearly items that continue to thematise the vexed history of nationhood. Closing the series of performance pieces clearly in a 'national' frame, the second part of the performance returns to *Háry János* for a brief orchestral Intermezzo.

It might legitimately be asked: Why it is even worth mentioning that the Ensemble's programme, as it is prepared for a set of performances abroad, reflects a national frame?

---

[19]Mr Mészáros contributed this sheet to the Ensemble's archives in conjunction with the preparations for the 50-year commemoration of the tour in 2006; I received it from the archive soon thereafter. This is a doubly invaluable document. Not only is it the only programme among the 104 performances I have found; it is the programme of the Ensemble's first performance, ergo it can be seen as the clearest reflection of the ways the Ensemble's artists envisioned, the ways in which they would perform Hungary to Chinese audiences before they had any chance to adjust their programmes based on audience feedback.

[20]I have not been able to find videos of the remaining five items.

[21]It is likely that it was written music that soon became popularised for its patriotic meanings. Apocryphal arguments suggest that it may have been 'written music' – but it is clear that it spread folklorically by the early nineteenth century. http://mek.oszk.hu/02100/02115/html/4-836.html (accessed 10 June 2015).

[22]Ferenc Erkel's musical score was submitted to an 1844 competition to set to music to Ferenc Kölcsey's 1823 poem, 'Hymnus.'

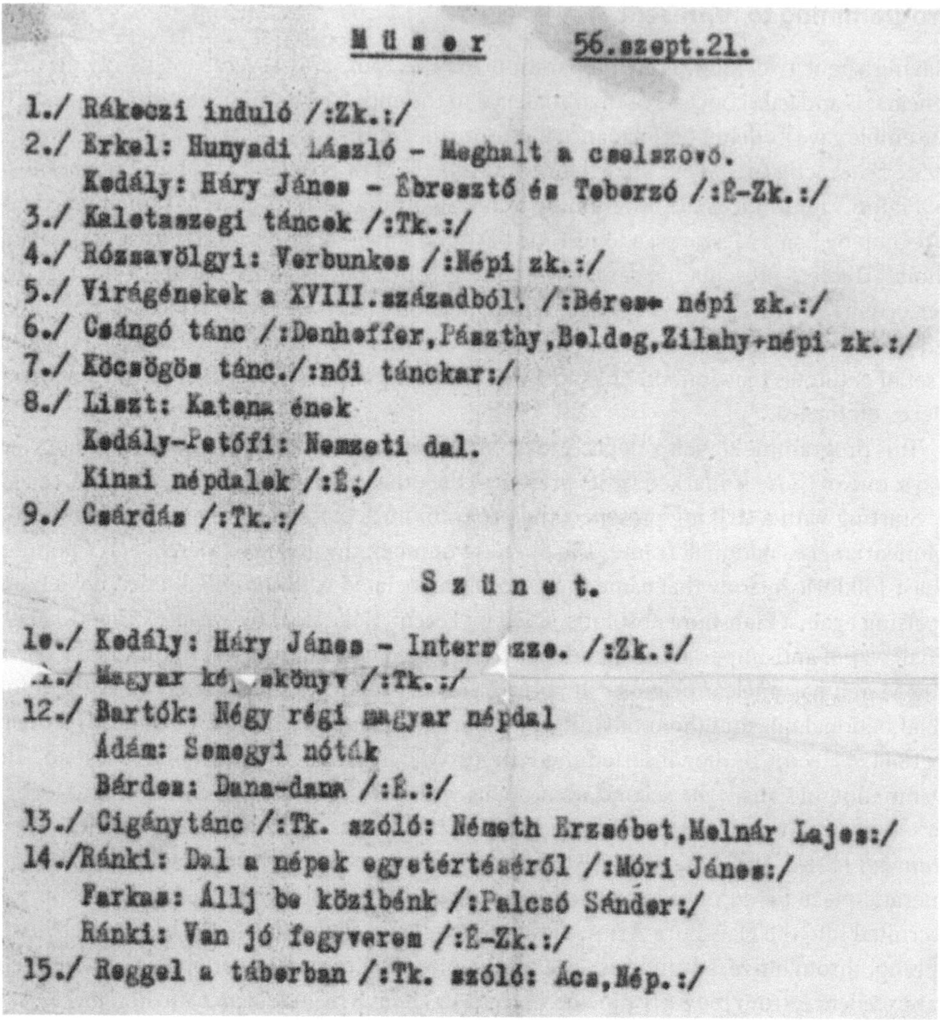

```
                    M ü s o r        56.szept.21.

 1./ Rákoczi induló /:Zk.:/
 2./ Erkel: Hunyadi László - Meghalt a caelszovó.
     Kedály: Háry János - Ébresztő és Teberzó /:É-Zk.:/
 3./ Kalotaszegi táncok /:Tk.:/
 4./ Rózsavölgyi: Verbunkes /:Népi zk.:/
 5./ Virágénekek a XVIII.századból. /:Béres+ népi zk.:/
 6./ Csángó tánc /:Denheffer,Pászthy,Beldeg,Zilahy+népi zk.:/
 7./ Köcsögös tánc./:női tánckar:/
 8./ Liszt: Katena ének
     Kedály-Petőfi: Nemzeti dal.
     Kinai népdalok /:É.;/
 9./ Csárdás /:Tk.:/


                         S z ü n e t.

 le./ Kedály: Háry János - Interm zze. /:Zk.:/
 .../ Magyar ké  akönyv /:Tk.:/
 12./ Bartók: Négy régi magyar népdal
      Ádám: Somogyi nóták
      Bárdes: Duna-dana /:É.:/
 13./ Cigánytánc /:Tk. szóló: Németh Erzsébet,Melnár Lajes:/
 14./Ránki: Dal a népek egyetértéséről /:Móri János:/
     Farkas: Állj be közibénk /:Palcsó Sándor:/
     Ránki: Van jó fegyverem /:É-Zk.:/
 15./ Reggel a táberban /:Tk. szóló: Ács,Nép.:/
```

Figure 1. 'M ü s o r' (Programme of the Début Performance in Shenyang), Hungarian original, 21 September 1956.

That frame is noteworthy, first of all, because the national is something that had been 'picked up' somewhere along the way in the Ensemble's – by September 1956, approximately eight-year-long – history. Although, as I mentioned above, there was a discernible 'national' character to the original framing of the ways in which the Ensemble was imagined at its inception, that was a feature of the narrative framework of the document in the sense that it was constructed as an 'inside-Hungary' conversation. Once the document's reader 'entered' that inside, however, there was absolutely nothing about nationhood there, except for the brief, and formulaic, derogatory dismissal of 'petty bourgeois nationalism.' In sharp contrast to that, the performance the Ensemble prepared for China in mid-to-late 1956, especially its first half, exuded a 'national spirit' of sorts. This is very likely to have had to do with the cultural-political positions the composer Zoltán Kodály – a towering figure in the classical-music, art, policy, and education field in Hungary since the interwar period,

Table 1. Programme of the Ensemble's Début Performance in Shenyang, on 21 September 1956.

	Author(s)	Title	Performer(s)
1	(Héctor Berlioz)	Rákóczi March[a] (from the opera *The Damnation of Faust*)	Symphony Orchestra
2	Ferenc Erkel	Meghalt a cselszövő[b] (Aria from the Opera *Hunyadi László*)	Men's Choir and Symphony Orchestra
	Zoltán Kodály	Wakeup Call and Recruitment[c] (from the *Háry János* suite)	Men's Choir and Symphony Orchestra
3	László Seregi – László Sásdi	Dances from Kalotaszeg[d]	Dance Troupe
4	Márk Rózsavölgyi	Recruitment Song[e]	Music Band of the Dance Troupe
5	(folklore adaptation)	'Flower Songs' from the eighteenth Century[f]	Ferenc Béres and Music Band of the Dance Troupe
6	(Sándor Fejes, choreography)	Csángó Dance	Dance and Singer Soloists and Music Band of the Dance Troupe
7	(Sándor Román, choreography)	Clay Pot Dance[g]	Women Dancers and the Music Band
8	Franz Liszt	Soldier Song[h] (from the *Faust* symphony)	Men's Choir
	Zoltán Kodály – Sándor Petőfi	'National Song'[i]	Men's Choir
		Chinese Songs	Men's Choir
9	(Sándor László-Bencsik, choreography)	Csárdás[j] (Hungarian folk-dance medley)	Dance Troupe and its Music Band
Intermission			
10	Zoltán Kodály	Intermezzo[k] (from the *Háry János* suite)	Symphony Orchestra
11	István Molnár	Hungarian Picture Book[l]	Dance Troupe and its Music Band
12	Béla Bartók	Four Old Hungarian Folk Songs[m]	Men's Choir
	Jenő Ádám	Songs from Somogy County	Men's Choir
	Lajos Bárdos	Dana-Don[n]	Men's Choir
13	(Dezső Létai, choreography)	Gypsy Dance	Erzsébet Német and Lajos Molnár, Solo Dancers
14	György Ránki	Song for the Agreement of Peoples	Men's Choir
	Ferenc Farkas	Join Us	Men's Choir
	György Ránki	I Have Good Arms	Men's Choir
15	László Sásdi – László Seregi	Morning in the Camp[o]	Dance Troupe and its Music Band

[a]https://www.youtube.com/watch?v=qflspYcnpeY (accessed 3 June 2015).
[b]https://www.youtube.com/watch?v=uUvsk9Hvm70 (accessed 5 June 2015).
[c]https://www.youtube.com/watch?v=b50eVcfXB0c (accessed 3 June 2015).
[d]https://www.youtube.com/watch?v=9IR2ALPaB_Q (accessed 3 June 2015).
[e]https://www.youtube.com/watch?v=8XVqpKA4Xwg (accessed 5 June 2015).
[f]https://www.youtube.com/watch?v=TDUgwz76kD4&list=PLsNdLc6Y_9UvT3Hsra3cbjg5ys2vEjCj3 (accessed 5 June 2015).
[g]Excerpt from the short film We Were China's Guests (Kína vendégei voltunk), by cinematographers Félix Bodrossy and Miklós Jancsó, released in 1957, which covers the Ensemble's tour in China for Hungarian audiences. The excerpt features the Ensemble's women dancers, on their tour in China. http://www.folkarchivum.hu/archivum/htsz/media.php?id=M0009&bel=1 (accessed 5 June 2015).
[h]https://www.youtube.com/watch?v=LW-6HMenF74j (accessed 5 June 2015).
[i]https://www.youtube.com/watch?v=LW-6HMenF74j (accessed 5 June 2015).
[j]http://www.kultura-muveszet.hu/szinhaz/tancszinhaz/honved-tancszinhaz-csardas.html (accessed 5 June 2015).
[k]https://www.youtube.com/watch?v=5D8t_L_J-70 (accessed 5 June 2015).
[l]https://www.youtube.com/watch?v=8qcq_mQmQ0I (accessed 3 June 2015).
[m]https://www.youtube.com/watch?v=s6uBN068oVI (accessed 5 June 2015).
[n]https://www.youtube.com/watch?v=SwEnLTQ-p_A (accessed 5 June 2015).
[o]Excerpt, performed by the dance troupe of the Ensemble. http://www.folkarchivum.hu/archivum/htsz/media.php?id=M0008&bel=1 (accessed 5 June 2015).

and the Ensemble's patron-cum-protector – 'navigated' in the complex relationship between various Soviet practices of nationalism/antinationalism at the turn of the 1950s in a debate with József Révai, the regime's main culture politician.[23]

---

[23]Lóránt Péteri, 'Kodály és az államszocializmus művelődéspolitikája (1948–1967),' *Forrás* (2007): 45–63, especially 50. See also Miklós Hadas, 'A nemzet prófétája. Kísérlet Kodály Zoltán pályájának szociológiai értelmezésére,' *Szociológia* 4 (1984): 469–90, and József Révai, *Marxizmus, népiesség, magyarság* (Budapest: Szikra, 1949).

Two things need to be added here, to help explain the choice of the national framing and, at the same time, to problematise it. First, of course there is something un-avoidable about foregrounding nationhood when it comes to quasi-operatic performances whose stated purpose is representation of one particular society to audiences of another. Arguably, the national frame has served, at least since the onset of modernity, and especially in East-Central and Eastern Europe, to some extent as the 'external form' that any society can present to outsiders. In that sense, the 'national presentation of self through performing arts' has a specific aesthetic character to it, and that character has its own history, both in Europe and, more specifically, in Hungary. On the other hand, however, insistence on invoking that 'European' tradition of national presentation-of-self has two consequences: it drives the representational process toward national purity that translates, all too easily, into a certain sense of 'national' exclusiveness.

In addition, the enforcement of the 'European' canon in national presentation-of-self in the context of an otherwise intra-socialist cultural contact situation becomes somewhat complicated. That is so partly because of the 'capitalist-bourgeois' character of the iconic forms of such self-representation, partly because it also reproduces, perforce, a certain nineteenth-century imagined West European standard of national essences as an implicit default, a powerful idea that had, to say the least, a very troubled history as it was transposed on the societies of Eastern/East-Central Europe, let alone societies outside the 'European' frame.

Second, there is something highly enticing about the spectacular character of the aesthetic presentation of 'the Hungarian nation' to non-European audiences. After all, the job of the Ensemble was to provide 'educative entertainment' – i.e. entertainment. And, as it turns out, what the Hungarian cultural tradition, especially the presentation-of-the-national-self to a foreign context has by way of visibly and audibly enjoyable, stage-worthy material actually happens to be closely linked into the early, 'progressive,' anti-Habsburg independence-seeking, romantic nationalist tradition. In this sense, the Ensemble's hands were somewhat 'tied.' If they wished to realise the performing arts imperative to invite, impress, and enchant their audiences, they had to work from the 'best' – read: most spectacular, most enjoyable – material they had, and that had to do, to a large extent, with the romantic nationalist period.

Indirect evidence suggests that this reliance on the romantic nationalist tradition might have actually worked. For a report filed by Ervin Havas, one of the journalists on the tour, with *Néphadsereg*, the Hungarian People's Army newspaper, narrates the following anecdote:

> Intermission. A young girl with a pigtail brings a message into the dressing room. Big excitement, running after the interpreters. And the message is read out in the dressing room: "To All Members of the Hungarian People's Army Performing Arts Ensemble. Thank you, thank you, once again thank you. I love your music very-very much because it reflects the character of the Hungarian people. I would like to request that the comrade pianist play Rhapsody II by Liszt. I wish you much success for your upcoming performances. Liu Zhoushin, worker of the Number 3 Shoe Factory."[24]

And yet, it is also hard not to notice, as it has been pointed out in the review of the Ensemble's China programme by Sándor Asztalos, that the programme does have a certain

---

[24]Ervin Havas, 'Az első napok a Kínai Népköztársaságban,' *Néphadsereg*, October 1956, n.d., 8.

historicising, 'music-philological' character to it.[25] That of course is not necessarily 'a problem' – after all, the pieces had to be put together in some sequence for there to have a gala performance – nevertheless, it is obvious that there is a certain level of meaning, lodged in the sequencing of the pieces, that is only accessible to the 'eyes and ears' of audiences intimately familiar with the musical, dance, not to mention social and political, histories of Europe, let alone specifically Hungary. In this sense, it is almost certain that there was a – perhaps unavoidable, but still palpable – sense in which the Ensemble communicated primarily with that small segment of the Chinese audiences that had training or at least basic familiarity with European histories, 'over the heads,' so to speak, of those who attended their performances without such preparation. In sum, the Ensemble's strong references to nineteenth-century romantic nationalism – while, most likely unavoidable – also carried what appears to be a rather unreflected 'regression' to a European artistic canon.

Or – was it fully unreflected? A tiny bit of evidence seems to suggest that it wasn't. The interview with the dance troupe's art director in the journal *Táncművészet* (*Dance Art*) makes a truly suggestive point here. In considering the long-term goals of the group, he makes a reference to a concept paper published by another prominent stage folk-dance art choreographer a few months before, as follows: I fully agree with Miklós Rábai's three-word motto (Modern, Magyar, European). This idea must be victorious at [our Ensemble] as well. I believe we have what it takes to realize this concept.[26]

Although he argued that the full realisation of this goal will have to wait until after the Ensemble's return from China, it is fairly clear that the debate is about the specific 'form language' the Ensemble would pursue within the overlap among the 'Modern, Magyar, European' domains, and simply not the predominance of those features.[27] In a certain way, pursuance of this particular dictum appears to have been unavoidable for the Ensemble.

Miklós Rábai's slogan, echoed by the art director of the Ensemble's dance troupe here, is a fairly sharp clue that helps clarify the character of just which of the many possible meanings of the idea of nationhood the Ensemble ended up aligning itself with. While artistic references to the late-eighteenth-to-late-nineteenth-century struggles for independence from Habsburg rule can of course be seen, perhaps with a large dose of good will, as ethnically somewhat comprehensive, two facts – both of which were of course amply available to the artists who created the Ensemble's profile – are undeniable. Namely, first, that the Habsburg Empire, including, very prominently, its larger, eastern part that was referred to as 'the lands of the Hungarian Crown,' was an intensely poly-ethnic space, i.e. it is hardly satisfactory to make the conventional slip of referring to it as 'Magyar.' The period treated in conventional 'schoolbook' history in Hungary proper as 'struggle for independence' featured, with Rogers Brubaker's useful formulation, a conceptual struggle between the 'poly-ethnic' and 'multi-national' readings of that reality – with the eventual political 'victory' of the latter scheme. As a result, second, in close conjunction with this, the state entity 'Hungary' was formed with the blatant exclusion of all the bewildering varieties of complex non-'Magyar' 'ethnic' categories from the political process. In other words, referring to the period of the

---

[25]It starts with a piece that indexes the 1703–11 uprising via Berlioz' 1846 elaboration, then we move on to Erkel's nineteenth-century opera, then it moves on to another nineteenth-century piece, to Liszt's late nineteenth century, late-romantic nationhood, to Kodály's mid-twentieth-century interpretation of the mid-nineteenth-century iconic romantic-nationalist poem 'National Song,' and so on.

[26]Gy. Cs., 'A kínai út előtt ...,' 391.

[27]Ibid.

late-eighteenth-to-mid-nineteenth century as 'national independence,' and then switching the conversation to a 'Magyar' national frame, involves a strongly ethno-nationalist, *ergo* by definition ethnically exclusive, interpretation of history.

That this is not idle speculation but, indeed, a feature of the Ensemble's work is reflected in two parallel facts regarding its artistic programme brought to China. The first one has to do with a presence – the inclusion of a 'Csángó Dance' in the programme, a folk-dance medley featuring ethnic Magyar materials from a micro-region called Bukovina/Bucovina/Bukowina, a borderland area between the Ottoman, Habsburg, and Russian Empires, part of the Ukrainian Soviet Republic of the USSR at the time. Throughout its momentous history of imperial control, Bukovina had never 'technically' been part of Hungary proper, definitely not as long as we conceive the latter as a state defined by its borders as of the mid-1950s. There is a strong convention in stage folk-art dance in Hungary to use Csángó materials because this small enclave of ethnic Magyar peasants lived so far away, and in such cultural isolation, from the main body of their fellow-Magyar co-ethnics that they preserved layers of their dance and musical heritage (as well as their distinctive language dialect, the only one in Magyar that poses comprehension difficulties for speakers of literary Magyar) that is found nowhere else. In other words, a defining feature of the Csángó – a subgroup of ethnic Magyars whose very name derives from a verb referring to 'wandering away' – is the very distance of Bukovina, their ethnic enclave, from Hungary. Inclusion of this material reveals that the Ensemble, just like much of the folk-dance movement in Hungary, thought about 'peasant' art along ethno-nationalist lines.

The other clue has to do with the underrepresentation of ethnically non-'Magyar' folk music or dance in the programme. If the Ensemble were to have conceived their understanding of 'Magyar'-ness along some other, ethnically more inclusive, lines, it remains to be explained why there was only one reference – the insertion of a 'Gypsy Dance' – to the 20 or so ethnic groups that lived in Hungary at the time, from Germans to Ukrainians, from Romanians to Slovaks, Serbs, Croats and Slovenes, Armenians and Greeks, not to mention the multiple layers of Jewish folkloric heritage in Hungary. This is noteworthy because one crucial aspect of the work of the Ensemble's un-questioned idol, Béla Bartók, was his avid interest in folklore beyond boundaries of the Magyar ethnic group (quite a blurred and complicated boundary, anyway), both in East-Central Europe and farther away.[28] The inclusion of a 'Gypsy Dance' is, again, something that works very much along the lines of the folk-dance movement in Hungary at the time (where the power of Roma folklore heritage was very strongly articulated and widely acknowledged), and raises questions about the presence of the Roma as well as the absence of all others. Be that as it may, the 'people' that the Hungarian People's Army Ensemble represented, were ethnic Magyars, with a small concession to the spectacular treasure of 'Gypsy' traditions – even as it was exoticised by virtue of being marked as 'Gypsy.'

It is indicative of the location of the fundamentally ethno-nationalist posture of the stage folk-art dance movement at the time that the question of ethno-national purity was raised

---

[28]For instance, Bartók conducted years of extensive fieldwork in Romanian folk music, he learnt Romanian, was a widely recognised contributor to the scholarly study of Romanian folk music, and composed a number of works based on Romanian folk melodies. See, e.g. Tiberu Alexandru, 'Bartók Béla és a román népzene,' *Korunk* 8 (1970): 1164–7; Ágnes Herczku, 'A folklore ereje. Bartók szemével látni és láttatni,' *Előadás a Charta XXI Megbékélési Mozgalom által szervezett 'Egymás szemében – Közép-Európai Identitások' című konferencián* (Brussels: European Parliament), 27 November 2013. http://www.hagyomanyokhaza.hu/page/11403/ (accessed 11 June 2015).

in slightly different terms as well. In the year of Stalin's death, when the first 'new winds started to blow' in the Soviet 'bloc,' choreographer Miklós Rábai, a stalwart of the stage folk-art dance movement in Hungary and director of the State Folk Ensemble for decades (whom I have quoted above for his programmatic three-word axiom for the movement) voiced his – given the nationalist space created by Kodály's manoeuvrings, rather damning – opinion, in a review of the dance troupe's one thousandth performance, that 'the Ensemble does not dance in Magyar,' a shortcoming he explained with their supposedly excessive focus on ballet training.[29]

Another subplot of the main story of national independence is the programme's repeated references to military themes. This of course is completely to be expected – after all, this is the performing-arts ensemble of the Hungarian People's *Army*, on an official visit hosted by the People's Liberation *Army* in China. And yet, this was a tender area for the Ensemble, a place where they had to tread gingerly. For, first of all, Hungary's military history did not exactly provide these artists with many examples of a glorious military past from which they could derive artistic inspiration. Add to that the recent dark historical cloud looming most heavily over the head of any artist who would look for rousing reminiscences of past glory, the fact that Hungary not only participated in World War II on the wrong side – as an ally of Nazi Germany – it fought actively against the Soviet Union, it also inflicted genocide against the civilian populations in those parts of the USSR which its army occupied, and members of the Hungarian armed forces participated actively in genocide against Hungary's own citizens. It is reasonable to assume that this experience – which the Hungarian military participated in a mere 11 to 17 years before the tour – was to be an elephant in the room for anyone trying to construct a 'positive,' rousing artistic portrayal of military life. Most likely for this reason, the various examples for the appearance of the 'military' theme in the programme – with one glaring exception to be addressed later – are located, again, Hungary's early-modern history, essentially as a subplot of the 'safely' distant romantic-nationalist master narrative.

As for the most glaring absence, it is remarkable how little the programme offers by way of explicitly Party-oriented, Stalinist propaganda art. The only item that qualifies under that heading is the penultimate block (number 14 in the list) comprising three choral works: 'Song for the Agreement of Peoples,' 'Join Us,' and 'I Have Good Arms,' the first and the third composed by György Ránki, the middle one by Ferenc Farkas. All three of these works were conceived to satisfy the official, Stalinist demand for directly political works, and they had been written between 1949 and 1955.

Although the placement of this block close to the finale could perhaps be interpreted as a sign of a somewhat elevated status, it is obvious that the programme as a whole provides the absolute minimum by way of Stalin-era propaganda art. Perhaps even more significant is the complete absence of what is referred to in the concept paper of 1948 as 'the choral art of the Hungarian working class movement which is at the cutting edge world-wide.'[30] It is also clear from the oral-history interviews I have conducted with members of the Ensemble – including members of the men's choir – that, during the first seven years of the Ensemble's existence, a very significant part of the choir's repertoire consisted of Stalin-era Soviet and Hungarian propaganda pieces, including highly prominent examples such as Alexander

---

[29]Vitézi Ének Alapítvány, *Honvéd Táncszínház (1948–2007)* [The Army Dance Theatre, 1948–2007] (Budapest: Vitézi Ének, n.d.). Alapítvány. http://www.folkarchivum.hu/archivum/htsz/dok/A_Honved_Tancszinhaz_rovid_tortenete.pdf (accessed 6 June 2015).

[30]'A honvédség központi ...'.

Vasilyevich Alexandrov's (the Red Army Choir's founder's) famous Cantata on Stalin, a 1938 piece frequently cited as a particularly poignant example of Stalinist propaganda music.[31] Considering the centrality of Stalinist propaganda art to the Ensemble's repertoire until 1956, the placement of the three relatively brief pieces, grouped in one block to make up a tiny fraction of the Ensemble's programme in China, it is possible to have the impression that it had been inserted in the most minimal way, almost as if to 'cover' the Ensemble from that political angle. Importantly, all three of the Stalinist works chosen were Hungarian. That no Soviet piece was included in the Ensemble's programme is another indication that the programme was put together with a subtle underlying intent not to foreground the USSR as a point of reference. It is hard to imagine that that absence would go unnoticed by the numerous Soviet diplomats, political emissaries, intelligence officers, technical experts, and exchange students who occupied a very exalted position in Beijing expatriate life in 1956.

Another factor that might have prompted the Ensemble to de-emphasise the Stalinist segment of its repertoire is that, of course, in order for the desired political mobilising effort to take place, the audience had to be able to understand the lyrics of the songs, which would not have been the case with most Stalin-era propaganda songs from Eastern or East-Central Europe. The propaganda songs without the words, whatever the *sui generis* value of their music may have been, definitely do not work as effective propaganda. On the other hand, it is also remarkable that none of the standard pieces of music widely associated with the Communist movement – 'The International,' the various 'labour movement songs' from around the world (including, by the way, those from China) made it into the Ensemble's programme in China.[32]

Overall, the rest of the material is aligned quite effortlessly with the plebeian-peasant-progressive-socialist character of the Ensemble's original charge. Practically all of the dance pieces, as well as the various works by Zoltán Kodály, Béla Bartók, and Jenő Ádám, match closely the main concept – with one slight deviation: a popular early-nineteenth-century piece by Márk Rózsavölgyi that qualifies as an example of *imitated* quasi-folk music. In sum, the prominence of the ethno-national 'angle' and the downplaying of Stalinist propaganda art, coupled with the programme's close adherence to the populist-socialist new aesthetic, suggest that the Ensemble's programme is intended as a socialist cultural statement with a distinct, post-Stalinist bent.

'Morning in the Camp' – twist at the end

The programme's finale, a dance choreography entitled 'Morning in the Camp,' fits none of the classification attempts developed thus far. Because of its distance from the staged folk-dance conventions, it is clearly neither 'folkloric,' nor Stalinist. It is very difficult to impute any direct, conventional-ethno-nationalist content to it either. So, what is it, then?

The piece was conceived in 1953 by László Seregi and László Sásdi, two soloists of the dance troupe at the time, set to a distinctly twentith-century, modern, stylised, post-folk music score by Gábor Barta. 'Morning in the Camp' was a tremendous success in Hungary, so much so that one of its co-choreographers, László Seregi – who would become, by the mid-to-late-1960s, the star creative choreographer and art director of the Ballet Troupe of

---

[31]See, for instance, https://www.youtube.com/watch?v=CQCAKgOwGNw (accessed 10 June 2015).
[32]Notice also the absence of both the Hungarian and the Chinese national anthems.

the State Opera House in Budapest – considered it one of the most successful choreographies of his life in the oral-history interview he was gracious enough to give me a few years ago. And that was so in spite of the fact that, in Seregi's words, it was just a 'ten-to-eleven-minute little sketch.'[33]

> It's morning, the birds are chirping, the orderly officer enters, we are open-air, in a grove, the trumpeter blows the wake-up signal, guys run onto the stage cheerfully, in tee shirts, to do the morning calisthenics, with a bouncy rhythm, and suddenly a little short character ambles on to the stage, ... his footcloth sticking out of his boots, he ambles in, then falls asleep, and then this nap causes all kinds of delays, he misses his breakfast. This is the basic idea, a little silly thing. At last, he pulls himself together, the commander forgives him, the platoon lines up and the Ensemble walks out lock-step, parade-style.[34]

It is easy to see why this piece would be popular with audiences, in Hungary as well as abroad. It tells a story, something that none of the Ensemble's other pieces can claim. It is a story that is very easy to relate to, having to do with a microscopic life experience most people had had. It is a story with a small, likeable central character, and all he is trying to do is rectify the initial mistake he had made. And, of course, the story has a happy ending.

Miklós Rábai (according to whom the Ensemble's dance group had too much ballet influence so that it was 'not dancing in Magyar' in 1953), linked what he saw in an early 1956 performance of 'Morning in the Camp' to the aesthetic project of transposing the 'spirit' of folklore to socialist art. He saw this work as a

> ... heartwarming composition. Soldiers of many a [military] camp, audiences at many garrison stages, as well as scores of 'civilians' have laughed their way through the case of the sleepy little soldier. This is the genre that is needed, this is the genre whose content can be placed next to, or even above, other compositions. Its forms of expression are strong. Even parts that had earlier come across as sapless appear new, strong, and beautiful [now]. This is not a new composition, and it appears to be true that the real value of a piece can only be measured after the thirtieth performance, as things fall into place by then and the momentum of the performance helps the dancers through the weaker parts as well.[35]

That 'sketch' was not 'only' popular with the audiences and colleagues; it was also noticed by the Hungarian People's Army high command. Hungary's Minister of Defence opined at the time that 'comrade Seregi solved the task of [presenting] the Hungarian soldier through a healthy [and] sympathetic [piece of] dance.'[36] Apparently not everybody agreed. On a tour in the USSR later, official complaints were lodged with the Ensemble's leadership: 'A socialist soldier is never late, and how can you even place a negative example in the centre of the dance?'[37]

'Morning in the Camp' was a strongly (self-)ironical piece of dance art, offering a whole series of allegorical readings. The soldier who is 'late' to 'wake up' for 'service' that is, then, helped by his 'comrades' to 'catch up' – it must have truly been difficult for the Hungarian viewer not to recognise in this piece a certain self-deprecating, comical collective self-representation, the self-image of a society whose historical development is 'belated' but one

---

[33] Oral-history interview with László Seregi, conducted by the author.
[34] Ibid.
[35] Miklós Rábai, 'A Magyar Néphadsereg Művészegyüttesének bemutatójához,' *Szabad Hazánkért* (April 1956): 22–3 (23).
[36] Oral-history interview with László Seregi, conducted by the author.
[37] Anecdote related by Tibor Vadasi, who would become art director of the Ensemble's dance troupe after 1957. Vitézi Ének, *A Honvéd Táncszínház*.

that eventually 'catches up.'[38] In that sense, the piece remains comfortably within the aesthetic-political ambit of official art. It concerns itself, after all, with 'catching up' through discipline, effort, and increased readiness: all those virtues extolled in the construction of socialism, especially given the army setting.

However, notions of (self-)irony, self-deprecating humour, self-belittling, the foregrounding of tiny, personal difficulties in performing one's tasks – these are ideas that were truly alien from the customary pathos, grand, unambiguous gestures and overall heaviness that characterise the official Stalinist variety of propaganda art. In other words – while 'Morning in the Camp' is, clearly, 'programme art,' and, clearly, socialist – it is socialist in a different, post-pathos, post-grand, post-unambiguous, and post-heavy, i.e. post-Stalinist way. It is a piece that manages to insert some of the attitudes and sensibilities of a collectivity that sees itself as part of a bigger entity, but in a highly complex, polysemic, partly reluctant, partly self-ironical fashion. The greater entity is unmistakably socialist, the individual contribution and the form language in which the narrative is told is unambiguously post-Stalinist.

Finally, it is important to notice that the irony of the piece cuts not only against the Stalinist propaganda tradition; it is also ironical vis-à-vis both of the other key aesthetic elements of the programme: the nineteenth-century, romantic-imagination of the independent nation, and the proclivity of the populist-socialist peasant-to-'high'-art tradition to romanticising such a complex and problematic class location as that of 'the peasant.' Whether or not the Ensemble's members realised this, placement of 'Morning in the Camp' at the very end – almost as if twisting a few drops of lemon juice on vanilla ice cream – opens up a set of possibilities to re-read the entire preceding programme as reaffirmation of a set of socialist commitments – in a different, more acerbic, way.

Conclusion: performing socialist Hungary

The reception of 'Morning in the Camp,' as that of the entire tour of the Ensemble, was astonishingly positive. József Maklári – one of the men's choir's conductors – who managed to send a report to the Budapest daily *Népszava* about the Ensemble's performance in Mukden describes the reception of 'Morning in the Camp':

> Never before have audiences laughed so much at this composition, built on situation comedy and a fresh sense of humor, as these always smiling people who are receptive of the smallest occasion of humor. The last parade March is accompanied by rhythmic applause ...[39]

In the materials prepared for the fiftieth anniversary commemoration of the China tour in 2006, the Ensemble's archive inserted the Hungarian translation (reproduced here in Figure 2) of the concluding section of one of the Chinese reviews of the Shenyang performances at the bottom of the sheet containing the programme list.[40] It reads:

> In addition, there were two lively, humorous folk dances. As the soldier dance entitled 'Morning in the Camp' began, I couldn't help but start smiling. I remembered the 'Soldier Dance' I saw in Bulgaria, the 'Defender's Dance' I saw in Poland, the 'Setting Off For Exercise' I saw in

---

[38]That one-to-one, allegorical reading is of course reinforced by the title of the piece where the 'camp' can be read as both the army camp depicted in the piece, and as a pun on the 'socialist/peace camp,' a centrepiece of geopolitical rhetoric in Eastern and East-Central Europe at the time.

[39]József Maklári, 'ÁTÜTŐ MAGYAR SIKER – MUKDENBEN,' *Népszava*, 9 October 1956. (Mukden is an older name of the town called, since the end of World War II, Shenyang. It is unclear why Maklári refers to it by its colonial name.

[40]Unfortunately this source contains no bibliographic reference.

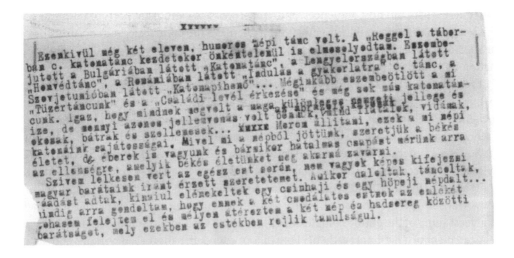

Figure 2. Review of the Shenyang Performances (Excerpt).

Romania, the 'Soldier's Rest' I saw in the Soviet Union ... And even more I recalled our 'Artillery Dance' and the 'Arrival of A Letter from the Family,' and our many other soldier's dances. It is true that each of them had their own quality and taste, but how many features they shared, they were youthful, cheerful, smart, brave and witty ... I daresay these are traits of our people's soldiers. Because we came from the people, we love peaceful life, but we are also vigilant and we are ready to deal a powerful blow on the enemy that would wish to disturb our peaceful life.

My heart beat with enthusiasm during the entire evening. I am unable to express the affection I feel toward our Hungarian friends. When they sang their songs, danced, when they gave their encore, when they sang a folk song from Jinhai and another from Hebei ... I kept thinking, I shall never forget the memory of these two wonderful evenings, and I felt deeply the friendship between the two peoples and armies that is lodged in these evenings.[41]

According to all accounts, the tour was a resounding success. Adding the anecdote of the fan mail delivered to the dressing room and the review quoted above, we have before us a possible summary of what we have learnt about the Ensemble's project of representation in China.[42] The Ensemble did the 'job' assigned to it—(1) representing (2) socialist (3) Hungary— with great efficiency, as the above review suggests. That is a particularly remarkable achievement since they accomplished that without resorting to any of the standard 'political propaganda' works that marked official international communications at the time. They also did so without even mentioning the USSR – but they also avoided, with surgical precision, the political and aesthetic traps of explicit anti-Soviet propaganda. The references to foreign rule/independence remained below several layers of symbolic and historical materials, as well as (self-)irony. As the story of the effusive 'thank you – thank you – thank you' note / request slip shows, the Ensemble managed to provide 'educative entertainment' along the lines of a national framing in such a way that it remained 'safe' for

---

[41]Review of the Ensemble's performances in Shenyang. For the Hungarian translation, see Figure 2.
[42]See, e.g. Rácz, 'Adalékok a magyar-kínai katinadiplomáciai kapcsolatok történetéhez,' quoting Gábor Mészöly, *50 év* (Budapest: Zrínyi, 1999), 24; *A Honvéd Táncszínház (1948–2007)*, 4, http://www.folkarchivum.hu/archivum/htsz/tortenet.php (accessed 22 November 2017); Kánya Andrea, 'Mikor felléptünk, szinte a csillárról is lógtak az emberek,' Honvédelem, 12 October 2009, http://www.honvedelem.hu/cikk/16792 (accessed 22 November 2017), as well as about a dozen oral-history interviews conducted with members of the Ensemble who were on the tour between 2006 and 2015, as part of this research.

both guest artists and host audiences, and 'went across' to significant parts of the audience. This was possible because the Ensemble's fundamental political, artistic, and social-historical 'project' of a plebeian-'peasant'-progressive – i.e. in that specific way 'socialist' – transformation remained intact.

The material of this tour is of course vastly richer than what a short paper can do justice to. But even this brief analysis shows that, in contrast to accounts of the Stalinist era of state socialism, widely portrayed as monolithic, the aesthetic practices considered here suggest a remarkable sense of *complexity*. First, we see a number of elisions and omissions (of both the Soviet and international revolutionary aesthetic and propaganda works). Second, we see oblique references (e.g. to the national 'shame and dirt' in Kodály's choice of the 'National Song' and his rhyming 'thank you' note) that rethink pressing national moral questions in a new, creatively juxtaposed way. Third, there are the open, albeit extremely partial, references to at least some of the ethnic complexities of Hungary's folklore traditions and the obvious reinstatement of a national aesthetic. Fourth is of course the allegorical critique-and-re-affirmation of socialism in the dance piece 'Morning in the Camp.' And, finally, fifth, there is the pervasive (self-)irony and playfulness of the same dance piece, an obvious contrast to Stalinist pathos. All five of those techniques helped move the Ensemble away from the Stalinist aesthetic dogma in ways that explain perhaps part of its success.

Disclosure statement

No potential conflict of interest was reported by the author.

Socialist exhibits and Sino-Soviet relations, 1950–60

Austin Jersild

ABSTRACT

Socialist bloc exhibits in China in the 1950s communicated ideas about the future prosperity and development to be brought to China in the wake of its alliance with the socialist world, the role of socialism in preserving and maintaining folk and traditional culture, and the role of the bloc in extending the virtues of European high culture to the East. The Soviets proudly displayed Russia's historic contribution to high culture as well as information about contemporary events at the Bol'shoi Theater and other cultural institutions in Moscow and St. Petersburg, and the East Germans and the Czechoslovaks similarly emphasized the prestige and quality of their past artists and composers as well as their contemporary symphonies and orchestras. The Chinese, however, were increasingly disappointed both with socialist bloc approaches to Chinese development as well as with depictions of Chinese culture that reminded them of the heritage of European imperialism. They complained in the exhibit "comment books" about methods, practices and technology that offered little to unique Chinese "conditions" and "peculiarities." They were frustrated by the inefficiencies of Soviet-style socialism, and they even complained about the food at the Moscow Restaurant. By the end of the decade, the exhibits served as yet another example of the miscommunication, frustration and dispute over models of development that contributed to the Sino-Soviet split.

General Secretary Nikita Khrushchev went to America in September 1959, accompanied by a Soviet display that was the companion exhibit to the American National Exhibition at Sokolniki Park in Moscow.[1] The American exhibit was sponsored by the United States Information Agency, formerly part of the Department of State, and featured the famous 'kitchen debate' between Khrushchev and visiting Vice President Richard Nixon. Khrushchev welcomed the competition, determined to show that the Soviet Union would indeed 'catch up and surpass' the Americans in yet another area of competition. That encounter has attracted the attention of numerous historians, who explore the episode as an example of American foreign-policy propaganda and public

---

[1]For commentary on previous drafts of this article, my thanks to Jan Zofka, Sören Urbansky, Beáta Hock, the Associates Writing Group of the Department of History at Old Dominion University, the participants at the conference on 'Beyond the Kremlin's Reach? Transfers and Entanglements between Eastern Europe and China during the Cold War Era', in Leipzig, Germany, 29 June-2 July 2015, and several anonymous reviewers engaged by *Cold War History*.

diplomacy, exhibit history, and the evolving nature of the Cold War.[2] Historians of the Soviet Union use Russian and East European archival materials to direct attention to the specific Soviet and socialist context shaping debates over consumerism, culture, and the Cold War.[3] The Soviet participation in the exhibit exchange illustrates the somewhat conventional notion of the Soviet vision. The Soviet exhibit, initially in New York from 30 June 1959, displayed the accomplishments of Soviet science and technology, the virtues of the Russian classical tradition, and the importance and possibilities of 'peaceful coexistence' with the United States. The Soviets brought leading ballerinas from the Bol'shoi Theatre, soloists from the Kirov Theatre, a ballet company, and the 900-voice Piatnitsky Choir.[4] Traditional forms of culture were also flourishing in the Soviet Union, emphasised exhibit organisers, who displayed Palekh lacquer boxes, porcelain, glassware, and traditional Russian shirts and tablecloths. Socialist bloc domesticity was restrained, reasonable, and tasteful, all in contrast to common socialist perceptions of a daily life in America marked by excessive materialism and the absence of culture.

The Chinese did not approve of this socialist effort to engage with the norms and practices of the West. They did not like that Khrushchev even visited the United States, as they told him in no uncertain terms when he stopped in Beijing on his way home via Vladivostok and the Russian Far East. Similarly, the many Chinese in Moscow in 1959 were not happy about the exhibit exchanges, and roundly criticised the American display. Chinese technical specialists in Moscow in the autumn of 1959 rejected an invitation from the Soviet-Chinese Friendship Society to attend the American National Exhibition. They were 'not the least bit interested in the United States', they claimed, surely disturbed by the large crowds assembling at Sokolniki Park.[5] The Chinese embassy that autumn set up a pictorial exhibit about post-revolutionary China, hoping

---

[2]See Robert H. Haddow, *Pavilions of Plenty: Exhibiting American Culture Abroad in the 1950s* (Washington, DC: Smithsonian Institution Press, 1997); Jane De Hart Mathews, 'Art and Politics in Cold War America,' *American Historical Review* 81, no. 4 (October 1976): 762–87; Walter L. Hixson, *Parting the Curtain: Propaganda, Culture, and the Cold War, 1945–1961* (New York: St. Martin's Press, 1997); Marilyn S. Kushner, 'Exhibiting Art at the American National Exhibition in Moscow, 1959,' *Journal of Cold War Studies* 4, no. 1 (2002): 6–26; Karal Ann Marling, *As Seen on TV: The Visual Culture of Everyday Life in the 1950s* (Cambridge, MA: Harvard University Press, 1994).

[3]Tomas Tolvaisas, 'Cold War "Bridge Building": U.S. Exchange Exhibits and Their Reception in the Soviet Union, 1959–1967,' *Journal of Cold War Studies* 12, no. 4 (2010): 3–31; Susan E. Reid, 'Who Will Beat Whom? Soviet Popular Reception of the American National Exhibition in Moscow, 1959,' *Kritika: Explorations in Russian and Eurasian History* 9, no. 4 (2008): 855–904; Susan E. Reid, 'Cold War in the Kitchen: Gender and the De-Stalinization of Consumer Taste in the Soviet Union under Khrushchev,' *Slavic Review* 61, no. 2 (2002): 211–52; Greg Castillo, *Cold War on the Home Front: The Soft Power of Midcentury Design* (Minneapolis: University of Minnesota Press, 2010). For Soviet treatments of exhibits, see Boris Brodskii, *Ves' mir na iugo-zapade* (Moscow: 'Znanie', 1961); K. A. Pavlov, 'Sovetskie universal'nye i spetsializirovannye vystavki za granitsei v period s 1946 po 1957 g.,' 61–84, and A. V. Saag, 'Inostrannye vystavki v SSSR,' 85–108; in M. V. Nesterov, eds., *Uchastie sovetskogo soiuza v mezhdunarodnykh iarmarkakh i vystavkakh* (Moscow, 1957); P. A. Cherviakov, *Vsemirnaia vystavka 1958 goda v Briussele* (Moscow: 'Znanie', 1958); I. G. Bol'shakov, *Na vsekh kontinentakh mira* (Moscow, 1963); I. G. Bol'shakov, *Pered litsom vsego mira* (Moscow, 1960). On Soviet contributions to major exhibits in the 1930s, see 1937, 'Predlozheniia,' f. 5673, op. 1, d. 8; Anthony Swift, 'The Soviet World of Tomorrow at the New York World's Fair, 1939,' *The Russian Review* 57 (1998): 364–79, Gosudarstvennyi arkhiv rossiiskoi federatsii (State Archive of the Russian Federation) (GARF), Moscow.

[4]1959, A. Shel'nov, et al., 306, op. 1, d. 389, l. 1-3, Rossiiskii gosudarstvennyi arkhiv ekonomiki (Russian State Archive of the Economy) (RGAE), Moscow; Stuart W. Little, 'Festival of Soviet Music and Dance Here in July,' *New York Herald Tribune* (1 May 1959), Records Relating to the American National Exhibition, Moscow, 1957-1959, 306/88/12/Box 3, Folders: Cultural, National Archives and Records Administration, Record Group (NARA RG), College Park, Maryland; David Caute, *The Dancer Defects: The Struggle for Cultural Hegemony During the Cold War* (Oxford: Oxford University Press, 2003), 481–2.

[5]29 July 1959, 'Priem,' G. Pushkin, f. 0100, op. 46, p. 187, d. 6, l. 4, Arkhiv vneshnei politiki rossiiskoi federadtsii (Archive of Foreign Policy of the Russian Federation) (AVPRF), Moscow.

to deflect attention from what was happening at Sokolniki. '[W]hen you compare the past to the present, the progress is very rapid,' offered officials from the Chinese Ministry of Foreign Affairs. 'The Chinese exhibit is much more beautiful than the American one,' supposedly concluded 'several Americans'.[6] Also to temper the American display, the Chinese reminded the Soviets of America's interethnic troubles. The photographs displayed at Sokolniki, they suggested, only confirmed that 'the life of white people [in America] is excellent.' American references to Asia and Africa depicted labouring peasants in a way that was 'insulting to our country'.[7]

Sino-Soviet relations were tense from 1958 and the beginning of China's radical developmental path in the form of the Great Leap Forward, which was accompanied by critiques of expertise, the visiting bloc advisers, and the Soviet model generally. Within a year of the exhibit at Sokolniki most of the socialist bloc advisers had left China; in less than a decade the Chinese were identifying 'Soviet revisionism' as a threat equal in danger to 'American imperialism'. High-level political disputes between the two states about the leadership of the socialist world, policy toward America, the socialist developmental model, and related topics clearly were central to the Sino-Soviet split, as Lorenz Lüthi, Sergei Radchenko, and others have described.[8] This was one of the more significant geopolitical realignments of the entire Cold War, with the Global South now courted by a new patron and model in the form of radical Chinese communism.[9] The polemical exchanges between the CPSU and CCP and the relationship between Khrushchev and Chairman Mao attract significant attention from scholars for good reason.

Attention to broader forms of cultural miscommunication and conflict, however, evident here in tensions over the exhibit exchanges and drawn from the reports of advisers, the exhibit 'comment books', and other sources, offers a different lens on Sino-Soviet tension and the complexities of international relations generally.[10] This article

---

[6]24 October 1959, 'Woguo shinian lai jianshe chengjiu ji tupian zai mosike zhanchu de qingkuang,' 109-01919-05, 83, Waijiaobu danganguan (Ministry of Foreign Affairs Archive) (WJBDAG), Beijing.

[7]30 July 1959, 'Baogao meiguo zai mo juben zhanlanhui qingkuang,' 109-00876-03, 7, WJBDAG.

[8]Lorenz Lüthi, *The Sino-Soviet Split, 1956–1966* (Princeton, NJ: Princeton University Press, 2008); Sergei Radchenko, *Two Suns in the Heavens: The Sino-Soviet Struggle for Supremacy, 1962–1967* (Stanford: Stanford University Press, 2009); Odd Arne Westad, ed., *Brothers in Arms: The Rise and Fall of the Sino-Soviet Alliance, 1945–1963* (Washington, DC and Stanford: Woodrow Wilson Centre Press and Stanford University Press, 1998); Chen Jian, *Mao's China and the Cold War* (Chapel Hill: University of North Carolina Press, 2001).

[9]On the global Sino-Soviet rivalry, see Jeremy Friedman, *Shadow Cold War: The Sino-Soviet Competition for the Third World* (Chapel Hill: University of North Carolina Press, 2015).

[10]For studies of Sino-Soviet cultural exchange, see Nicolai Volland, 'Translating the Soviet State: Cultural Exchange, National Identity, and the Socialist World in the Early PRC,' *Twentieth-Century China* 33, no. 2 (2007): 51–72; Nicolai Volland, 'Soviet Spaceships in Socialist China: Reading Soviet Popular Literature in the 1950s,' *Modern China Studies* 22, no. 1 (2015): 191–214; Tina Mai Chen, 'Internationalism and Cultural Experience: Soviet Films and Popular Chinese Understandings of the Future in the 1950s,' *Cultural Critique* 58 (2004): 82–114. For an innovative approach to Russian-Chinese relations before 1949, see Elizabeth McGuire, *Red at Heart: How Chinese Communists Fell in Love with the Russian Revolution* (Oxford: Oxford University Press, 2017). On socialist bloc advisers and the Sino-Soviet relationship, see Shen Zhihua, *Sulian zhuanjia zai zhongguo (1948–1960)* (Beijing: Zhongguo guoji guangbo chubanshe, 2003); Austin Jersild, *The Sino-Soviet Alliance: An International History* (Chapel Hill: University of North Carolina Press, 2014). On Soviet advisers in India, see David C. Engerman, 'Learning from the East: Soviet Experts and India in the Era of Competitive Coexistence,' *Comparative Studies of South Asia, Africa and the Middle East* 33, no. 2 (2013): 227–38. On GDR advisers in the Global South, see Ulrich van der Heyden, 'FDJ-Brigaden der Freundschaft aus der DDR— die *Peace Corps* des Ostens?' and Berthold Unfried, 'Instrumente und Praktiken von "Solidarität" Ost und "Entwicklungshilfe" West: Blickpunkt auf das entsandte Personal,' in Berthold Unfried and Eva Himmelstoss, eds., *Die eine Welt schaffen: Praktiken von Internationalen Solidarität und Internationalen Entwicklung* (Vienna: Akademische Verlagsanstalt, 2012), 99–122, 73–98; Berthold Unfried, 'Friendship and Education, Coffee and Weapons: Exchanges between Socialist Ethiopia and the German Democratic Republic,' *Northeast African Studies* 16, no. 1 (2016); Young-Sun Hong, 'Through a Glass Darkly: East German Assistance to North Korea and Alternative Narratives of the Cold War,' in Quinn Slobodian, ed., *Comrades of Colour: East Germany in the Cold War World* (New York: Berghahn, 2015), 43–72.

explores socialist bloc exhibits –within the bloc about China, international displays, and Soviet exhibits in the major cities of China – in order to illustrate these emerging tensions in Sino-Soviet relations. The history of the production of the exhibits and their reception in China reveals Chinese frustrations with the attitudes and practices of the socialist bloc, as well as an inability on the part of East Europeans and Soviets even to recognise or understand this Chinese response. These tensions were evident well before the public disputes of 1958–60, and plagued the 'Great Friendship' from the very proclamation of the alliance in February 1950.

Socialist bloc exhibits

Socialist bloc exhibits were similar to the American National Exhibition at Sokolniki and other international exhibits in terms of propaganda and the display of new achievements and a superior 'way of life'. They also had a distinctive history, however, that emerged from their function within a world shaped by economic practices unique to socialism. Socialist bloc exhibits had a practicality and workmanlike purpose directly related to the emerging world of postwar bloc collaboration. Their primary purpose was to extend, deepen, and facilitate 'socialist' forms of exchange, and they thus included the arrangement of trade agreements and contracts between ministries, factories, universities, work units, and so on. The exhibits intersected with distinctly socialist norms concerning planning, the division of labour, resource allocation, and related matters. Administrators, managers, and experts and specialists in a wide variety of fields accompanied the exhibits, expecting to foster productive relationships with their counterparts in the other socialist bloc countries. Accompanying advisers journeyed beyond the exhibit hall, to lecture, advise, learn, and trade in industrial, agricultural, and educational settings. The exhibit was in part an example of 'socialism' in practice, and therefore different from the way the United States Information Agency encouraged American companies to display their many products, or rounded up young Russian-speaking Americans to serve as 'guides' and converse with the Soviet public.[11]

Very practical socialist exhibits in Sofia, Prague, Budapest, Leipzig, and other places might typically include attention to such mundane matters as heavy industrial equipment, milk separators, and grain threshers.[12] The very manner of preparing, constructing, and displaying the exhibits followed the format of socialist bloc exchange and cooperation.[13] Exhibit officials procured numerous items and goods through the various Soviet industrial ministries for display throughout the bloc. Factory directors in the Soviet interior provinces, for example, were expected to respond to a ministerial demand for equipment and goods for an exhibit in Eastern or Central Europe in the same way they might fulfil an 'order' for any other economic exchange, either within the Soviet Union or the larger bloc.[14] Exhibits were opportunities for Soviet technicians, engineers, and officials to arrange direct economic relationships, and also to inform socialist bloc colleagues of Soviet practices and manners of handling economic exchange. They also became an opportunity for Soviet industrial and technical experts to acquire more advanced forms of knowledge and technology in places like East Germany,

---

[11] 14 August 1959, Report on Training Programme for Guides, Paul R. Conroy, 306, 1957-59, 306/88/12/Box 7, Folder: Reports, NARA RG: Records Relating to the American National Exhibition, Moscow.

[12] 1948, 'List;' 1951, 'List,' f. 8123, op. 3, d. 1110, 1. 5, RGAE.

[13] 28 April 1950, P. Stepanov, f. 8123, op. 3, d. 1110, l. 56, RGAE.

[14] 16 October 1951, P. Bulgakov, f. 8123, op. 3 d. 1124, l. 14, RGAE.

Czechoslovakia, Poland, and Hungary. The relationship with China established in February 1950 was viewed with excitement by exhibit organisers, who took it as an opportunity to foster and deepen bloc collaboration with the important new member of an alliance that stretched from Europe to Asia.

In matters of cultural promotion and display the exhibits possessed a flavour characteristic of the Soviet and socialist world. This was a world of traditional cultural hierarchy in which the West (Eastern Europe, Moscow, St Petersburg) was viewed as more advanced than the East (the Far East, the Caucasus, Central Asia, North Korea, North Vietnam, China), and part of the purpose of Soviet cultural projects as well as intrabloc cultural projects was for the West to uplift and help the East. The vision made sense of Russia's historical experience and its vast multi-ethnic space, and served to congratulate Russians in the present, who were the 'leading people' of the Soviet Union and pleased to provide access to all of this to the presumably less developed peoples of the socialist world.[15] A key term, especially in the eastern areas of the Soviet Union, was *kul'turnost'*, a notion suggesting the process of acquiring culture, something particularly important to lesser educated people distant from the West.[16] East Europeans in particular had an important role to play. As the Sino-Soviet relationship deteriorated in 1959–60, alarmed Soviet and East European embassy officials remained determined to expedite visits from institutions sure to represent the best of European high culture, such as the Dresden Philharmonic Orchestra and the Prague Philharmonic Orchestra.[17] East Germans, Czechoslovaks, Poles, and others were proud to offer their contribution to the uplifting of culture in once backward China, eager to help the Soviets accomplish some of the same forms of cultural uplift in China that they believed had already been accomplished in the far corners of the Soviet Union.[18] The notion of *kul'turnost'* even pertained to daily life, where officials emphasised notions of a proper 'cultured consumerism', again a contrast to what was routinely depicted as the excessive materialism of the Americans.[19] All of these notions were on display in exhibits about China and in Soviet exhibits in China during the 1950s.

Exhibiting China within the socialist world

The revival of tradition, minus its exploitive and negative characteristics, was part of the socialist vision throughout Eastern Europe and the Soviet Union. Numerous exhibits

---

[15]Terry Martin, *The Affirmative Action Empire: Nations and Nationalism in the Soviet Union, 1923–1939* (Ithaca: Cornell University Press, 2001), 430. On the 'developmental hierarchies' of the socialist world, see Gyÿorgy Péteri, 'The Oblique Coordinate Systems of Modern Identity,' in Gyÿorgy Péteri, ed., *Imagining the West in Eastern Europe and the Soviet Union* (Pittsburgh: University of Pittsburgh Press, 2010), 1–12.

[16]Vadim Vokov, 'The Concept of *kul'turnost'*: Notes on the Stalinist Civilising Process,' in Sheila Fitzpatrick, ed., *Stalinism: New Directions* (New York: Routledge, 2000), 210–30; Catriona Kelly, *Refining Russia: Advice Literature, Polite Culture, and Gender from Catherine to Yeltsin* (Oxford: Oxford University Press, 2001), 230–393. For a Soviet explanation, see T. Kudrina, 'K voprosu o kul'turno-vospitatel'noi funktsii sovetskogo gosudarstva v usloviiakh razvitogo sotsializma,' in T. A. Kudrina, ed., *Aktual'nye voprosy kul'turnogo stroitel'stva v period razvitogo sotsializma* (Moscow: Ministerstvo kul'tury RSFSR, 1977), 6–22.

[17]10 December 1959, 'Zpráva o zájezdu české filharmonie,' 073159, 1955-1959, ČLR, krabice 2, obal 4; 'Dogovor druzhby i bratstva,' *Novoe vremia* 7 (12 February 1960), Archiv Ministerstva zahraničních vící České republiky (Archive of the Ministry of Foreign Affairs) (MZVTO-T).

[18]'Ist die Sowjetunion eine Kolonialmacht? Die Entwicklung der zentralasiatischen Sowjetrepubliken auf dem Gebiete des Gesundheits—und Bildungswesens,' *Deutsche Aussenpolitik*, 4 (April 1958), 416–22.

[19]Lewis H. Siegelbaum, 'Introduction,' in Siegelbaum, ed., *The Socialist Car: Automobility in the Eastern Bloc* (Ithaca: Cornell University Press, 2011), 3; Sheila Fitzpatrick, *Everyday Stalinism: Ordinary Life in Extraordinary Times: Soviet Russia in the 1930s* (Oxford: Oxford University Press, 1999), 79–83.

throughout the bloc celebrated the artistic and cultural traditions of the Chinese past, now informed with a new content and vision. The classical heritage of Chinese culture, historically assaulted by the imperialists, as commentator A. Vinogradov argued, would now be rescued by the socialist world and simultaneously infused with a 'different content'.[20] Exhibit organisers often pushed their Chinese colleagues to send more examples of tradition eagerly appreciated by their respective publics, from East Germans interested in traditional Chinese woodcuts to Muscovites interested in embroidery from Suzhou and silk-making in Hangzhou.[21] Soviet artists, painters, and sculptors travelled to China in order to create works inspired by examples of what they took to be traditional Chinese culture (rickshaws, peasants carrying water, old winding streets in Shanghai and Guangzhou, tiled roofs in Suzhou, the lakes in Hangzhou, historic architecture), which they then displayed in exhibits sponsored by the Union of Artists in Moscow.[22] Similar to the Soviet visualisation of small and Eastern peoples on its frontier, it was socialism that promised the resurrection and restoration of a historic culture long suffering exploitation in the more recent past.[23]

The revival of tradition was complemented by exposure to European high culture, to which the Soviets were proud contributors. It was self-evident to publics and exhibit organisers throughout the bloc that the Chinese were now fortunate to have better access to the great works of Russian literature or performances of the Warsaw Philharmonic. Cultural exchange with China flourished throughout the 1950s. The 'Great Friendship' was an opportunity for China to enjoy the benefit of cultural exchange and cultural tutelage from Russians, Czechoslovaks, Germans, Poles, and others, who routinely sent their cultural delegations, exhibits, instructors, and teachers to work in Chinese institutions, participate in exchanges, and collaborate on numerous cultural projects from film festivals to orchestra performances. The Czechoslovaks, for example, enthusiastically shipped their best examples of the European classical tradition to China, and Prague in turn played host to Chinese renditions of traditional folk music, opera, and dance. To celebrate the tenth anniversary of the Chinese revolution in Prague, the Czechs hosted an arts festival dedicated to traditional Chinese landscape painting, regional variations of Chinese opera, Chinese porcelain and ceramics, and examples of contemporary Chinese literature and film. The Czech Philharmonic played Dvořak, Smetana, Borodin and other classical works, followed by Chinese folk music.[24] The Soviet Ministry of Culture routinely chose highly trained and accomplished classical musicians for the exchanges in China. Soviets contributed to traditions

---

[20]A. Vinogradov, *V strane velikoi iantszy: Ocherki* (Kurgan: Izdatel'stvo gazety 'Sovetskoe zaural'e,' 1959), 7.

[21]Joachim Krüger, 'Das China-Bild in der DDR der 50er Jahre,' *Bochumer Jahrbuch zür Ostasienforschung* 25 (2001), 266; 18 November 1961, 'Informatsiia,' F. Konstantinov, f. 9518, op. 1, d. 133, l. 218-19, GARF; Karl Heinz Hagen, 'Die Kulturellen Beziehungen der DDR zu den Ländern des sozialistischen Lagers,' *Deutsche Aussenpolitik* 11 (1957), 955; Aleksandr N. Tikhomirov, *Iskusstvo sotisalisticheskikh stran* (Moscow: 'Znanie', 1959); S.V. Gerasimov, 'Iskusstvo stran sotsializma,' *Tvorchestvo* 12 (1958): 1–2; 1953, 'Al'bom vystavki,' f. 635, op. 1, d. 272, l. 17-27, RGAE; 13 August 1957, Ge Baoquan to N.G. Erofeev, f. 5283, op. 18, d. 207, l. 36, GARF.

[22]V. V. Bogatkin, et al., *Sto dnei v Kitae (dekabr' 1956-fevral' 1957): Katalog* (Moscow: Soiuz khudozhnikov SSSR, 1957), 9–10, 17–26.

[23]The rescue of a once glorious antiquity from more recent forms of cultural decline is a trope long explored by scholars of 'Orientalism'. See Edward Said, *Orientalism* (New York: Vintage, 1978), 92; John M. MacKenzie, *Orientalism: History, Theory and the Arts* (Manchester: Manchester University Press, 1995), 58–67.

[24]17 December 1959, 'O účasti čínských umělců a vědců na oslavách 10. Výročí ČLR,' Jaromír Štětina, 033.857/59, 1955-1959, ČLR, krabice 8, obal 1, MZVTO-T; 25 September 1959, 'Záznam pro I náměstka s. Dr. Gregora,' 028.351/59, 1955-1959, ČLR, krabice 1, obal 1, MZVTO-T.

established by famous pre-revolutionary musicians, giving the Chinese an introduction to the best 'Russian classical and Soviet composers'.[25] The East Germans as well were intensely interested in China and eager promoters of exchange, and also engaged in their own effort to 'harmonise transformation and tradition', or to explore and develop 'heimat culture' while constructing socialism, as Jan Palmowski explains.[26] The alternative version of modernity offered by the bloc respected and maintained indigenous Chinese cultural tradition, but was accompanied by hierarchical ideas about Europe and Asia. The many advisers and cultural figures who travelled to China generally assumed the Chinese should be grateful to be exposed to the world of socialism and its culture, and believed they had more to teach than to learn. Socialist publics throughout the bloc felt the same way.

The exhibits in China

These assumptions about China were similarly evident in the huge exhibits that took place in Beijing, Shanghai, and Guangzhou. The East and Central Europeans were very much part of these events, which were extensive forms of exchange far beyond the exhibits that sent advisers, technicians, instructors, administrators, and others to local enterprises, factories, universities, and related locations.[27] The exhibits also included 'continually functioning circles' of advisers and interpreters who branched out to local factories and enterprises well beyond these three major cities, to Xian, Wuhan, Nanjing, Hangzhou, and other cities.[28] A big and grandiose display in China was symbolic of China's importance to the bloc, and high officials in both countries devoted significant attention to the huge production that opened in Beijing on 2 October 1954 (a day after the five-year anniversary of the Chinese revolution) and moved to Shanghai and Guangzhou the following year. Top officials such as politburo member Anastas Mikoyan were heavily involved in the planning process, and Soviet Ambassador Pavel Iudin followed matters relating to the exhibit very closely, attending both the opening and closing ceremonies in each of the three major locations.[29] Chairman Mao noted the significance of the exhibit in an address to the Central Committee on 27 August 1954, in which he thanked the Soviets for their support and 'brotherly aid'. 'The showing of the Soviet exhibit will serve as a great inspiration for the Chinese people, having now accomplished socialist construction and socialist transformation,' he intoned.[30] Zhou Enlai and other leading Chinese officials attended the opening ceremony in the nation's capital. Nikita Khrushchev was there as well, having been invited by Zhou Enlai the previous January to China's capital for the anniversary celebrations and the opening of the exhibit.[31] Chairman Mao paid a personal visit to the exhibit on 25 October 1954.

---

[25]31 December 1954, 'Perepiska s deiateliami kul'tury i iskusstva Kitaia,' B. Belyi, f. 2077, op. 1, d. 1121, l. 13, Rossiiskii gosudarstvennyi arkhiv literatury i iskusstvo (Russian State Archive of Literature and Culture) (RGALI); 6 December 1957, 'Zasedaniia biuro inostrannoi komissii soiuza kompozitorov SSSR,' f. 2077, op. 1, d. 1432, l. 3 RGALI.

[26]Jan Palmowski, *Inventing a Socialist Nation: Heimat and the Politics of Everyday Life in the GDR 1945–1990* (Cambridge: Cambridge University Press, 2009), 60.

[27]28 August 1954, 'Kratkaia kharakteristika sovetskoi vystavki v Pekine,' I. Bol'shakov, r. 5113, f. 5, op. 28, d. 187, l. 174, Rossiiskii gosudarstvennyi arkhiv noveishii istorii (Russian State Archive of Contemporary History) (RGANI).

[28]1955, 'Otchet,' K. Smol'ianov, f. 635, op. 1, d. 299, l. 129-30, 142, 158, RGAE.

[29]1955, 'Otchet,' K. Smol'ianov, f. 635, op. 1, d. 299, l. 152, RGAE.

[30]27 August 1954, Chairman Mao to CC, f. 5, op. 30, d. 76, l. 32, RGANI.

[31]Vladislav Zubok and Constantine Pleshakov, *Inside the Kremlin's Cold War: From Stalin to Khrushchev* (Cambridge, MA: Harvard University Press, 1996), 170.

The enormous Exhibition Centre in Beijing attempted to illustrate the strength, stability, and significance of the Sino-Soviet relationship. The building in Beijing was divided into three sections, devoted to industry, agriculture, and culture, with some 11,500 items on display in 27 different halls ranging some 33,000 square metres. There was a theatre for 3200 people. The 'Moscow Restaurant' that was part of the exhibit was especially ornate in Beijing, with a high dome, crystal chandeliers, handsome wood floors, tall windows, and gigantic pillars.[32] The Shanghai exhibit drew 3,828,608 people, including a 'Friendship' film theatre that featured 288 events for 242,818 visitors.[33] After Guangzhou a smaller version of the exhibit went to Wuhan, which included forms of outreach to other more provincial locations, and its composition was changed somewhat to focus more on agriculture. The size and scope of the Soviet exhibit in Beijing (313,000 square metres) was well known to Soviet exhibit organisers throughout the globe.[34] The exhibit director for a 1955 display in Argentina, for example, was proud to report that his pavilion was second only to the massive effort in China.[35] China was the new jewel of the socialist bloc, and Soviet and East European organisers went to great lengths to make sure visitors understood this.

The socialist bloc exhibits in China also had to address the question of America and the general affluence and technological sophistication of the West. Many educated Chinese in the 1950s possessed memories of European and American technology and forms of expertise from the pre-revolutionary era. One of the primary pedagogic purposes of the exhibit was to reeducate Chinese who might possess different conceptions of the merits of the Soviet experience in comparison to the West. 'Before I thought poorly about the Soviet Union,' wrote Wu Kezong in the comment book,

> I considered Soviet goods to be poorly made. I thought the Soviet Union was boasting. Today I see with my own eyes that all the exhibits of the great Soviet Union are wonderful and beautiful. I am convinced that the Soviet Union is not as they say.

Ma Junliang offered similarly comforting comments about the 'valuable' and 'leading' economic experience of the Soviet Union.[36] As 'Worker Guo' in Guangzhou put it: 'Before I saw this exhibit, I greatly admired America and the western countries.' But now he knew that the Soviet Union had 'overtaken in many respects' the world of the West. Numerous Chinese cultural and other officials offered similar testimonies.[37] Some came from overseas Chinese (*huaqiao*), who returned to declare their respect for post-revolutionary accomplishments, or confirm, as Li Wang from Hong Kong said, that 'Soviet cars in fact were better than English and American [cars].'[38] The question of the efficiency and viability of the socialist world was especially sensitive after 1956, when even Communist Party members and officials complained about Soviet 'great-power chauvinism', the weaknesses of the economy,

---

[32]Yan Li, 'Building Friendship: Soviet Influence, Socialist Modernity, and Chinese Cityscape in the 1950s,' *Quarterly Journal of Chinese Studies* 2, no. 3 (2014): 48–66.

[33]1955, 'Otchet,' K. Smol'ianov, f. 635, op. 1, d. 299, l. 121-3, 158, RGAE.

[34]July 1954, I. Bol'shakov, f. 5, op. 28, d. 186, l. 174, RGANI.

[35]September 1955, 'Otchet,' G. Virob'ian, f. 635, op. 1, d. 299, l. 1, RGAE.

[36]1955, 'Otchet,' K. Smol'ianov, f. 635, op. 1, d. 299, l. 153, RGAE.

[37]4 January 1956, 'Otchet,' K. Smol'ianov, f. 635, op. 1, d. 300, l. 99-105, RGAE; 9 March 1955, 21–22 March 1955, 25 March 1955, 'Perevod otzyvov,' f. 635, op. 2, d. 283, l. 9, 139, 135, RGAE.

[38]4 January 1956, 'Otchet,' K. Smol'ianov, f. 635, op. 1, d. 300, l. 103, RGAE.

the character of the Soviet advising programmes, and the quality of Soviet science and technology.[39]

Culture, however, was an area where socialist bloc theorists were confident about their ability to compete with the Americans. The exhibits in China devoted a huge section to 'Culture' (4250 square metres), where the East Europeans and Soviets communicated their notion of culture as *kul'turnost'*, the virtues of European high culture, and the role of socialism in facilitating the cultivation of tradition. The collection of musical instruments included five concert pianos and five upright pianos.[40] A fine-arts display featured examples of Soviet portrait painting, landscapes, and sculpture. Charts with ascending figures compared book publication numbers of the works of Pushkin, Lermontov, Gogol, Tolstoy, and Chekhov from 1888–1917 with those of 1918–53.[41] There were displays on radios and classical music, institutions of higher education such as Moscow State University, and photographs and information pertaining to the experience of Chinese studying in the Soviet Union, as if to remind the Chinese that the fruits of high culture were now available to them by virtue of their incorporation into the bloc. Some 4000 people attended a discussion about schooling in the Soviet Union.[42] There were numerous cultural events in the Chinese capital that accompanied the exhibit, such as 50 different performances of classical operas and ballets in the autumn of 1954 by the K.S. Stanislavskii State Musical Theatre, as well as attention to traditional Chinese culture.[43] Academics gave lectures on Soviet cultural theory, sculpture, opera, music, and historic Russian painters such as I. E. Repin, V. I. Surikov, and V. V. Vereshchagin.[44]

The sections on culture attempted to show that the world of traditional high culture was accessible to the larger population, and easily integrated into the daily lives of average Soviet citizens. At the Beijing exhibit the area devoted to the 'culture of everyday life' featured musical instruments, televisions and radios, household appliances, furniture, carpets, crystal, porcelain, glass, and Palekh lacquerware. Photomontages and displays explored Soviet classical orchestras, soloists, opera, and ballet. Everyday Soviet life was presumably a world informed and shaped by the sublime elements of classical music and high culture. Classical instruments and music, including a grand piano, were part of the 'Hall of Musical Instruments, Radio, Furniture, and Objects of Daily Life' in Shanghai. Traditional crafts and artisanal work also endured in Soviet life, organisers emphasised, in spite of the transformations of industrial modernity. Qing Yuanxian was exposed to Russian porcelain and lacquer products, and learned that we Chinese must 'develop the production of porcelain and lacquer and preserve our glorious traditions, and compete with you in a friendly fashion'.[45] As a gift in Beijing, the Soviets presented to the Chinese an enormous Palekh lacquer box, an example of the 'folk culture of Ancient Rus', supported by four polished porphyry legs

---

[39]16 July 1956, 'Muqian sulian baozhi xuanchuan zhongde yizhong zhongyao renwu,' 109-01617-16, 119, WJBDAG; 8 December 1956, 'Dui bolan shijian de chubu guji,' 109-00762-01, 6, WJBDAG; Shen Zhihua, *Sulian zhuanjia zai zhongguo (1948–1960)*, 253–60, 291, 340, 367; Jersild, *The Sino-Soviet Alliance*, 109–31.

[40]26 August 1954, P. Kriukov, f. 5, op. 30, d. 72, l. 80, RGANI.

[41]7 September 1954, 'Tematicheskii plan,' I. Shiriaev, f. 5, r. 5113, op. 28, d. 187, l. 195, RGANI.

[42]1955, 'Otchet,' K. Smol'ianov, f. 635, op. 1, d. 299, l. 140-, RGAE.

[43]1954, 'Otchet,' f. 635, op. 1, d. 278, l. 98-103, RGAE.

[44]1955, 'Otchet,' K. Smol'ianov, f. 635, op. 1, d. 299, l. 145, RGAE.

[45]1955, 'Otchet,' K. Smol'ianov, f. 635, op. 1, d. 299, l. 148, RGAE.

and adorned with gold leaf. The five-pointed star made of ears of rice and wheat was fastened to a backdrop of ruby red glass with Russian precious stones, and located above an image of the Tiananmen Gate.[46] Revolution was compatible with national tradition, and the Soviets encouraged the Chinese to think about the matter in the same way.

The section on culture and everyday life that pertained to living conditions (*byt*) was restrained and proper, illustrating the way *kul'turnost'* supposedly informed everyday life in the socialist world. One display was devoted to Soviet furniture, complemented by an example of Soviet dining rooms, living rooms, and bedrooms. A quiet reading room was presented as an example of a 'study of a professor or scientific worker'. A display highlighted a speech of Nikolai Bulganin, who was proud of the new '183 million square metres of living space' constructed for urban workers since the war.[47] The party and ruling elite in the socialist bloc projected a vision of a refined and cultured everyday life that contrasted significantly with the practicality, materialism, and fun that would be suggested by the American exhibit at Sokolniki Park in Moscow in 1959.

East Europeans contributed to the exhibits as advisers and lecturers, and East European achievements in culture, technology, and also consumer culture were proudly promoted by the Soviets. The Soviet Exhibition Centre in Beijing featured a second exhibit in April 1955, devoted to Czechoslovakia, but also other Central European countries such as Hungary, Poland, and East Germany as examples of consumer achievements under socialism was becoming a familiar part of socialist bloc self-presentation.[48] Czechoslovaks were especially useful in this endeavour, with previous experience exhibiting the virtues of their country in Marseilles, Utrecht, Helsinki, Kodani, Milan, and Toronto.[49] The best known international example of this would be the Czechoslovak Pavilion at the Brussels World Fair in 1958, with impressive displays of industrial technology, classical music, and also consumer products from clothing to Pilsner Urquell beer to Škoda motor scooters.[50] The explicit promotion of consumer culture, however, worried some Communist Party critics more inclined to traditional orthodoxy, and the Chinese were soon to voice similar frustrations.[51]

---

[46]3 March 1954, N. Chesnokov, f. 5, op. 30, d. 72, ll. 69-72, RGANI.

[47]7 September 1954, 'Tematicheskii plan,' I. Shiriaev, f. 5, r. 5113, op. 28, d. 187, l. 191, RGANI.

[48]Rachel Applebaum, 'The Friendship Project: Socialist Internationalism in the Soviet Union and Czechoslovakia in the 1950s and 1960s,' *Slavic Review* 74, no. 3 (2015): 500–6; Jiří Pernes, *Krize komunistického režimu v Československu v 50. Letech 20. století* (Brno: Centrum pro stadium demokracie a kultury, 2008), 36–44; Giustino, 'Industrial Design and the Czechoslovak Pavilion at EXPO '58,' 200.

[49]7 March 1955, J. Veselý, 11.43.5/55; 21 February 1955, Ludmila Jankovcová, 11.43.7/55; 13 June 1955, Ludmila Jankovcová, 11.43.8/55; 7 May 1955, Ludmila Jankovcová, 11.43.15/55, krabice 2373, folder 12/1.37.3/59 (Svetová výstava v Bruselu), Národní archiv (National Archive) (NA) Uřad předsednictva vlády (Office of the Chairman of the Government)

[50]On Soviet and East European exhibits at Brussels, see Lewis Siegelbaum, 'Sputnik Goes to Brussels: The Exhibition of a Soviet Technological Wonder,' *Journal of Contemporary History*, 47, no. 1 (2012): 120–36; György Péteri, 'Transsystemic Fantasies: Counterrevolutionary Hungary at Brussels Expo '58,' *Journal of Contemporary History* 47, no. 1 (2012): 137–60; Cathleen M. Giustino, 'Industrial Design and the Czechoslovak Pavilion at EXPO '58: Artistic Autonomy, Party Control and Cold War Common Ground,' *Journal of Contemporary History* 47, no. 1 (2012): 185–212. For a series of primary source collections on the Czechoslovak exhibit in Brussels prepared by the National Archive in Prague, see *Expo '58: Československá restaurace: Příběh československé účasti na Světové výstavě v Bruselu* (Prague: Národní archiv, 2008); *Expo 58: Zápisy z porad: Příběh československé účasti na Světové výstavě v Bruselu* (Prague: Národní archiv, 2008); *Expo 58: Scénář: Příběh československé účasti na Světové výstavě v Bruselu* (Prague: Národní archiv, 2008); *Expo '58: Přísně tajné: Příběh československé účasti na Světové výstavě v Bruselu* (Prague: Národní archiv, 2008).

[51]'Informační zpráva,' Köhler and Hendrych, *Expo 58: Scénář*, 9–11.

China's response and alternative path

Virtually every aspect of the alternative path of development (the Great Leap Forward of 1958–60) that reshaped China was a critique in some way of the socialist bloc and its assumptions and practices. The reaction covered agricultural development, the reliance on expertise, the acceptability of social hierarchy and wage differentiation, the role of planning, and other topics.[52] The Chinese were increasingly convinced that socialist bloc assumptions and the Soviet model were being inappropriately imposed upon a very different and unique society.

The Sino-Soviet relationship deteriorated quickly after 1958, but many of these Chinese concerns and frustrations were evident throughout the 1950s. The exhibits in China illustrated some of these tensions, and served as yet another example of the weaknesses of the broader Soviet Union and of socialism in practice. Numerous technological devices failed to work, the radios in several Soviet automobiles did not function, televisions arrived with broken screens, tennis rackets arrived with broken strings, one-half of the sports jerseys had been eaten by moths, dishes and crystal were broken, and so on. Such problems were a product of an economic system where suppliers did not face the anger of the frustrated consumer if merchandise were delivered in that fashion. Chinese officials and visitors to the exhibit did not frame the problem in this way, but they did complain quite a bit. Similar to every other aspect of the socialist economy, Soviet industrial ministries fulfilled 'orders' from the exhibit organisers and did not worry about the quality of the final product. The exhibit staff in China could only routinely lament the problem of 'careless packing'.[53] The Chinese even complained about the food, the 'inconsiderate' staff, and the disorganisation of the 'Moscow Restaurant'. The restaurant hardly served as an advertisement for socialism. 'It's good that at that time there were not any foreign guests [in the restaurant],' complained a Chinese visitor to the exhibit in Guangzhou, 'as it would have made a very bad impression.'[54] Soviet exhibit inadequacies and inefficiencies came to the attention of politburo member and mayor of Beijing, Peng Zhen, who frequently complained about the matter to Soviet Ambassador Pavel Iudin.[55] Chinese frustration with the mechanics of the exhibit mirrored the general Chinese frustration with their overall encounter with the socialist system.

More significant was a general Chinese frustration with a programme and system that did not seem to understand the Chinese or address their particular needs and concerns. Soviets themselves often seemed ignorant of China, complained contributors to the 'comment books', and unable to offer useful advice.[56] At the exhibits Soviet

---

[52]Dali L. Yang, 'Surviving the Great Leap Famine: The Struggle over Rural Policy, 1958–1962,' in Timothy Cheek and Tony Saich, eds., *New Perspectives on State Socialism in China* (Armonk, New York: M. E. Sharpe, 1997), 262–302; Zhihua Shen and Yafeng Xia, 'The Great Leap Forward, the People's Commune and the Sino-Soviet Split,' *Journal of Contemporary China*, 20 (72) (2011), 861–82; Li Jie, *Mao Zedong yu xin zhongguo de neizheng waijiao* (Beijing: Zhongguo qingnian chubanshe, 2003), 100–5, 148; Frank Dikötter, *Mao's Great Famine: The History of China's Most Devastating Catastrophe, 1958–1962* (New York: Walker, 2010), 13–57.

[53]1954, 'Otchet,' 635, op. 1, d. 278, l. 111, RGAE; 3 September 1955, 'O nekotorykh nedostatkakh v organizatsii kul'turnykh i nauchnykh sviazei,' S. Rumiantsev, f. 5, r. 5136, op. 28, d. 286, l. 183-184, RGANI.

[54]9 October 1955, 'Otzyvy posetitelei,' f. 635, op. 2, d. 247, l. 32, 23, RGAE.

[55]3 March 1954, 'Zapis' besedy,' P.F. Iudin and Peng Zhen, f. 0100, op. 47, p. 379, d. 7, l. 48, AVPRF. For other Chinese complaints, see 9 October 1955, 'Otzyvy posetitelei,' f. 635, op. 2, d. 247, l. 32, 23, RGAE.

[56]3 September 1955, 'O nekotorykh nedostatkakh i organizatsii kul'turnykh i nauchnykh sviazei,' S. Rumiantsev, f. 5, r. 5136, op. 28, d. 286, l. 183, RGANI.

lecturers charged ahead with instructions on the proper organisation and management of numerous areas of experience that seemed foreign to Chinese ways and habits, from food preparation and culinary technology to public hygiene.[57] Zhou Jianglong noted that much of the Soviet agricultural equipment displayed in Guangzhou was of limited use in water-covered rice fields, and Huang Ganghong suggested the displayed agricultural equipment needed to be demonstrated in actual fields in provincial Guangdong. Zhou Wenzuo, Qiu Jianglin, and Cheng Yichen also posed practical questions about irrigation, rice fields, Russian seed varieties, and terrace agriculture on slopes and mountains. A local party official pondered a Soviet combine: 'I thought about how we sow rice here. This combine is very useful for the harvest. But would it be suitable for the way we do our planting?'[58] Li Bohui posed similar questions concerning the suitability of Soviet technology in Chinese factories.[59] The encounter with the exhibit, like the general encounter with the Soviet system, thus encouraged the Chinese to develop their ideas about the applicability of the Soviet model to the 'peculiarities' of the Chinese revolution and its society, as interpreter Li Yueran suggested in his memoirs.[60] And these Chinese frustrations were expressed during the so-called 'honeymoon' of the relationship, well before the more public disputes of 1958–62.

The socialist bloc preoccupation with high culture raised similar questions for the Chinese. Socialist bloc teachers and cultural figures found themselves suspect for their inability to understand the significance of uniquely Chinese cultural traditions. This was a debate between the advisers and the Chinese developing in numerous areas, over the virtues of 'village knowledge' to appropriate topics for filmmakers.[61] The East Europeans in particular seemed prone to what the Chinese would soon denounce as 'revisionism' and an unhealthy interest in Western-style consumerism. In 1957, Chinese officials informed Czechoslovaks and Soviets at the Central Conservatory of Music in Beijing that their course of musical instruction was 'divorced' from both 'national tradition' and 'practice'. The students were better off, they claimed, engaged in manual labour and the instruction of reading to peasants.[62]

The Chinese were correct that 'revolution' was far from the minds of socialist bloc officials and visitors associated with international exhibits. When 'peaceful coexistence' allowed for the display of English cultural exhibits in the Soviet Union, for example, Soviet organisers eagerly sought out the finest examples of English music and painting, sure to be 'well-known and highly-valued by the Russian public'.[63] When they went

---

[57]1954, 'Otchet,' f. 635, op. 1, d. 278, l. 104, RGAE.

[58]9 October 1955, 'Otzyvy posetitelei,' f. 635, op. 2, d. 247, l. 71, 74, 101, 112, 130, RGAE.

[59]9 October 1955, 'Otzyvy posetitelei,' f. 635, op. 2, d. 247, l. 32, RGAE.

[60]Li Yueran, *Zhongsu waijiao qinliji: Shouxi eyu fanyi de lishi jianzheng* (Beijing: Shijie zhishi chubanshe, 2001), 51.

[61]'Gongren jieji shehuizhuyi jiaoyu xuezhe cunke,' *Gongren ribao* (29 January 1958), 3; Quanmin de jieri quanmin de shengli,' *Xinmin ribao* (1 October 1958), 3; 6 November 1959, 'Sulian tongzhi tan woguo dianying yishu de fazhan,' 2 April 1959, 'Wo guo dianying zai sulian shangying de qingkuang,' 109-01919-05, 74-76, 67-69, WJBDAG; 3 July 1958, 'Připomínky čínské strany, k cs. Filmu 'Bratr ocean,'' 018.219/58, MZV, Teritoriální odbory - Tajné 1955-1959,' ČLR, krabice 2, obal 5. On Chinese film in the 1950s, see Tina Mai Chen, 'Internationalism and Cultural Experience;' Paul G. Pickowicz, 'Acting Like Revolutionaries: Shi Hui, the Wenhua Studio, and Private-Sector Filmmaking, 1949–52,' in Jeremy Brown and Paul G. Pickowicz, eds., *Dilemmas of Victory: The Early Years of the People's Republic of China* (Cambridge, MA: Harvard University Press, 2007), 256–87.

[62]14 December 1959, 'O návštěvě ústřední konservatoře hudby v Pekingu,' Jaromír Štětina, 033.355/59, 1955-1959, ČLR, krabice 8, obal 1, MZVTO-T.

[63]1956, 'Iskusstvo Anglii,' f. 652, op. 10, d. 81, l. 32, RGALI.

abroad, Soviet cultural workers assumed high-quality renditions of notable works from the Russian classical tradition would best bring prestige to the Soviet state. Cultural radicals from around the world were routinely disappointed, evident in their many ignored suggestions and even desperate pleas they sent to various cultural ministries in Moscow.[64] This aspect of the Cold War was shaped in part by the character of transnational exchange within the bloc: East Europeans routinely coached the Soviets about the importance of high-quality Soviet performances before audiences both familiar with the best of Western high culture and sceptical of Russia's accomplishments in this and other areas.[65] The East Europeans generally encouraged the Soviets to cultivate more cultural exchange with the West, eager to be allowed more access to the world of the West and also to illustrate their usefulness to the Soviets in the Cold War competition.[66]

Chinese frustration with the cultural assumptions of the visiting Soviets and East Europeans was also evident at the exhibits in China. Chinese visitors such as 'former soldier' Jian Qingyun communicated their enthusiasm for Stalin-era films, and depicted contemporary examples of Soviet film, sculpture, and painting as insufficiently decisive and radical.[67] As the Sino-Soviet relationship deteriorated, the Soviets and East Europeans remained immune to this line of reasoning. Soviet Ambassador Stepan Chervonenko expressly reminded his colleagues in the Soviet Union in late 1961 that the current political climate demanded the arrival in China of only the 'highest quality' Soviet violinists and ballerinas.[68]

Conclusions

During the time of the Sino-Soviet alliance, Soviets and East Europeans shared similar assumptions about the cultural and technological achievements of the socialist world, as well as similar assumptions about the important role they played in promoting progress in China. These views were on display in socialist bloc exhibits, both in domestic East European and Soviet exhibits, and in the large exhibits in China in the 1950s. Many Chinese, however, were not impressed, and drew different conclusions about the character of the bloc and its future direction. The socialist bloc was intersecting with and indeed contributing to an internal debate within China about culture and revolution. In December 1959, Liu Shaoqi could still comfortably applaud and emphasise the virtues of a version of 'Swan Lake' performed at the Bol'shoi Theatre Ballet.[69] Just seven years later, of course, he would be removed from his position and soon after no longer

---

[64] 20 June 1957, Iouko Tolonen to Ministry of Culture; June 1957, Minoru Ochi to Mikhail Chulaki; 29 July 1957, S. Oreshnikov to V. T. Stepanov, f. 648, op. 7, d. 258, l. 26, 19, 50, RGALI.

[65] 23 December 1961, M. Zimianin, f. 9518, op. 1, d. 145, l. 11-12, GARF; 30 September 1961, Aristov to E. A. Furtseva, f. 9518, op. 1, d. 133, l. 179, GARF. On transnational connections within the socialist world, see Patryk Babiracki and Kenyon Zimmer, eds., *Cold War Crossings: International Travel and Exchange across the Soviet Bloc, 1940s–1960s* (College Station: Texas A&M University Press, 2014); Patryk Babiracki and Austin Jersild, eds., *Socialist Internationalism in the Cold War: Exploring the Second World* (London: Palgrave Macmillan, 2016).

[66] 27 March 1962, M. Zimianin to G. A. Zhukov, f. 9518, op. 1, d. 145, l. 65, GARF.

[67] 4 November 1954, 'Otzyvy posetitelei,' f. 635, op. 2, d. 217, l. 155, RGAE.

[68] 23 December 1961, 'Materialy o kul'turnykh sviaziakh OSKD s OKSD,' S. Chervonenko, f. 9576, op. 18, d. 113, l. 212-13, GARF.

[69] 30 January 1960, 'Zapis' besedy,' S. V. Chervonenko, Chen Yi, and Li Fuchun; and 18 January 1960, 'Zapis' besedy,' S. V. Chervonenko and Liu Shaoqi, f. 0100, op. 53, p. 454, d. 8, l. 31, 1, AVPRF.

be alive. Chairman Mao, by contrast, supposedly changed his room at the Kremlin in November 1957 because he was put off by its traditional Russian flavour and decoration.[70] In 1958 the Soviet Exhibition Centre in Beijing was renamed the Beijing Exhibition Centre, and the Moscow Restaurant became the Beijing Exhibition Centre Restaurant.[71]

The exhibits about China in the socialist world and the exhibits in China after 1954 were conceived and formulated in the spirit of the early slogan, 'Learn from the Soviet Union' (*xuexi sulian*). The exhibit organisers, as well as the many Soviet and East European advisers and cultural figures in China, were confident of their purpose and programme, especially in a land they considered part of the historic 'East'. K. Smol'ianov, the Soviet exhibit director in Shanghai, described exhibit outreach activities as 'the primary channel for the transport of the leading technological experience of the Soviet Union to the Chinese People's Republic'.[72] Chinese visitors and collaborators, however, were increasingly sceptical of the applicability of the socialist model and practices in China, believed bloc planners and advisers had failed to appreciate adequately uniquely Chinese sources of strength, and wondered about the global competitiveness of Soviet technology. In matters of culture, as in questions of planning, hierarchy, the use of expertise, and other areas, the socialist world remained traditional and conservative, oblivious to debates about these topics in China. Most frustrating to the Chinese was the Soviet determination to engage with the culture and practices of the West rather than the radical alternatives developing in China. Other developing notions, such as 'socialist consumerism' and 'peaceful coexistence', further left the Chinese frustrated with a socialist world that they concluded had lost its way. After the CCP pursued the radical Great Leap Forward from 1958, common ground between the two sides was increasingly difficult to find. The exhibits did not cause the Sino-Soviet split, but remind us of the difficulties of intrabloc exchange that shaped the socialist world from start to finish.

The Soviets looked West, preoccupied with their competition with the United States rather than the politics of revolutionary culture in China. This in part was how the Soviets viewed the purpose of international exhibits in the Khrushchev era of reform. Foreign exchange and trade, noted Anastas Mikoyan in Leipzig in 1955, was now possible 'irrespective of a country's social system'.[73] On 30 December 1959, Soviet official G. M. Pushkin advised Chinese foreign-affairs officials in Moscow that on the question of standards of living and competing with the West, 'in this regard we can study the experience of the capitalist countries.'[74] That general posture was evident in the displays and activities of the Czechoslovaks, Poles, and Hungarians at the Brussels World's Fair in 1958. For the Chinese, by contrast, the very effort to engage with the West in this way was an example of the 'revisionism' of the socialist world.[75]

---

[70]Quan Yanchi, *Mao Zedong yu Heluxiaofu* (Huhe: Nei menggu renmin chubanshe, 1998), 89–92.
[71]Yan Li, 'Building Friendship,' 63.
[72]1955, 'Otchet,' K. Smol'ianov, f. 635, op. 1, d. 299, l. 158, RGAE.
[73]8 August 1955, 'Otchet,' S. Tochilin, f. 635, op. 1, d. 299, l. 83, RGAE.
[74]30 December 1959, 'Puxijin tan suguo neiwai xingshi,' 109-02064-01, 2, WJBDAG.
[75]8 December 1959, 'Bo bao pingjia aisenhaoweier chuguo fangwen,' 109-01393-03, 55, WJBDAG.

Disclosure statement

No potential conflict of interest was reported by the author.

Sino-Czechoslovak cooperation on agricultural cooperatives: the twinning project

Daniela Kolenovská 🆔

ABSTRACT
The Czechoslovak Communists officially declared the People's Republic of China second most important ally after the Soviet Union in 1949. The onset of collectivisation in both countries opened opportunities for exchange of experience in agriculture. Taking a twinning bilateral project between two agricultural cooperatives as an example, the article analyses various dimensions of Sino-Czechoslovak relations. Based upon Czechoslovak archival documents and an interview with the Czech participant in the twinning, it argues that while top political and economic contacts remained Soviet-supervised, on the personal level positive impression survived the Sino-Soviet split although the Czechoslovak Communists stayed loyal to Moscow.

Introduction

After the communist *coup d'état* in 1948, Czechoslovak foreign policy easily succumbed to the ideological Marxist-Leninist vision of the world divided into two hostile camps and isolated itself in the Soviet-led bloc. Moscow promoted its own agenda in Czechoslovak foreign policy in relation to the rejected West, but also towards the allied countries within the Communist bloc. The position of the Soviet Union was decisive. It dictated the Czechoslovak ranking of individual Soviet allies according to geographical location, strategic importance for the Eastern bloc, and current political situation. Furthermore, the Czechoslovak economy was one of the most developed in the bloc, and as such it was expected to contribute to the progress of all socialist states, as well as of various left-wing radical movements worldwide. Czechoslovakia also provided a cover for Soviet contacts with international revolutionaries where a direct connection to Moscow would weaken the revolutionaries' domestic or international position. Among these supported forces, Czechoslovak communists enlisted their Chinese comrades in early 1949 and a Xinhua News Agency office was opened in Prague to become the first bases of the Chinese communists' voice in Europe. Finally, the relation started to develop at the governmental level after the proclamation of the People's Republic of China (PRC) in October 1949. In line with its communist ideology, Prague focused on the economic problems and offered support for Chinese industrialisation.

Starting from 1950, political and economic cooperation was broadened and both countries attempted to share their experience in reforming society according to the model of the glorified Soviet system of governance. Collectivisation was one of the priorities. To ensure the closest information on the impact of the related changes in the countryside, another Soviet receipt was used: a twinning project between the agricultural cooperatives of Vinařice in Czechoslovakia and Cangzhou in China was established. However, the unique project failed as the international development drew the PRC away from the key Czechoslovak ally – Moscow. After the Sino-Soviet split, both Beijing and Prague adopted a purely pragmatic approach towards their relations. In this context, the Sino-Czechoslovak cooperation on agricultural cooperatives proved no longer necessary. But to what extent did central policies reach down to ordinary people? What was the social dimension of Czechoslovak-Chinese rapprochement?

Until today, there has not been any in-depth research into the relationship of both countries. Czechoslovakia had a traditional, romantic vision of the Orient. In the aftermath of the Second World War, the revolutionary ethos of the heroic struggle of the Chinese people for liberation easily matched the older construct. The most prominent Czechoslovak sinologist, the president of the Czechoslovak-Chinese Society (Společnost československo-čínská, 1945–1951) Jaroslav Průšek, was a convinced communist himself and his works did not contradict the image of China created by the prevailing translated Soviet literature.[1] Czechoslovak citizens, working in China since the interwar expansion of Czechoslovak industrial companies into the Asian markets, could have offered a different view on Chinese events. However, on their return they were systematically ordered to work in professions and regions from which they could not influence current politics.[2] Furthermore, Rudolf Fürst's insight into Czech stereotypes about China revealed that unrealistic perceptions of Chinese politics prevail among Czechs even at the beginning of the twenty-first century.[3] Until now Czech historical research on Czechoslovak-Chinese and Sino-Czechoslovak relations has predominantly concentrated on the period up to 1949;[4] the only two exceptions are Vladimír Nálevka's description of Stalin's, Mao Zedong's, and Gottwald's talks about Korea[5] and Aleš Skřivan's detailed analysis of Czechoslovak exports to China during the twentieth century.[6] Most recently, Lenka Krátká has enriched Skřivan's findings in her monograph on Czechoslovak seafaring and described the default of Sino-Czechoslovak cooperation in it after 1960.[7]

Drawing on materials from newly opened Chinese, Russian, and Eastern European archives, the international scholars described the Soviet-bloc political context of

---

[1] Jaroslav Průšek, *Čínský lid v boji za svobodu* (Prague: Naše vojsko, 1949); Ladislav Šimovič 'Z československo-čínských stykov,' in *Ve veliké čínské zemi. Sborník statí čs. vládní delegace v ČLR r. 1952*, ed. František M. Komzala (Prague: Orbis, 1953), 121–36.

[2] Archive of the Ministry of Foreign Affairs of the Czech Republic (Archiv Ministerstva zahraničních věcí, AMZV ČR), fond Porady kolegia ministra, Book 4, 17 March 1954; Daniela Kolenovská, 'Magdalena, hrdinka čínské revoluce,' *Dějiny a současnost* 37, no. 9 (2015): 30–3.

[3] Rudolf Fürst, 'Politické vnímání Číny v Čechách: mezi věcností a nevěcností, orientalismem a okcidentalismem,' *Mezinárodní vztahy* 40, no. 3 (2005): 24–43.

[4] Ľubica Obuchová, ed., *Po stopách krajanů ve starém Orientu: soubor studií* (Prague: Česká orientalistická společnost, 2009); Ivana Bakešová, *Legionáři v roli diplomatů: československo-čínské vztahy 1918–1949* (Prague: Filozofická fakulta Univerzity Karlovy, 2013).

[5] Vladimír Nálevka, 'Stalin, Mao Ce-tung, Gottwald a začátek války v Koreji,' in *Dvacáté století*, ed. Vladimír Nálevka (Prague: Filozofická fakulta Univerzita Karlova v Praze, 2006), 99–114.

[6] Aleš Skřivan, *Československý vývoz do Číny 1918–1992* (Prague: Scriptorium, 2009).

[7] Lenka Krátká, *A History of the Czechoslovak Ocean Shipping Company, 1948–1989: How a Small, Landlocked Country Ran Maritime Business During the Cold War* (New York: Columbia University Press, 2015).

Czechoslovak contacts with China. They confirmed that the PRC's relationships with Eastern Europe followed the dynamics of Sino-Soviet relations.[8] Whereas this interconnection had devastating consequences on Sino-Czechoslovak cooperation on governmental and ideological levels, the twinning villagers became rare footholds for diplomats dispatched in an otherwise unfriendly environment. This article analyses scarce material from the Czech archives and local press and makes use of an interview with the Czech participant in the twinning on agricultural cooperatives. It shows that – thanks to the versatile nature of the twinning project – on the level of ordinary people good relations continued for years after the Sino-Soviet split and preserved the memory of positive Sino-Czechoslovak contacts. As such, it could be exploited to foster the Czech position in the PRC even in the twenty-first century.

Collectivisation as a means of strengthening fraternal solidarity

The outset of collectivisation in Czechoslovakia and China opened opportunities for deeper involvement of local people in bilateral cooperation. By that time, Prague was already well practised in centralising the 'friendship between peoples of fraternal socialist countries' into uniform pro-Soviet organisations which could be easily managed and controlled from above. These organisations were first to follow prescribed rules which the Czechoslovak Communist Party deduced from the Soviet experience in their discipline. To keep in touch with reality but also demonstrate loyalty and general agreement between the working people, they built twinning partnerships with their Soviet counterparts. The same pattern was used in agricultural contacts with the Chinese.

In May 1952, the journey to Beijing of the Czechoslovak Minister of Information, Václav Kopecký, culminated in the signature of the Cultural Agreement and Agreements on Scientific and Technological Cooperation, Postal Services, and Telecommunications. Within the framework of cultural agreements, Chinese students, doctors, and journalists came to Czechoslovakia and every year there was a delegation of Czechoslovak cultural professionals visiting the PRC.[9]

According to a story later passed on in Vinařice, the Kopecký delegation, on behalf of the Czechoslovak president Klement Gottwald, thanked the villagers of Cangzhou[10] in Hebei province for their birthday greetings and promised them to find a twinning partner in Czechoslovakia to exchange letters and experience. The search was mandated to Jan

---

[8]Mikhail Prozumenshchikov, 'Pekin-Moskva-Praga: put' ot 'kul'turnoy revolyutsii' k 'prazhskoy vesne' i obratno,' in *Prazhskaja vesna i mezhdunarodnyj krizis 1968 g.: stat'i, issledovaniya, dokumenty*, ed. Natalia G. Tomilina, Stefan Karner, and Aleksandr O. Chubaryan (Moscow: Mezhdunarodnyy fond Demokratiya, 2010); James Hershberg, Sergey Radchenko, Péter Vámos, and David Wolff, 'The Interkit Story: A Window into the Final Decades of the Sino-Soviet Relationship,' Cold War International History Project. Working Paper 63 (2011); Niu Jun, 'China and Eastern Europe from the 1960 Moscow Conference to Khrushchev's Removal,' Cold War International History Project e-Dossier 58 (2014) at https://www.wilson-center.org/publication/china-and-eastern-europe-the-1960-moscow-conference-to-khrushchevs-removal#intro; Austin Jersild, 'Central Europeans and the Sino-Soviet Split: The "Great Friendship" as International History,' Cold War International History Project e-Dossier 46 (2014) at https://www.wilsoncenter.org/publication/central-europeans-and-the-sino-soviet-split-the-great-friendship-international-history#sthash.PFQnYGeG.dpuf.

[9]František Zupka, *Všečínská federace práce: Asijské národy v boji za svobodu* (Prague: Práce 1951), 5–12 and 330–5.

[10]As there existed no transcription rule, forms of the name of the original twinning village in Cangzhou varied in the Czechoslovak documents and press. The most frequent were: Tiang-Kuo-Čchuan; Tiang-Kuo-Tchuan; Cchang-čou; and Čang-kuo-čuang.

Tauber, an agricultural expert, geographer, and sinologist, who picked Vinařice, a village in the region of Kopecký's hometown Mladá Boleslav, north of Prague. Altogether, there were 320 inhabitants living in Vinařice, of which 80 individuals were members of the Communist Party. The cooperative was founded in 1949, on the grounds of a large confiscated farm estate. According to Tauber, some 48 cooperative farmers worked there and cultivated all the typical Czechoslovak crops.[11] Another added value was a stately renaissance home, confiscated together with the farm estate, which offered presentable premises. The inhabitants of Vinařice probably also drew attention due to their three ministerial diplomas for the fastest undertaking of agricultural works. At the outset, Vinařice was four times smaller than its Communist Party dictated Chinese partner. The cooperative farm in Cangzhou was officially set up in 1953 by amalgamating 34 peasant farms. The number of its members reached thousands in a few years and the farm swiftly ranked among the best cooperatives of the Beijing area.

In the presence of film cameras, the ceremony that connected the uneven partners took place on 23 April 1953. The event was carefully organised by the government to present the PRC as the second most important of the Czechoslovak allies. It emphasised that the whole of Czechoslovak society was devoted to the progress of the socialist world and presented the village of Vinařice as the honoured and trusted Czechoslovak representative. Antonín Herman, the president of Vinařice cooperative, chronicled in 1956:

> [a]ll of those who love the great nation of China and all of those who had something to say came to Vinařice … on the stage, under the flag of the PRC, Czechoslovakia and the Soviet Union, and under the picture of Mao Zedong and our president, the ministers, the representatives of the Chinese embassy … poets, researchers gathered … and called upon us (the members of the Vinařice cooperative) to take a lead in the twinning between the Czech, Slovak and Chinese nations.

Herman added that, 'at the other end of the great camp of socialist nations and on the same day, you were, our friends, also celebrating the start of twinning relations with us.' The cultural room of Vinařice began to fill up with Chinese paintings and art objects brought by the delegations and work teams organised by the Chinese Embassy.[12]

The last year of Gottwald's five-year plan, which in respect to the countryside emphasised the inevitability of the path to collective farming, was marked by extensive social changes in Czechoslovakia. The consequences of the liquidation of Rudolf Slanský were still perceptible, both Stalin and Gottwald had died, and along with the expected abolition of the ration-coupon system, monetary reform was declared. To contribute to socialism in such conditions, the agriculturists were encouraged by the military rhetoric: 'Socialisation of the countryside is a "combat task" for all of us!'; 'Each of our successes will consolidate the world peace front and will deliver a blow to the warmongers.' According to the rhetoric, the enemies were closely watching every setback in the process of laying down the foundations of socialism, and international workers' solidarity offered resistance to them.[13]

---

[11] Jan Tauber, *Vinařičtí družstevníci píší o své práci do Číny* (Prague: SZN, 1956), 21.

[12] Jan Tauber, *Vinařičtí družstevníci píší o své práci do Číny* (Prague: SZN, 1956), 22. The film 'Vinařice 1953' documenting the ceremony in Chinese was remastered and digitised by Freesam in 2014 to be used as a part of its project 'Je nám spolu dobře' [Happy together] (www.freesam.org/cz/projekty/159-happy-together).

[13] 'Do posledního roku Gottwaldovy pětiletky,' *Družstevní noviny* 8, no. 1 (1 January 1953), 3; František Šimáček, 'Socializace vesnice je bojový úkol nás všech!,' *Družstevní noviny* 8, no. 7 (28 February 1953), 2.

To demonstrate the Chinese friendship, a visit to Vinařice became part of a cultural programme for Chinese delegates and diplomats in Czechoslovakia. The villagers enjoyed a privileged position when compared to other collective farms in the region. The presents brought by each Chinese delegation and extraordinary cultural events organised by the visitors in Vinařice relieved the monotony of everyday hard work. For example, the Chinese donated a television to the cultural room of Vinařice in July 1953. Even after decades, memories of watching it belong to the happiest childhood experiences of the local population.[14] The friendship with the Chinese also stimulated courtesy and attention of the Czechoslovak central authorities on Vinařice and opened opportunities for the farm leadership to demand additional support for the cooperative efforts.

The social life of the village intensified and five dozen cooperative members in Vinařice had to improve their social graces very quickly. Combining agricultural works with the constant presence of official visitors was very demanding. Annual celebrations of the twinning anniversaries took place in April, the month of important spring agricultural works; other events were organised during harvests. The preparations took days and waiting for the arrival of the guests sometimes lasted for several hours. For example, 279 members of the choir of the Chinese People's Liberation Army arrived at Vinařice to support the cooperative members in working hard for the communist future in August 1954 with a three-hour delay. Nevertheless, they were greeted by school children with flowers. The Czechoslovak press and film-makers were present as well. The president of Vinařice cooperative Herman showed the guests around the village and handed them presents for Cangzhou villagers: a crystal vase, honey, and a photograph album with local motifs. The letter from Cangzhou coop members was read in return. Following the live performance of the Chinese choir, the unforgettable experience for many villagers, the guests left for Prague early in the evening.[15]

The events resulting from the friendship sometimes also disturbed the private lives of the villagers: on 22 December 1954, two weeks after arriving in Czechoslovakia and two days before Christmas, the new PRC ambassador to Prague, Cao Ying, brought his wife and colleagues to see the early social and political results of Czechoslovak collectivisation in Vinařice. Only three weeks later, the Chinese writer Ai Wu spent two days in Vinařice. His sudden unannounced visits to local houses embarrassed several families but were accepted without a protest. They were explained as an attempt to learn about the true life of the Czechoslovak cooperative in order to describe it later in Cangzhou.[16]

In order to secure the propagandistic impact of the example of collectivised Vinařice, Czechoslovak central and regional authorities strove for better efficiency of its cooperative farm. In July 1953, a new bilateral Agreement on the Cooperation of the Czechoslovak Republic and the PRC in the Quarantine and Protection of Plants from Pests and Diseases opened up a new dimension for the friendship between the members of the cooperatives. The direct participation of Czechoslovak researchers was to contribute to the mobilisation of the countryside; doctors and nutritionists, experts of the Czechoslovak Academy of Agricultural Sciences, agronomists, and zoo technologists were all sent to Vinařice to oversee

---

[14] 'JZD – televize na vesnici' in Fotobanka České tiskové kanceláře (9 July 1953). Interviews with the head of Vinařice local administration and great-grandson of former president of the agricultural cooperative Jiří Kohout (born 1975) and the direct participant in the twinning Petr Sobotka Sr. (born 1943), conducted in June 2015.

[15] 'Čínští hosté,' Nová vesnice 3, no. 29 (2 August 1954).

[16] 'JZD Vinařice a československo-čínská družba,' in The Chronicle of Vinařice (January 1955).

the cooperative farm in the autumn of 1954.[17] In March 1955, Vinařice also came under the aegis of the regional garrison of nearby Luštěnice. From that time, the enthusiastic soldiers spent their leisure time working as agricultural labourers so that the cooperative farm would fulfil the plan five days ahead of schedule. They were also engaged in repairing the agricultural machinery. Within several weeks, the garrison made fences around the cooperative's property, reconstructed the sugar beet warehouse and built a sump. Soldiers were obliged to participate in celebrations of Czechoslovak-Chinese friendship in Vinařice as well; they promised to provide cultural programmes during the festivities, political training for the villagers, and organisational background for the cooperative's management. Members of the cooperative committed themselves to sell vegetables to the garrison in return.[18]

Thus, the second anniversary of the twinning could be celebrated with dignity on 26 April 1955. The Minister of Agriculture, Marek Šmíd, and his subordinates, together with representatives of the Ministry of Foreign Affairs and members of the Chinese Embassy led by Ambassador Cao Ying, were satisfied with improvements in the cooperative's organisation as well as in its production of meat, milk, and eggs. Vinařice was proudly declared a pioneer of collectivisation in Czechoslovakia and Minister Šmíd stressed that its success was being carefully observed by their Chinese colleagues. Again, the press and filmmakers were sent to document the event. The international fame of Vinařice was deemed to grow and the Czechoslovak government ordered further research to make Vinařice the key example of a new socialist village.[19] Two weeks later, high-ranking Chinese participants in Czechoslovak May celebrations held on the 10th anniversary of the liberation from Nazism paid a visit to Vinařice. They drew the audience's attention to the danger of American imperialism and remembered the greetings and presents from Cangzhou in the context of peaceful efforts of Chinese people. The secretary of the Central Committee of the Czechoslovak Communist Party Václav Pašek referred to his recent journey to Cangzhou. He assured the villagers of Vinařice that a tractor, which they had sent to China in 1953, contributed to rapid voluntary collectivisation of Cangzhou because its efficiency was widely convincing.[20]

Direct contact between the villagers of China and Czechoslovakia remained limited. Both countries had sufficient labour forces for their economies and their massive exchange was unrealistic.[21] The Chinese students, who showed up in Vinařice to help with agricultural works from time to time, represented nothing more but the will of the PRC Embassy in Prague to develop contacts with the locals. Cooperation in agriculture stayed on the edge of the interests of both parties. Under the Agreement on the Scientific and Technological Cooperation of 1952, only experts could come to help to transmit Czechoslovak technologies to Chinese industry. Starting from June 1953, the Czechoslovak government cooperated with Beijing on the basis of a top-secret Protocol on the Development of Maritime Transport.[22] The initial Czechoslovak motive to support Chinese industrialisation as a matter of international communist solidarity changed only slightly after Khrushchev's ideological revision of Soviet foreign policy. According to Khrushchev, the political and military struggle between

---

[17] Jan Tauber, *Vinařičtí družstevníci píší o své práci do Číny* (Prague: Státní zemědělské nakladatelství, 1956), 23.

[18] *Nová vesnice 4*, no. 12 (30 March 1956).

[19] *Nová vesnice 4*, no. 16 (27 April 1956); *The Chronicle of Vinařice* (April –July 1955). 'JZD Vinařice,' in Fotobanka České tiskové kanceláře, 27 April 1955.

[20] *The Chronicle of Vinařice*, May 1955.

[21] 'Event. nábor prac. sil z ČLR – rozbor situace' A MZV, fond Teritoriální odbor – tajné (TO-T), Čína 1955–1959, box 2, file 7 (30 November 1956).

[22] Krátká, *A History of the Czechoslovak Ocean Shipping Company, 1948–1989*, 38–40.

the communist and capitalist worlds was to continue in the economic sphere. This confirmed the Czechoslovak preference of industrial exports in cooperation with the PRC as Prague oriented its economy towards heavy industry and arms production.[23]

After several years, cooperation on agricultural reform retreated from the main Czechoslovak tasks to maintain Chinese growth. It was obvious that the conditions of Cangzhou and Vinařice differed greatly. The practical execution of twinning between the village of Cangzhou and the Vinařice cooperative in China was assisted from Beijing by the Czechoslovak Embassy. Being isolated in dependence on information and its interpretations from Soviet envoys in China, the Czechoslovak diplomats took advantage of the exceptional opportunity to contact local people. The embassy also actively informed the Chinese newspapers, provided them with articles sent for this purpose from Prague, distributed films and other promotional material and also issued its own monthly bulletin in Chinese. The first official delegation of Czechoslovak cooperative members arrived in China to attend the Congress of Chinese colleagues in July 1954. The delegation visited various towns and villages and was most impressed by Shanghai.[24]

Similarly, it was the Chinese Embassy in Prague that was particularly interested in the results of the members of the Vinařice cooperative. Searching for authentic information, the diplomats visited families in Vinařice in their homes and built personal contacts with them. Official delegations kept coming only to record any positive changes of the cooperative farm and their help was mainly demonstrative. In August 1955, a group of 30 Chinese opera singers was brought to Vinařice to celebrate its successful wheat harvest. Before performing, the artists took part in binding the last sheaves and they were shown round the farm to observe its success. The vice-chairman of the PRC government, Marshal Zhu De, did not pay a visit to the cooperative of Vinařice during his stay in Czechoslovakia in January 1956. But he sent his representatives with presents to Vinařice. In addition, four of the cooperative members had an opportunity to participate at the reception for 489 guests held in his honour at Prague Castle on 18 January 1956.[25] At this point, the Chinese presents to the villagers of Vinařice changed their character as the experience of mutual interaction grew. Things for personal use prevailed over propagandistic material. On the other hand, it was obvious that the farm served the same propagandistic purposes as the Czechoslovak cultural exhibitions or tours of Czechoslovak artists to the East: they were projected to promote an unknown small European country in fraternal communist China.

The twinning was expected to contribute to Czechoslovak trade with China as well. On 24 April 1956, the cooperative farm in Cangzhou was renamed the Cooperative Farm of the Chinese-Czechoslovak Friendship, in evidence of the successfully developing mutual aid. The ceremony was attended by the Chinese vice-minister of agriculture, the vice-mayor of Beijing, the Czechoslovak ambassador, and the vice-minister of foreign trade. At that time, the farm had already cultivated more than 4000 hectares of land, out of which 1700 hectares were arable. For this reason, Czechoslovakia provided it with 600 pieces of agricultural machinery, in total amounting to 7.9 million Czechoslovak crowns (approx. 1.1 million

---

[23]Skřivan, *Československý vývoz do Číny 1918–1992*, 177–9.

[24]Václav Novák, 'Na sjezdu čínských družstevníků,' *Družstevní noviny* 8, no. 19 (16 September 1954); Václav Novák, 'Na sjezdu čínských družstevníků,' *Družstevní noviny* 8, no. 20 (30 September 1954).

[25]'Seznam hostí pozvaných na recepci 18. 1. 1956,' The Archive of the President's Office (Archiv kanceláře prezidenta republiky, AKPR), fond Tajné - Čína.

dollars). Apart from 35 Zetor tractors, the intended flagships of future Czechoslovak export to China that had been introduced to Chinese customers thanks to the coop twinning in 1953, new items were sent such as cars, trucks, a mobile service station, ploughs, and seed gates.

The name of the cooperative farm in Vinařice was also broadened to the 'Cooperative Farm of Czechoslovak-Chinese Friendship' during a similar ceremony with the participation of the representatives of the Ministries of Agriculture and Foreign Affairs and the representatives of the state administration. The ceremony to commemorate the third anniversary of the twinning was attended by a Chinese diplomat, Chargé d'Affaires Ke Puhai, who brought presents for the children and women of Vinařice from the mayor of Beijing. These included toys, drums, or cymbals for children and silk and wool fabrics for women. Ke Puhai's announcement that the Chinese partner of Vinařice obtained a new symbolic name was received by the villagers with enthusiasm.

However, the official delegation of the All-China Federation of Supply and Marketing Cooperatives, which was at that time on a three-week tour of Czechoslovakia to reciprocate the 1954 visit, did not include Vinařice in its programme. Maintaining contacts with Czechoslovak industry was of higher priority for the Chinese than strengthening agricultural cooperation.[26] In December 1956, when the delegation of the National People's Congress of the PRC, headed by the Mayor of Beijing Peng Zhen, visited Czechoslovakia, a journey to the Vinařice cooperative was only the third option offered by the Ministry of Foreign Affairs for the fourth day of their programme.[27]

In the summer of 1956, the Ministry of Foreign Affairs began preparations for the journey of the Czechoslovak government delegation to China, Mongolia, and Korea. However, shortly before the planned date, at the end of October 1956, the arrangements were suspended.[28] On both sides, priority was given to the dramatic events in Poland and Hungary. At this moment, the Chinese leadership was becoming increasingly discontent with Khrushchev's international strategy. Antonín Novotný, representing both the Czechoslovak state as well as the Communist Party of Czechoslovakia during a Moscow meeting with the Soviet officials in January 1957, did everything to support Khrushchev, his constant protector in Moscow. Czechoslovak governmental officials as well as the delegates of the Czechoslovak Communist Party pointed out that the weakening of the leading role of the Communist Party of the Soviet Union could only have a negative impact on the international communist movement. They expressed their loyalty to Moscow, reaffirmed their commitment to the Marxist-Leninist tenets of socialist construction, and proclaimed unity to be the main interest of all socialist countries.[29]

During 1957, interest in developing mutual cooperation continued to wane further on both sides. China started slowly to abandon its role as a grateful recipient of Czechoslovak

---

[26]'Přehled československo-čínských styků za II. čtvrtletí 1956.' AMZV, TO-T 1955–1959, box 2, file 10; 'Hosté z daleké Číny,' *Družstevní noviny* 9, no. 9 (27 April 1956): 2; 'Z pobytu čínských družstevníků u nás.' *Družstevní noviny* 9, no. 10 (11 May 1956); *Nová vesnice 5*, No. 18 (4 May 1956).

[27]'Seznam hostí pozvaných na recepci. Minutovník návštěvy delegace.' AKPR, fond Tajné – Čína.

[28]'Záznam z porady 25 October 1956, Stav příprav odjezdu čs. vládní delegace do ČLR, MLR a KLDR.' AMZV, fond Porady kolegia ministra, Book 22.

[29]'Zpráva o průběhu jednání delegace ÚV KSČ s delegací ÚV KSSS.'The National Archives of the Czech Republic (Národní archiv České republiky, NA), fond Antonín Novotný II., box 192, file 119, 15. Programme, correspondence related to the conference in NA, fond Antonín Novotný II., box 192, file 118; 'Společná československo-sovětská deklarace' (corrected by Koucký according to the Soviet text) in NA, fond Antonín Novotný II., box. 192, file 122.

48 BEYOND THE KREMLIN'S REACH?

industrial assistance. The Czechoslovak machinery was not adapted to the severe and dusty Chinese climate in Cangzhou and many claims occurred. Another problematic factor for Czechoslovak deliveries to China was inaccuracy in the trade agreements. The economists in Prague worried about financial loss and debated which of the parties was to pay the freight and packing costs. Nor was the emerging Czechoslovak seafaring able to take over unanticipated expenses in the second half of the 1950s.[30]

In the developing conflict with Moscow, Beijing argued for more open debates and solutions independent of the Soviet example or point of view. During the Moscow Conference of representatives of communist and workers' parties in November 1957, the Czechoslovak delegation confirmed the validity of Khrushchev's domestic and international policies. The primary importance of the Soviet Union for Czechoslovakia was demonstrated during the 11th Congress of the Communist Party of Czechoslovakia in June 1958. In contrast to previous occasions, the Chinese delegate was seated on the side tribune. The main themes of the Congress were the Soviet slogans: struggle for peace, peaceful coexistence, and determination to compete with the capitalist world on the economic level.[31]

As a result of the Great Leap Forward and the policy to establish people's communes in the Chinese countryside, the Sino-Czechoslovak Friendship Cooperative Farm in Cangzhou merged with three other estates and one township into the Chinese-Czechoslovak Friendship People's Commune in August 1958. It was managed by an administrative committee and subdivided into five brigades competing between themselves for the red flag of the commune. According to Czechoslovak diplomats, out of 74,000 inhabitants, 1769 were members of the Communist Party. Some 31,000 inhabitants worked in agriculture. They were successfully growing wheat, peanut vine, and fruit, as well as breeding thousands of pigs and cattle, and tens of thousands of poultry. Manufacturing was the key industry. There were several health centres in the commune and in total 45 primary schools for almost 10,000 pupils. The difference in geographical, political, and social conditions between Cangzhou and Vinařice was abysmal, and this naturally affected the intensity of mutual contacts. Over the years, the twinning relationships became more and more formal. The commune then limited itself to sending congratulation letters for important Czechoslovak anniversaries.[32]

China tried to offer Czechoslovakia a new partner. On 30 September 1958, the Chinese-Czechoslovak Friendship Society was established. It was presided over by the Chinese Deputy Minister of Culture, Xia Yan, with representatives of all-important Chinese mass organisations sitting on its 20-member Council. The Friendship Society planned to set up branches in all the bigger cities to inform the Chinese people about the life and work of Czechoslovakia. The general secretary of the Friendship Society suggested that it would be convenient to form a similar organisation in Czechoslovakia.[33] Prague's response was strict: it did not see founding a similar institution as purposeful. Czechoslovak authorities wanted to focus on the all-round support of the Union of Czechoslovak-Soviet Friendship.

---

[30]Krátká, *A History of the Czechoslovak Ocean Shipping Company, 1948–1989*, 48 and 58.

[31]*Mezinárodní postavení a zahraniční politika ČSSR v období mezi XI. a XII. sjezdem KSČ*, (Prague: Oddělení propagandy a agitace ÚV KSČ, 1962).

[32]'Základní údaje o komuně čínsko-československého přátelství v Pekingu. 24. 6. 1959.' AMZV, fond TO-T 1955–1959, box 2, file 4.

[33]'Zpráva o jednání s generálním sekretářem Společnosti čínsko-československého přátelství.' AMZV, TO - T, Čína 1955–1959, box 2, file 5, 11 October 1958.

In relation to China it envisaged using only the existing international agreements. Thus, no new organisational platform for bilateral cooperation was created.[34]

Nevertheless, Prague still tried to send its experts to Chinese industry in order to support, apart from world socialism, its own exports. The task of these experts was also to spread propaganda for Czechoslovakia. But by the beginning of 1959, the Ministry of Foreign Affairs was not maintaining the necessary close contact with them and was unable to provide them with Czechoslovak press or party material. The embassy organised a joint programme, but preference was usually given to other types of activities, such as an excursion to Xiangshan Gongyuan in Beijing (Fragrant Hills Park in Beijing), a meeting with Czechoslovak athletes Dana and Emil Zátopek, or tours of steelworks, over the visit to the brigade in Cangzhou. There were also agricultural delegations visiting China, but their members were officials or academics.[35] No Czechoslovak agricultural group or team was sent to work in China.[36] There was a similar lack of interest in continuing to share experience in agricultural reforms on the Chinese side. Political and economic delegations took turns in Czechoslovakia, but the Chinese coop members were represented, at most, by officials oriented toward consumer interests and trade.[37]

Other specific goals of Czechoslovak-Chinese cooperation in agriculture were defined by the so called 'Berlin' multilateral agreement on direct cooperation between the central research institutions of socialist states in the field of agriculture and forestry in 1956, and the subsequent bilateral agreement on research cooperation between the Czechoslovak and Chinese Academies of Agricultural Sciences in 1959.[38] It was then that the relationship between Vinařice and China culminated. On 10 May 1959, Vinařice received the delegation of the Chinese People's Army, which was visiting Czechoslovakia at the time. After the demonstration of Soviet and Czechoslovak airplanes and the work of the border guards the delegation was received by the agriculturists of Vinařice, and participated in a presentation of their farming.[39]

The celebrations of the tenth anniversary of the foundation of the PRC represented the last important moment of mutual relations for two decades ahead. On 28 September 1959, Antonín Novotný finally made his visit to China, which had been postponed one year. He spoke about the long tradition of comradely solidarity of both countries, which based its revolutionary paths on the enduring legacy of the Great October Socialist Revolution and contributed to the promotion of socialism in the world. Novotný paid tribute to the Chinese industrial efforts as observed at the Brno Fairs, and acknowledged the contribution of the PRC's intransigence in crushing 'revisionism' and 'imperialism'.[40]

---

[34]'Založení Spol. čs. - čínského přátelství – informace.' AMZV, TO - T, Čína 1955–1959, box 2, file 5.

[35]Martin Slobodník, 'Východný vietor prevláda? Čínsky Veľký skok vpred v Československu,' in *Podoby globalizácie v Oriente*, ed. Martina Bucková and Gabriel Pirický (Bratislava: Slovenská orientalistická spoločnosť – Ústav orientalistiky SAV, 2015), 9–30.

[36] 'Zpráva o politickém a společenském životě čs. občanů v ČLR za IV. čtvrtletí 1958.' AMZV, TO - T, Čína 1955–1959, box 2, file 2, 28 January 1959.

[37]'Prehľad stykov s ČLR za II. čtvrtročie 1957.' AMZV, TO - T, Čína 1955–1959, box 2, file 10.

[38]'Informace o spolupráci na úseku zemědělského výzkumu s Čínskou lidovou republikou.' AMZV, fond Teritoriální odbory - obyčejné (TO – O), Čína 1965–1968, box 1, file 151/69 Zemědělství, 24 April 1967.

[39]'Minutovník návštěvy čínské delegace.' AKPR, Tajné - Čína.

[40]'Podklady k cestě a korespondence mezi A. Novotným a Mao Ce-tungem.' AMZV, fond TO-T, Čína 1955–1959, box 2, file 2; Projev Antonína Novotného z 28. září 1959, in *Dokumenty československé zahraniční politiky*, nos. 10–11 (1959), 347.

On this occasion, Prague prepared two exhibitions, a TV appearance of the Chinese ambassador, and a series of newspaper articles on the successes of the constructive Chinese efforts. Prague was also looking forward to the visit of the Sichuan Opera.[41] The friendship towards the Chinese people was demonstrated by schools, military troops, or industrial facilities, which declared their willingness to handle Chinese orders as a priority. Vinařice was also expected to send an official greeting.[42] Unfortunately, while the assessors of President Novotný were considering the suitability of donating a medical X-ray machine to Cangzhou,[43] Vinařice missed its opportunity. The embassy in Beijing urged an explanation and rectification. It expected the cooperative to inform regularly the twin commune on its successes. As officials from the Czechoslovak Academy of Agricultural Sciences wrote:

> The celebrations in Vinařice were carried out with dignity and the failures to send congratulations were caused by the loss of the resolutions and telegrams, which were approved at the end of the manifestation, and further delayed by the preparation of a photo album which will form part, together with the opening letter, of a decent congratulation, albeit belated.[44]

The embassy in Beijing proved to be the subject most concerned with the persistence of the cooperatives' relationship. It took advantage of the first occasion in order to blot out the unpleasant omission of the Vinařice farmers. As early as 20 November, the members of the Czechoslovak Philharmonic Orchestra visited the Chinese-Czechoslovak Friendship Commune during their tour in China. After a short welcome, the deputy secretary of the People's Commune accepted the letter and photo album from Vinařice. Subsequently, the members of the Philharmonic Orchestra performed, and then listened to, several folk songs; in two hours they had left the commune.[45]

Impact of the Sino-Soviet dispute

The development of the Soviet-Chinese dispute did not favour Czechoslovak-Chinese relations. In September 1959, ironically during the top-level visit of Antonín Novotný in China, the Ministry of Foreign Affairs called upon the embassy in Beijing to thoroughly educate the Czechoslovak citizens, who were sent to China within the framework of cultural agreements, with the aim of preventing infiltration of improper views among them.[46] Trade, however, reached its post-war maximum. On the occasion of the fifteenth anniversary of the liberation of Czechoslovakia, China organised celebrations with the participation of a Czechoslovak delegation. The Beijing Embassy took this opportunity and proposed to set up a maintenance workshop in Cangzhou by the Czechoslovak-Chinese Friendship Factory, which was founded earlier in China thanks to the licence of the Czechoslovak

---

[41]'Návrh plánu akcí ve vztahu k Čínské lidové republice nárok 1959.' AMZV, fond Porady kolegia ministra, Book 41, 25 March 1959 and 9 April 1959, 15–18.

[42]'Plán akcí ve vztahu k Čínské lidové republice na r. 1959.' AMZV, fond TO-T, Čína 1955–1959, box 2, file 3, 16 March 1959. 'Programme pobytu vládní vojenské delegace Čínské lidové republiky v Československé republice' AMZV, fond TO-T, Čína 1955–1959, box 2, file 2, 29 April 1959.

[43]'Návštěva I. tajemníka ÚV KSČ a prezidenta republiky s. Antonína Novotného v Čínské lidové republice.' AMZV, fond TO-T, Čína 1955–1959, box 2, file 2, 25 November 1958.

[44]'Velvyslanectví Peking, Telegram.' AMZV, fond TO-T, Čína 1955–1959, box 2, file 3, 17 October 1959. 'Odpověď vedoucího odboru.' AMZV, fond TO-T, Čína 1955–1959, box 2, file 3, 10 November 1959.

[45]'Záznam z návštěvy části České filharmonie v LK čínsko-československého přátelství.' AMZV, fond TO-T, Čína 1955–1959, box 2, file 10, 21 November 1959.

[46]AMZV, fond Porady kolegia ministra, book 53, 15 September 1959.

Machine Tools Works (TOS) company to repair Czechoslovak machinery sold to the PRC. The Ministry of Foreign Affairs appreciated the proposal, but added that the personal and telephonic contact with Chinese comrades declined after the critique of their foreign-policy views at the Bucharest meeting of fraternal parties in June 1960. The Chinese, however, kept visiting the Czechoslovak-Chinese Friendship Collective Farm and kept going there for voluntary work.[47]

The key moment came in April 1960, when China expressed its reservations about Soviet politics in the pamphlet '*Long Live Leninism*', shortly after Khrushchev's visit to Southeast Asia. Beijing offered its own revolutionary model and interpretation of international politics. Nevertheless, Prague believed that Beijing ignored the opinion of the majority of communist parties; in domestic politics it 'pursued a strange version of Marxism-Leninism based solely on the Mao Zedong writings' and underestimated the natural character of the interests of the working class. In terms of foreign policy, it broke up the unity of the socialist camp, complicated its success and took the side of contemporary leftism.[48] As the documents preserved at the Czech Foreign Ministry Archive and National Archive show, the disagreement on the political level led to a drastic reduction of Sino-Czechoslovak economic and cultural contacts in 1960. In two years, the trade volume with China decreased to 15% of the level reached in 1959. Both countries limited the movement of diplomats of each other's country outside the embassy, further formalised the cultural cooperation, and sought to limit its ideological influence on the public.[49]

Although the decrease in mutual contacts was also related to the economic setbacks of the politics of the Great Leap Forward, the Czechoslovak diplomats in China were reported to have become gradually isolated. They complained about worse access to authorities and a lack of information. With the increasing conflict between Moscow and Beijing, the interest of Czechoslovakia and China in mutual twinning relations decreased further. The political barriers could not be overcome by time-limited study trips, concerts or lectures, nor tours by sports teams. Several-month-long stays in China by the Czechoslovak army music ensemble or of Czechoslovak writers and researchers remained confined to the beginning of the 1950s.[50] The bilateral cultural plans (each year more modest) were carried out, but the events did not attract the attention of the wider public. The previously mentioned Professor Průšek, who was then president of the Oriental Institute of the Academy of Sciences, complained that his subordinates had become, as interpreters, involuntary witnesses of unacceptable embarrassments. According to Průšek, Chinese cultural delegations had to cope with inappropriate accommodation, sudden changes in their programme, or no public response to the events.

In Vinařice, the level and frequency of Chinese visits deceased. The village started to be promoted more as an example of successful socialist transformation to other sympathisers of the Soviet Union. Andrew Rothstein, member of the Communist Party of Great Britain

---

[47]'Současná politická situace v Čínské lidové republice a československo-čínské vztahy.' AMZV, Porady kolegia ministra, book 53, 15 September 1960. AMZV, Porady kolegia ministra, book 53, 26 September 1960.

[48]'Současná politická situace v Čínské lidové republice a československo-čínské styky.' AMZV, fond Porady kolegia ministra, Book 53, 15 September 1960.

[49]'Zahraničněpolitické vztahy, vnitropolitická situace ČLR a současné vztahy ČSSR a ČLR.' AMZV, TO-T 1955–1959, box 2, file 1, 23 April 1966; 'Informace k posledním opařením vůči činnosti ZÚ ČLR.' AMZV, TO-T 1955–1959, box 2, file 2, 5 February 1958.

[50]Jaroslav Čech, Vojtěch Jasný, and Karel Kachyňa, *Byli jsme v zemi květů* (Prague: Naše vojsko, 1954); Adolf Hoffmeister, *Pohlednice z Číny. Malá knížka o velké Číně* (Prague: Československý spisovatel, 1954).

and the correspondent of the Czechoslovak Trade Union newspaper *Práce*, came in October 1958, a group of Warsaw Pact military attaches visited in March 1960, and a Cuban veterinarian, Pedro Valerino Fernandez, in June 1964. Chinese presents in the cultural room of Vinařice were shifted behind the newest gifts slowly. And when children from Vinařice started to correspond with their counterparts in the socialist abroad, the Chinese were not among them.[51]

In December 1961, the collegium of the Minister of Foreign Affairs stated that through the fault of the Chinese comrades' position on key ideological issues, mutual relations had been limited on all levels.[52] This state lasted for 20 years. In 1965, celebrations of the twentieth anniversary of Czechoslovakia's liberation consisted mainly of sporting competitions in the PRC; one year later, the only activities were organised by the Czechoslovak Embassy. It was characteristic that on behalf of the Chinese-Czechoslovak Friendship Commune it was mainly children who participated, holding the minor investiture ceremony of tying red scarves to new members. Meanwhile, the leadership of the Commune sent only a greeting letter. A similar greeting letter was delivered from the Chinese-Czechoslovak Friendship Society and the Chinese-Czechoslovak Friendship Factory. The only Chinese initiative on this occasion was a film showing and a brief cocktail party.[53]

In the developing conflict between Moscow and Beijing, Prague's position was clearly pro-Soviet.[54] The situation was further complicated in 1968, when China first rejected the Czechoslovak reforms as revisionism and later condemned the invasion of Czechoslovakia by the Warsaw Pact armies. At the same time, the Czech broadcasting of Radio Beijing was launched as a means of supporting the Chinese disapproval of what was seen by the PRC as Soviet revisionism. The Prague normalisation government regarded the Beijing position as an attempt to use the Czechoslovak development against Moscow. It took scrupulous care not to offer a pretext to the PRC to destroy the unity of the Soviet bloc. On the other hand, Beijing focused on developing contacts with the Czechoslovak left-wing exiles.[55]

By the decision of the Vinařice Cooperative members and after the approval of the regional administration in Mladá Boleslav, the Czechoslovak-Chinese Friendship Cooperative of Vinařice merged on 7 March 1973 with another nearby cooperative and formally ceased to exist.[56] The direct relations of the agricultural coop members were brought to an end and the development of Czechoslovak-Chinese twinning relations was limited to inviting its former representatives to the social events held at the embassy of the CSSR in Beijing and at the

---

[51] *The Chronicle of Vinařice*, October 1958–June 1964.

[52] AMZV, fond Porady kolegia ministra, Book 66, 13 December 1961.

[53] 'Oslavy Zpráva o průběhu oslav státního svátku 1966 na ZÚ Peking.' AMZV, fond TO-O, Čína, 1965–1968, Čína, box 1, file 151/74 13 May 1966. 'Oslavy. Promítání ZÚ–ČLR.' AMZV TO-O, Čína 1965–1968, box 1, file 151/74 18 October 1967.

[54] 'Cizí ZÚ v ČSSR. Záznam z návštěvy III. Tajemníka velvyslanectví ČLR na ministerstvu školství.' AMZV, fond TO-O, Čína 1965–1968, box 1, file 151/16, 28 February 1967.

[55] 'Stanovisko ČLR k obsazení ČSSR.' AMZV, fond TO-T, Čína 1965–1969, box 2, file 4, 7 September 1968, 'Čínský ohlas na události v Československu – informace.' AMZV, fond TO-T, Čína 1965–1969, box 2, file 4, 31 October 1968; 'Čs.-čínské vztahy.' AMZV, fond TO-T, Čína 1975–1979, box 5, file 151/311 Politické zprávy, 3 February 1975; 'Zaměření a současné úkoly čs. zahraniční politiky vůči Čínské lidové republice.' AMZV, fond Porady kolegia ministra, book 177, 11 January 1977; 'Zaměření a hlavní úkoly československé zahraniční politiky vůči Čínské lidové republice.' AMZV, fond Porady kolegia ministra, book 205, 20 November 1979; 'Zaměření a hlavní úkoly československé zahraniční politiky vůči Čínské lidové republice.' AMZV, fond Porady kolegia ministra, book 245, 2 March 1984.

[56] Business register ARES, Výpis dat Obchodního rejstříku k Zemědělsko-obchodnímu družstvu Týnec, IČ: 00105821. 'Osobnost obce Petr Sobotka,' *Vinařické listy*, no. 3 (June 2013) (http://www.obecvinarice.cz/e_download.php?file=data/messages/obsah10_1.pdf&original=cerven2013.pdf).

embassy of the PRC in Prague. In the 1980s, 'the formally enduring twinning relations … were commemorated by the visits of the representatives of the embassies organised through the Ministry of Foreign Affairs.'[57] Apart from the Communist Party, the Czechoslovak diplomats considered the central Chinese People's Association for Friendship with Foreign Countries the most influential partner. However, at home it made sustained efforts to eliminate the influence of the PRC Embassy on the Czechoslovak public.[58]

In China, Cangzhou maintained its character based on collective ownership but transformed into a city with over 100,000 inhabitants and with industry surpassing agriculture as the primary sector of economic activity. Sharing experiences with several dozen members of the Vinařice Cooperative was definitely beyond their interests. In the mid-1980s, as Czechoslovak-Chinese relations improved, Vinařice was replaced as a twinning partner of Cangzhou by the holder of the Czechoslovak Order of Labour, the Slušovice Cooperative Farm. This cooperative had farmed the foothills of Central Moravia (the Gottwaldov region) since 1954, and had gradually become one of the most productive state farms. Some 4000 coop members worked on its 8000 hectares of land, out of which some 3500 hectares were arable. The overall productivity increased each year. Thanks to the authority of its leading agronomist František Čuba among the Communist Party leadership, the cooperative was exclusively allowed not only to carry out agricultural activities, but was also involved in the processing of agricultural products, developing machinery manufacturing, agricultural biochemicals and chemicals, and even engaged in the construction sector. They also produced their own computers and built their own racing stable. According to Čuba, all these successes were naively presented to the Chinese during the mid-1980s and the Chinese copied it all.[59]

Conclusion

The Czechoslovak-Chinese cooperation on agricultural cooperatives emerged in the formative period of the Soviet bloc. In the atmosphere of assumed threat from the West, it was intended to prove the Chinese peoples' approval of Czechoslovak agricultural reforms. The Czechoslovak politicians put much effort into being able to promote Vinařice as the key example of successfully realised collectivisation. At the same time, strict centralisation, institutionalisation, and subordination to the principles of proletarian internationalism were unable to encourage strong cooperation in agriculture between Czechoslovakia and China. Soon it was obvious that the collectivisation policies of the two countries differed to a great extent and the twinning project for the Czechoslovak and Chinese cooperative members became a matter of public diplomacy. The small cooperative of Vinařice was not an equal partner to the expanding Chinese agro-industrial conglomerate and the choice itself indicated that Prague was not very interested in exporting its agricultural experience. After all, at that time Prague was only beginning to learn from the Soviet collectivisation experience. The Czechoslovak position within the Soviet bloc did, as well as the

---

[57]'Zaměření a hlavní úkoly československé zahraniční politiky vůči Čínské lidové republice. Příloha IV.' AMZV, fond Porady kolegia ministra, book 177, 11 January 1977.

[58]'Zaměření a hlavní úkoly československé zahraniční politiky vůči Čínské lidové republice.' AMZV, fond Porady kolegia ministra, book 245, 2 March 1984.

[59]*Jednotné zemědělské družstvo Slušovice. Nositel řádu práce. Základní informace účastníkům II. celostátní konference Agroenerg ´86* (Slušovice: Agropublik, 1986); František Čuba, 'Nové zemědělství', no. 3, http://www.naseekonomika.cz/frantisek-cuba-nove-zemedelstvi-3/ (27 October 2013).

requirements of Czechoslovak economy, give preference to exports of machinery. Thus, the twinning between Vinařice and Cangzhou was exploited to promote Czechoslovak tractors and agricultural machinery in the PRC. Unfortunately, these were not ready for the Chinese climate. At the end of the day, it was easier for Czechoslovak economists to deal with their Chinese counterparts directly.

As the Soviet-Chinese dispute deepened, Czechoslovak-Chinese relations abandoned the poetic level of slogans about providing mutual assistance or the exchange of experience in building socialism and put more emphasis on sharing experience from partisan work and state governance. Preference was also given, together with the emphasis on the working character of cultural events, to activities with tangible results and minimal impact on the domestic population. After the Moscow consultation in 1960, Czechoslovak-Chinese relations followed the deteriorating level of Soviet-Chinese relations. Any political problems had immediate impact on the sensitive economic cooperation of Czechoslovakia with China and consequently on the Czechoslovak economy. In July 1961, however, Novotný managed to convince Khrushchev to purchase part of the Czechoslovak machinery ordered and then refused by the Chinese. Novotný argued that this would be a necessary Soviet payment for the Czechoslovak political support of Moscow. Under Novotný's leadership the Communist Party of Czechoslovakia preferred the Soviet 'liberator' and perceived Chinese politics primarily through its lens. The documents of the leadership of the Communist Party of Czechoslovakia and the materials of the Archives of the Ministry of Foreign Affairs of the Czech Republic show that it has been this way from the very beginning of its relations with the Chinese communists. The low level of Sino-Czechoslovak mutual contacts and reduction of goods exchange also affected contacts among ordinary citizens of both countries. Built artificially as a side effect of mutual political and trade cooperation, these served as grounds to demonstrate close relations between the two people, both externally and internally. In the situation where the institutionally based cooperation lost its support from the centre it did not flourish. The dissolution of the later Chinese partner, the Slušovice Cooperative, added to the loss of Czech memory of the relations between Czechoslovak and Chinese agriculturists. It was the Czechoslovak Embassy in Beijing that most contributed to the contacts with Cangzhou as it considered them a priority of its kind and a unique source of information. However, it was probably just this diplomatic marginality of the twinning relations between the cooperatives which helped them to survive inconspicuously into the next century. Despite different political ideals and goals, it was possible for the Czech Republic to build on previous relations. A monument of Chinese-Czechoslovak Friendship was unveiled in Cangzhou in 2006. The diplomats decided not to make any contact with the farmers of Vinařice and, interestingly, failed to capture the proper year to celebrate the sixtieth anniversary of the twinning. Several years later, an unofficial journey of the village of Vinařice representatives to Cangzhou revealed insuperable distinctions between their memory-based expectations, efforts of contemporary economy-driven Czech diplomacy, and the real situation. Nevertheless, the Chinese-Czechoslovak Friendship Farm became a stronghold for Czech business in China. It bought the Czech pavilion from the Shanghai Expo in 2010 and consequently commissioned a replica of the Charles Bridge by the same Prague company which had designed the monument and the pavilion. Although the field, character, and scope of the cooperation have changed, Czechoslovak public diplomacy has confirmed its long-term effect in China.

Disclosure statement

No potential conflict of interest was reported by the author.

ORCID

Daniela Kolenovska http://orcid.org/0000-0003-1019-098X

Kremlinology revisited: the nuances of reporting on China in the Eastern bloc press

Sören Urbansky and Max Trecker

ABSTRACT
Based on the assumption that the media was part of the intra-bloc diplomacy in eastern Europe, we explore the official portrayal of China in the East German, Hungarian and Polish press. Focusing on the Great Leap Forward, Sino-Indian War and Cultural Revolution, we analyse not only what was reported, but also how news were structured and what language was used. Disparities indicate that the uncertainty of future relations between Moscow and Beijing, combined with disagreements between Moscow and its satellites, forced the leaderships to adapt to new circumstances but simultaneously created leeway for their own political agendas.

The state socialist press and intra-bloc relations

To demand interviews with representatives of [the Chinese – *authors*] party and state, as you suggested in your last telegram, is not possible under the current circumstances. So many phrases would be uttered if I were allowed to conduct such an interview that in Berlin you … would have to cross out almost everything. The publication of such a truncated interview would not only mean nothing good, but would most likely lead to a breakdown in the relationship of our two countries. Not to publish it would be even worse …. I urge you not to send me any more telegrams asking me for interviews. Such requests could lead to the impression amongst the Chinese that the 'good people' are sitting in the headquarters in Berlin while this Beijing correspondent is sabotaging their 'good' intentions and thus no longer deserves to be granted access to anything.[1]

The East German China correspondent Gerda Lindner was well aware of the tension between the central party directive and her work as a journalist in Beijing. By September 1962, when Lindner cabled this message to East Berlin, reporting on China had become a delicate task. With the Sino-Soviet conflict escalating, party newspapers in Moscow and in its socialist satellite states states had to toe a fine line between open support for the Kremlin's position and upholding an image of China that had not (yet) broken away from the socialist ecumene.

---

[1]'Auszug aus einem Bericht unserer Korrespondentin in Peking,' 14 September 1962, Bundesarchiv Berlin-Lichterfelde (Barch), DY/30/IV 2/2.028/82.

Correspondents in Beijing acted as more than just brokers between their host country and editors back home. Their news and stories often fulfilled another function too: as part of the state-controlled propaganda machinery, they conveyed the official picture about China to their readers at home and abroad, not least the many so-called 'Kremlinologists', who compared newspaper articles and drew conclusions about Soviet decision-making leading to a better understanding of the framework of intra- and inter-bloc relations.[2] Kremlinology can mean either to focus on the standing of individual politicians inside their country's hierarchy or to focus on the relations between the socialist countries. We refer to the latter in this article. Zbigniew Brzezinski was among the most distinguished Kremlinologists. Early on in his academic career he focused on tensions inside the Soviet sphere.[3] What Brzezinski and his fellow Kremlinologists had in common was their reliance on published sources which they had to interpret. Their methods overlapped with the work of journalists and was sought after by politicians.

With the opening up of archives in Russia and the former socialist bloc in the early 1990s this method fell out of fashion. It was prone to bias and sometimes produced unreliable results, like the 'insight' that the Soviet Union wanted to use the intervention in Afghanistan to establish a communist government in India.[4] Nevertheless, we argue that Kremlinology can still provide fruitful insights into the Cold War period, if combined with archival material from the respective Politburo departments and editorial offices. Kremlinology matters because the party press was more than a mere instrument of propaganda. It was also an important tool for communication with the outside world, especially within the socialist bloc. This is often overlooked, even in post-1990 literature focusing on the state socialist press.[5] It constituted a means of diplomacy in the transnational socialist web and should therefore not be seen in isolation.[6] Lastly, it is also important to recall what the average newspaper reader in Szeged, Poznań or Magdeburg would have been able to know or deduce as far as the stories behind the headlines were concerned.

In contrast to what the name suggests, the socialist bloc was at no time a uniform entity. As frictions inside the bloc were rarely communicated openly, foreigners and natives alike had to read between the lines in order to get a decent insight into the events of the day. Details such as who was invited to which meeting and who was not, who featured prominently in an article or how congratulatory telegrams were positioned within a particular newspaper were more than just a matter of protocol. Such details were important metrics in a bloc where tensions were often communicated implicitly to avoid the possible communication of a discord between the allies. Though the press only exhibits traces of such changes on the surface, Kremlinology as a supplementary method provides additional analytical value for our work, especially when conducted comparatively. The communication of important decisions and policy turns by newspapers had a long tradition in the communist movement that predated the Cold War, one of the most prominent examples

---

[2]On Kreminology as a method, cf. Alec Nove, *Was Stalin Really Necessary? Some Problems of Soviet Political Economy* (London: Allen & Unwin, 1964), 40–51.

[3]Cf. Zbigniew K. Brzezinski, *The Soviet Bloc: Unity and Conflict* (Cambridge, MA: Harvard University Press, 1960).

[4]As argued by Rosanne Klass, 'The Great Game Revisited,' in Rosanne Klass (ed), *Afghanistan: The Great Game Revisited* (New York: Freedom House, 1987), 1–30.

[5]See Michael Minholz/Uwe Stirnberg, *Der Allgemeine Deutsche Nachrichtendienst (ADN): Gute Nachrichten für die SED* (München: Saur, 1995).

[6]In his study, *The Sino-Soviet Alliance*, Austin Jersild also urges the community of Soviet historians to adopt a more transnational approach. See Austin Jersild, *The Sino-Soviet Alliance: An International History* (Chapel Hill: University of North Carolina Press, 2014), 21.

being Stalin's article 'Dizzy with Success.'[7] When the communists came to power in Eastern Europe after 1945, though the respective parties became identical with the state, they did not cease to be political movements.[8] As such, each of the ruling communist parties had a central newspaper organ that expressed the 'official' voice of the party as well as the government. In communicating with their sister parties and party state leadership, the ruling communist parties were able to build on their own and Soviet traditions that often defied 'classical' diplomacy as exercised in the West.

The following study is an analysis of different ways of reporting on China between the mid-1950s and late 1960s in Eastern Europe. We consider not only 'what' but also 'how' the press reported on China, with a particular focus on the use of language, the arrangement of articles on the pages, and the discrepancies and omissions in the China coverage of the party newspapers.[9] Following Stalin's death and the 20th Congress of the CPSU, the Chinese leadership started to interfere more assertively in Eastern European affairs, thereby challenging increasingly Moscow's supremacy. Although the political elites in the socialist states of Eastern Europe often watched the radical changes in China with great concern, they used the evolving opportunities that stemmed from the rivalry between Beijing and Moscow for their own ends.[10] Close reading of contemporary newspapers supports this view of heterogeneous opinions in East Berlin, Budapest and Warsaw with regards to relations with Beijing and Moscow. Particularly in the years between 1957 and 1962, the portrayal of China was neither consistent throughout the bloc nor guided by Moscow. Only after 1962 can one again observe a gradual harmonisation of the image of China in those countries.

That concerted press campaigns to intimidate and weaken perceived ideological enemies inside the transnational socialist hemisphere were a viable political option in the 1950s and 1960s is emphasised by an argument between Nikita Khrushchev and the East German leader Walter Ulbricht over the difficulties in Hungary and Poland in a meeting of the Praesidium of the CPSU Central Committee on 24 October 1956:

> Comrade Ulbricht emphasized … that in his view the situation had arisen because we did not act in time to expose all the incorrect opinions that had emerged in Poland and Hungary. He assumed that it would behoove each party to give a response in the press to certain incorrect opinions. Comrade Khrushchev recommended that they think about the problems in greater depth. We must realize that we are not living as we were during the CI [Communist International] when only one party was in power. If we wanted to operate by command today, we would inevitably create chaos. It is necessary to conduct propaganda work in each party, but we cannot permit this to turn into polemics between fraternal parties because this would lead to polemics between nations.[11]

---

[7]Sheila Fitzpatrick, *Stalin's Peasants: Resistance and Survival in the Russian Village after Collectivization* (New York: Oxford University Press, 1994), 62–5.

[8]On Sovietization, see E. A. Rees, 'Introduction: The Sovietization of Eastern Europe,' in Balázs Apor et al. (eds), *The Sovietization of Eastern Europe: New Perspectives on the Postwar Period* (Washington: New Academia Publ., 2008) 1–28.

[9]On the socialist press in general, and Soviet press in particular, see Jukka Pietiläinen, *The Regional Newspaper in Post-Soviet Russia* (Tampere: Tampere University Press, 2002) 99–119.

[10]Austin Jersild, 'The Soviet State as Imperial Scavenger: "Catch Up and Surpass" in the Transnational Socialist Bloc, 1950–60,' *The American Historical Review*, Vol. 116, No. 1 (2011) 110. There are, however, different opinions on the extent to which European communist states used this disagreement between Moscow and Beijing to gain leverage for their own political goals. Cf. Péter Vámos, '"Mi történt a kínaikkal?" A magyar-kínai kapcsolatok 1956–66 között,' *Kül-Világ*, Vol. 6, No. 1 (2009) 1–25.

[11]'Document No. 27: Jan Svoboda's Notes on the CPSU CC Praesidium Meeting with Satellite Leaders, October 24 1956,' in Csaba Békés, Malcolm Byrne, and János M Rainer (eds), *The 1956 Hungarian Revolution: A History in Documents* (Budapest: Central European University Press, 2002) 226.

Such discrepancies help to explain why it was only in 1967 that a thorough coordination mechanism vis-à-vis China had emerged in the Eastern Bloc.[12] The period between 1957 and 1962, when simmering tensions between Moscow and Beijing came to a head, not only provided opportunities for bloc member states, but the circumstances also forced them to react, as China could hardly be set aside, and because ignoring China was a statement in its own right. Due to Khrushchev's doubts about Mao's intentions in those years, policy coordination was far from smooth.

In this article we examine this dilemma by looking at the press in Hungary, Poland and East Germany and by combining the findings with sources from German, Hungarian and Indian archives. We thus analyse to what extent, at which stages in time and for what reasons, the governments in Budapest, Warsaw and East Berlin distanced themselves from Moscow publicly in their policy towards Beijing, how such dissonances were communicated in the press and what consequences such publicly transmitted opinions had for intra-bloc relations.

We base our analysis on the major daily newspapers of the communist parties of Hungary, Poland and East Germany: *Népszabadság* ('People's Freedom'), *Trybuna Ludu* ('People's Tribune') and *Neues Deutschland* ('New Germany'). The propaganda transmitted via these three party mouthpieces is a useful indicator of the respective governments' publicly communicated, official positions.[13] Building on the limited research on the portrayal of China in the Soviet bloc media already published, we restrict our analysis to three major themes that reveal the differences between the relations among the People's Republic of China and Eastern bloc states in relation to the Soviet Union in times of increasing tensions between Moscow and Beijing.[14] First we analyse the differences in the perception of the Great Leap Forward (1958–61) as China's definitive departure from the Soviet Union's model of development.[15] The second part examines the Sino-Indian conflict that evolved into the war of 1962. In many ways, this war can be seen as one of several turning points: China had not yet fully broken with the Soviet Union, while Jawaharlal Nehru's India was still to become a close partner of the Kremlin. The final part explores the early years of the Cultural Revolution and its ramifications for the deterioration of Sino-Soviet relations as seen from Warsaw, Berlin and Budapest.

When speech is golden: the Great Leap Forward

Since its foundation in 1949, Hungary, Poland and East Germany established the PRC as motivational example in public discourse, an image that gradually assumed more firm contours in the press over the following years due to intensifying contacts in political, cultural and economic spheres.[16] This process did not stop with the Hungarian Revolution or the

---

[12]1967 was the year 'Interkit', a policy coordination effort with China experts from the USSR, its Warsaw Pact allies, and other nations aligned with the Kremlin, was established. Cf. James Hershberg et al., 'The Interkit-Story: A Window into the Final Decades of the Sino-Soviet Relationship,' *Cold War International History Project Working Paper*, No. 63 (February 2011).

[13]*Pravda*, the organ of the Central Committee of the CPSU, will be used only as a reference point to assess the autonomy of reporting. Chinese newspapers will be left aside.

[14]David Tompkins recently examined images of China in East Germany and Poland. David Tompkins, 'The East is Red? Images of China in East Germany and Poland through the Sino-Soviet Split,' *Zeitschrift für Ostmitteleuropa-Forschung*, Vol. 62, No. 3 (2013) 393–424.

[15]Thomas P. Bernstein, 'Introduction: The Complexities of Learning from the Soviet Union,' in Thomas P. Bernstein/Hua-Yu Li (eds), *China Learns from the Soviet Union* (Lanham: Lexington Books, 2010) 17.

[16]Tompkins, 'The East is Red?,' 400–8.

60   BEYOND THE KREMLIN'S REACH?

Polish October of 1956.[17] When Chinese Prime Minister Zhou Enlai visited the new Polish leader Władysław Gomułka in January 1957, the Polish press hailed him as a 'messenger of friendship.'[18] This comes as no surprise given that both parties pursued common interests. The new Polish leadership sought Chinese support against the tough Soviet stance and both governments lamented aspects of Soviet hegemony.[19] Premier Józef Cyrankiewicz's subsequent state visit to China in April 1957 was presented in a similarly positive light.[20]

Despite such high praise in the press, Sino-Polish relations did not develop as imagined by Beijing during the summer of 1957. In the emerging discrepancies over socio-economic and foreign policy issues and the ideological course between China and the Soviet Union, Warsaw would side firmly with Moscow.[21] At the same time, the Chinese leadership was concerned about the loyalty of both the Poles and the Hungarians in the wake of 1956.[22] For some time, the Polish press concealed such disagreements from the public. Throughout 1957, *Trybuna Ludu* continued to publish extensively on Chinese social, economic and cultural issues.[23] The paper continued to uphold the façade of amicable Sino-Polish and Sino-Soviet relations for some time. However, first-hand observations and other genres of journalistic writing beyond the compulsory reporting on state visits, cultural exchange, economic cooperation and congratulatory messages on national holidays almost disappeared in the years following 1957.[24] Though Sino-Soviet controversies were not yet public, studying what was written between the lines, the observant reader would have understood that this standardised propaganda language was a warning sign of disagreement.

The quintessentially positive image of China lasted longer in Hungary. On 1 October 1959, the PRC celebrated its tenth anniversary. With the Hungarian leadership participating in the festivities, October 1959 became a month of celebration in *Népszabadság*. Editorials, Telegraph Agency of the Soviet Union (TASS)-articles and intimate reports written by Hungarian journalists on China and its ties to Hungary filled half the pages of the 1 and 2 October issues, while Prime Minister Ferenc Münnich presided over the festivities at home.[25] Reports of a Hungarian party delegation led by István Dobi, chairman of the Presidential Council of the People's Republic of Hungary, on tour through China conveyed an immensely positive image at odds with the tide of the devastating Great Leap Forward and rising tensions between Moscow and Beijing.[26] Ten days after the visit of a people's

---

[17]Cf. Andrzej Werblan, 'The Polish October of 1956: Legends and Reality,' in Jan Rowinski (ed), *The Polish October 1956 in World Politics* (Warsaw: Polski Instytut Spraw Miedzynarodowych, 2007) 13–42.

[18]E.g. 'Posłannik przyjaźni,' *Trybuna Ludu*, 11 January 1957, 2.

[19]For Zhou's visit, cf. L.W. Gluchowski, 'Poland, 1956: Khrushchev, Gomulka and the "Polish October",' *Cold War International History Project Bulletin*, No. 5 (1995) 43–5.

[20]E.g. 'Spotkanie delegacji polskiej z tow. Mao Tse-tungiem,' *Trybuna Ludu*, 9 April 1957, 1.

[21]Lorenz M. Lüthi, 'China and East Europe, 1956–1960,' *Modern China Studies* 22, No. 1 (2015) 243–9; Zhihua Shen/ Danhui Li, 'The Polish Crisis of 1956 and the Polish-Chinese Relations Viewed from Beijing,' in Jan Rowinski (ed), *The Polish October 1956 in World Politics* (Warsaw: Polski Instytut Spraw Miedzynarodowych, 2007) 75–113 *passim*; Tompkins, 'The East is Red?,' 413–5.

[22]Jersild, *Sino-Soviet Alliance*, 20.

[23]E.g. 'Jak wygląda kwestia małżeństwa w Chinach,' *Trybuna Ludu*, 4 September 1957, 2; 'Daleko od Pekinu,' *Trybuna Ludu*, 30 September 1957, 4.

[24]For example reports on increases in trade, e.g. 'Polsko-chińska współpraca gospodarcza,' *Trybuna Ludu*, 13 February 1958, 2; cultural exchange, e.g. 'Sukces "Mazowsza" w Pekinie,' *Trybuna Ludu*, 9 February 1960, 1; or Poland's support of China's admission to the United Nations that appeared regularly in the paper, 'Poska domaga się natychmiastowego przyznania ChRL należnego jej miejsca w ONZ,' *Trybuna Ludu*, 7 December 1960, 3.

[25]'Díszünnepség a Kínai Népköztársaság megalakulásának 10. Évfordulója alkalmából a Csepeli Sportcsarnokban,' *Népszabadság*, 1 October 1959, 1.

[26]'A magyar párt és kormányküldöttség látogatása egy Peking környéki népi kommunában,' *Népszabadság*, 4 October 1959, 5.

commune, an article authored by the Minister of the Interior Béla Biszku sounded enthusiastic. His account invokes the impression of an elderly, paternalistic Hungarian friend looking with hindsight at his young, energetic Chinese ally, and, in doing so, also attempts to strengthen the domestic legitimacy of the Hungarian leadership. Within this hierarchy of the socialist bloc, and with Beijing acknowledging Moscow's hegemony, Biszku foresaw a glittering future for China.[27]

The Hungarian communist leadership had reasons to be grateful to its Chinese comrades.[28] Just one year after the revolution, once the Kádár-group had gained full control and could be sure that the old-style Stalinists would remain in exile in the USSR, Hungary's new strong man made his second trip to China in fall 1957. The Chinese willingly supported his new regime. Zhou Enlai's visit to Budapest in January 1957, just weeks after the fighting was over, provided a big boost to Kádár at exactly the moment when he was in need of help.[29] Zhou's diplomatic activities increased significantly the political influence of Mao's China in Eastern Europe and would challenge Moscow's exclusive position.[30] Soon the contrasting positions of Beijing and Moscow became undeniable and the socialist satellite states found themselves sandwiched between the two. Beijing tried actively to split up Moscow's allies by giving benefits to states that were ready to have closer ties to China.[31]

The hard stance against counter-revolution, backed by Mao, helps to explain why the Hungarian leadership held onto the image of an intact socialist family for so long.[32] *Népszabadság* worked hard to propagate this claim. On 27 October, *Népszabadság* released a highly visible report on the Great Leap Forward citing Chinese sources.[33] The party newspaper did not necessarily have to claim anything negative with regards to the campaign, but could have simply decided to stop reporting on the Chinese economy – as the Polish press did. Also, István Dobi, who met Mao on 19 October in Beijing, gave a speech in which he praised the Great Leap Forward.[34] Two weeks after his return, he published an enthusiastic article on the people's communes in *Népszabadság*.[35]

Given that Hungary ultimately stayed loyal to the Soviet Union, the question is why the Hungarian people were, up to 1960, mainly able to read flattering propaganda articles on China and how the subsequent turn-around was staged? The communist leadership in Budapest, though still admiring its comrades in Beijing, became cautious about expressing its own opinion and republished Soviet articles on China in *Népszabadság*, in particular after Beijing's first comprehensive counter-attack on Moscow's ideology in April and more so after the Bucharest Conference of the World Communist and Workers' Parties and the meeting of the World Federation of Trade Unions in Beijing (both in June) and the withdrawal of

---

[27]'Látogatásunk a baráti Kínában,' *Népszabadság*, 13 October 1959, 3.

[28]Cf. Jersild, *Sino-Soviet Alliance*, 109 and 119–20; Zhihua Shen/Yafeng Xia, 'New Evidence for China's Role in the Hungarian Crisis of October 1956,' *The International History Review*, Vol. 31, No. 3 (2009) 558–75.

[29]Péter Vámos, 'Sino-Hungarian Relations and the 1956 Revolution,' *Cold War International History Project* Working Paper 54 (November 2006) 9, 20–2.

[30]Vámos, 'Sino-Hungarian Relations,' 23; Hermann Wentker, *Außenpolitik in engen Grenzen: Die DDR im internationalen System 1949–1989* (München: Oldenbourg, 2007) 167.

[31]Vámos, 'Mi történt a kínaikkal?,' 3.

[32]Cf. Kádár's first visit to China as Hungarian leader. 'Nagygyűlés Pekingben a magyar kormányküldöttség tiszteletére,' *Népszabadság*, 4 October 1957, 1.

[33]'A kínai népgazdaságban folytatódik az ugrásszerű fejlődés,' *Népszabadság*, 27 October 1959, 4.

[34]'Dobi István elvtárs beszéde Pekingben,' *Népszabadság*, 20 October 1959, 3.

[35]'Kínai barátainknál,' *Népszabadság*, 8 November 1959, 3.

Soviet advisers in August.[36] Though these events changed the level of hostility in Sino-Soviet relations considerably and made 1960 a watershed moment, it was only in 1963 that the Hungarian leadership would no longer allow articles from Xinhua to be published without comment. From then on, China was criticised in a more radical way than in the Soviet press, thus reversing the great enthusiasm of the late 1950s.

The relationship between the GDR and the PRC was a very special one right from the beginning. Both states were arguing for reunification with the 'non-liberated' parts of their nation and both were on the frontlines of the Cold War battlefield. Beijing signed a mutual treaty on friendship and cooperation with East Berlin in 1955 – earlier than with other socialist countries in Eastern Europe. China and East Germany profited from each other, particularly in the economic sphere. The importance of the emotional bonds between the two countries as endangered places on the bloc's outer rim was also stressed in *Neues Deutschland*. On 22 January 1959, the day that marked the arrival of an East German delegation led by the Prime Minister Otto Grotewohl to China, the paper published a front-page article by Paul Wandel, the East German Ambassador to Beijing:

> For all the spatial distance between the People's Republic of China and the German Democratic Republic, we are intertwined in an all the more special way. Both republics have the same birth date, October 1949, and in 1959 they celebrate their tenth anniversary together. ... United, determined and successful, they fight – the PR China in the Far East, the GDR in the heart of Europe – against the war policy of the imperialists and their minions, for the preservation of peace as the decisive need of humanity. In 1958 both republics entered a new important period in their fight for the accelerated buildup and the completion of socialism in a historically short time ... Our delegation will learn about the results of the Great Leap in 1958, the iron will, the enthusiasm, and the capability with which the Chinese people under the leadership of the Communist party are preparing for the another, even bigger Leap Forward in 1959.[37]

Wandel is referring indirectly to the collectivisation of agriculture that had occurred at roughly the same time in his country as the formation of people's communes in China. The delicate balancing act, mirrored in the state press, came to an end in the GDR when *Neues Deutschland* took a sharp and unique anti-Chinese turn concerning the people's communes in June 1960, after the director of the Chinese pavilion at the agricultural exhibition in Markkleeberg had given an interview to a provincial newspaper stating that people's communes were the best form of collectivisation.[38] For Ulbricht this must have felt like treason, as this suggestion could be seen as a tacit call for him to introduce people's communes in the near future, too. The East German leadership only reacted after West German newspapers had taken up the issue. Without consulting Moscow, the Politburo introduced a whole range of measures on 14 June 1960 to make a clear statement: a letter of protest was written to the director of the Chinese pavilion and a Politburo member lectured the Chinese Ambassador on the damage that Chinese behaviour had done to the East German collectivisation campaign. Moreover, a *Pravda* article on falsifications of Lenin by the Chinese was published

---

[36]The text 'Long Live Leninism' appeared in *Hongqi* (*Red Flag*) on 16 April 1960. On the ideological warfare in Beijing and Bucharest, cf. Lorenz M. Lüthi, *The Sino-Soviet Split: Cold War in the Communist World* (Princeton: Princeton University Press, 2008) 167–74.

[37]'Mächtiger Verbündeter und Freund,' *Neues Deutschland*, 22 January 1959, 1.

[38]The interview appeared on 4 June 1960 in *Thüringische Landeszeitung*.

BEYOND THE KREMLIN'S REACH?

immediately in *Neues Deutschland* and critical remarks on people's communes by Ulbricht himself appeared in the same paper.[39]

Though in Hungary the positive reporting on China continued for the rest of 1959,[40] sympathy for Beijing was beginning to decline by the end of the year. *Népszabadság* gave the Chinese delegation a warm welcome to the VII. Congress of the Hungarian Socialist Workers' Party in early December 1959.[41] But the reprint of Kádár's opening speech can be seen as an indicator for rebalancing ties with Beijing and Moscow: he only mentioned China in a short paragraph on the transformation of a former colony into a 'socialist world power.' In Kádár's eyes, the Soviet Union was the guardian of socialism and victor over fascism, now technologically advanced and years ahead of the United States.[42] The positioning and length of the published speeches by Khrushchev and the Chinese delegate Tan Zhenlin support this increasing inclination towards Moscow.[43]

Polish media coverage of the Great Leap Forward was scant compared to that of the Hungarian press. Initially, *Trybuna Ludu* reported on the key decisions taken by the party leadership, in 1958, that prepared for rapid collectivisation and industrialisation during the Great Leap Forward using affirmative language and going into great detail.[44] The paper lent its voice to Zhou Enlai's paean to the people's communes, dubbing them 'the best of all forms to increase production and speed up the construction of a socialist society on the path to communism.'[45] The Polish press was blinded by the impressive statistics which claimed that, in 1959, many goals of the Second Five-Year Plan (1958–62) had already been fulfilled.[46]

Yet *Trybuna Ludu* remained silent at the peak of the crisis. This policy was maintained when Khrushchev criticised people's communes, for the first time in public, at a rally in Poland on 18 July 1959. The Polish press simply did not publish his remarks; but *Pravda* did, causing a scandal with China.[47] In the following years, Polish newspaper subscribers could only guess at the disastrous outcome of the Great Leap Forward by interpreting the silence and reading between the lines: 'Better harvest in the PRC than in previous years,' ran a headline in September 1962.[48] And hidden away in a report on the Chinese New Year in January 1963 was a reference to a 'visible recovery in the stores that are now much better stocked with products than in the past.'[49] With empty shelves not uncommon in European socialist states either, the press would usually not report on such shortages. However, no

---

[39]Barch, DY/30/J IV 2/2/709, 'Protocol 28/60 Politburo meeting 28.06.1960.' The Soviet article 'Eine geistige Waffe des Kommunismus' appeared in *Neues Deutschland*, 15 June 1960, 5. An article condemning any notion that the GDR was considering the introduction of people's communes followed two days later: 'Zur Klärung einer Frage,' *Neues Deutschland*, 17 June 1960, 3. For a more general picture on the different layers of bilateral relations see Nicole F. Stuber-Berries, *East German China policy in the Face of the Sino-Soviet Conflict: 1966–1966* (PhD dissertation: Geneva University, 2004).

[40]E.g. reports on cultural and sporting events 'Tömegverseny ötvenezer részvevővel – Pekingben,' *Népszabadság*, 13 November 1959, 12.

[41]The arrival of the Chinese delegation was celebrated with a picture on the front page: 'Pénteken 14 ország testvérpártjának küldöttsége érkezett Budapestre az MSZMP kongresszusára,' *Népszabadság*, 28 November 1959, 1.

[42]'A Magyar Szocialista Munkáspárt Központi Bizottságának beszámolója és a párt feladatai,' *Népszabadság*, 1 December 1959, 3–11.

[43]'Őszintén kívánjuk a magyar népnek, arasson új győzelmeket a szocializmus építésében,' *Népszabadság*, 2 December 1959, 1–4. The speech delivered by the CCP central committee secretary was much shorter. 'Tan Csen-lin, Kína Kommunista Pártja Központi Bizottságának titkára,' *Népszabadság*, 3 December 1959, 1–2.

[44]E.g. 'Decyzje plenum KC Komunistycznej Partii Chin,' *Trybuna Ludu*, 18 December 1958, 1–2.

[45]'Obrady parlamentu chińskiego,' *Trybuna Ludu*, 18 December 1959, 1–2.

[46]'Plan rozwoju gospodarczego Chin,' *Trybuna Ludu*, 31 January 1960, 1.

[47]Zhihua Shen/Yafeng Xia, 'The Great Leap Forward, the People's Commune and the Sino-Soviet Split,' *Journal of Contemporary China* 20, No. 72 (2011): 874–5.

[48]'Zbiory w ChRL lepsze niż w latach ubiegłych,' *Trybuna Ludu*, 18 September 1962, 2.

[49]'Nowy Rok w Chinach,' *Trybuna Ludu*, 26 January 1963, 3.

64 BEYOND THE KREMLIN'S REACH?

one – not even in the West – would have imagined at this time that the campaign had cost millions of lives.[50]

Trybuna Ludu celebrated the Chinese path of quick transformation, only in its infancy. The behaviour of Hungary can be explained by way of the events of 1956 and their aftermath. Before 1956 the Hungarian leadership felt somewhat undervalued by the Chinese in comparison to the East Germans and other socialist bloc member states. This was not to change until the old Stalinist leader Mátyás Rákosi stepped down. The real take-off in Sino-Hungarian relations only occurred under Kádár.[51] Officially, this development was crowned by a mutual friendship and support treaty signed in May 1959, in China, by Prime Minister Ferenc Münnich, and was celebrated in the press.[52]

Changing friend-foe mindsets: the Sino-Indian War of 1962

By the early 1960s, bilateral cooperation between the USSR, its East European allies and China had almost ceased. The Sino-Indian struggle over state borders inherited from colonial times placed Moscow and its allies in a difficult situation.[53] The attentive *Trybuna Ludu* reader would perhaps have been caught by surprise in April 1960 to read about a territorial dispute between China and India since that had in fact erupted eight months earlier when Chinese troops captured a new Indian military outpost. Until then, the Polish paper had depicted the two Asian giants as good neighbours and friends.[54] This strategy changed only when Beijing's communists accused their Moscow comrades of ideological revisionism in April 1960. Obviously, with the clear intension of following Moscow's prudent stance, *Trybuna Ludu* did not speak on behalf of either of the warring parties when it reported about Zhou Enlai's landmark visit to India and the efforts to ease tensions on their shared border.[55]

The East European press propaganda also continued to follow Moscow's neutrality after the conflict escalated into a major border war. A Chinese unit attacked an Indian post on 8 September 1962 and crossed the McMahon Line on 20 October. News appeared with great delay – only after the worst fighting had already ceased.[56] On 26 October, *Trybuna Ludu* published a *Pravda* reprint, which associated the McMahon Line with the British colonial legacy and suggested the cause of the conflict was this history of colonial intrusion. By stressing 'unwavering friendship' with China and the 'deep satisfaction caused by the development of cooperation' with India, Moscow and Warsaw's awkward position became apparent in the press. Instead of fighting imperialism as their common enemy, the border clash weakened both countries.[57] This was almost the only news about the actual fighting.[58]

---

[50]Frank Dikötter, *Mao's Great Famine: The History of China's Most Devastating Catastrophe, 1958–1962* (New York: Walker & Co., 2010).

[51]Vámos, 'Sino-Hungarian Relations,' 7–9, 19–20.

[52]Vámos, 'Mi történt a kínaikkal?,' 4; 'Közlemény a magyar párt és kormanyküldöttségnek a Kínai Népköztársaságban tett látogatásáról,' *Népszabadság*, 7 May 1959, 1.

[53]For a general view of the border dispute, see Xuecheng Liu, *The Sino-Indian Border Dispute and Sino-Indian Relations* (Lanham: University Press of America, 1994).

[54]E.g. quoting Mao Zedong on the occasion of an official Indian state visit to China, 'Mao Tse-tung o stosunkach chińsko-indyjskich,' *Trybuna Ludu*, 20 September 1957, 2.

[55]'Premier Czou En-lai przybył z wyzytą do Indii,' *Trybuna Ludu*, 20 April 1960, 1; 'Wspólny komunikat o rozmowach Czou En-lai – Nehru,' *Trybuna Ludu*, 26 April 1960, 2; 'Chiny – Indie,' *Trybuna Ludu*, 28 April 1960, 2.

[56]Reasons why Moscow remained neutral in the border war are given in Lüthi, *Sino-Soviet Split*, 144–6.

[57]'"Prawda": Porozumnienie ChRL i Indii wykazałoby siłę zasady pokojowego współistnienia,' *Trybuna Ludu*, 26 October 1962, 2.

[58]A single article, relying equally on information from the two major press agencies Xinhua and Press Trust of India about the warfare, was the only exception. 'Sytuacja na granicy chińsko-indyjskiej,' *Trybuna Ludu*, 1 November 1962, 2.

BEYOND THE KREMLIN'S REACH? 65

Later *Pravda* reprints demanded an immediate end to the military operations and the start of negotiations.[59]

During the subsequent weeks and months, *Trybuna Ludu* closely followed the diplomatic resolution of the border dispute. It sided with Moscow, eventually portraying India as the victim of Chinese aggression. In the exchange of open letters and notes between Zhou and Nehru that followed, New Delhi's position was portrayed as strong, rightful and insisting on the *status quo* ante whereas Beijing was presented as almost docile, acknowledging its mistakes. *Trybuna Ludu* placed particular emphasis on the initiative of six non-aligned states, which convened in Colombo to seek a solution in a Bandung spirit.[60] The final word, however, rested with *Pravda*. The Soviet paper informed its Polish readers that in recent times the Chinese press had been filled with slander aimed against the Soviet position in the Sino-Indian dispute and that China was reluctant to accept the negotiating proposal of the non-aligned states.[61]

In Hungary, the coverage on the Sino-Indian War had started even more reluctantly. Just like *Trybuna Ludu*, *Népszabadság* reprinted a piece from *Pravda* on 26 October, accompanied by a short article based on a report by the Hungarian news agency's Beijing correspondent. Both articles were urging a peaceful solution to the conflict and emphasised the Chinese desire for peace.[62] As far as India is concerned, the focus was instead on the exploitation of the conflict by 'reactionaries', if the Indian government did not seek peaceful measures. Judging by the tone of these publications, the Hungarian press – in contrast to its Polish and Soviet counterparts – leaned towards the Chinese side. There was also a pro-Chinese misbalance in terms of sources in *Népszabadság*.[63]

Reporting changed over the course of the conflict. *Népszabadság* increasingly relied on articles from the Soviet press, much less on reports from Chinese media outlets. Articles by Hungarian correspondents were hardly published and reprinted articles were not placed as prominently in the Hungarian newspaper as in their original sources. An interpretational change occurred in early November 1962 with a reprint of a *Pravda* article blaming western imperialists trying to weaken progressive forces in India.[64] Indo-Soviet relations were seen as exemplary due to the peaceful coexistence of the two countries, according to a second article in the same issue.[65]

In 1959 the East German press was still supportive of the Chinese, while the Soviet media had remained neutral.[66] This even led to a major faux pas when Grotewohl claimed in a speech in Beijing in September 1959 that Indian forces had – for no reason – invaded Chinese territory. His statement shows the ideological sympathies of the East German leadership for China that prevailed until the Markkleeberg incident in June 1960, though

---

[59]'"Prawda" o konieczności uregulowania w drodze rokowań konfliktu indyjsko-chinskiego,' *Trybuna Ludu*, 6 November 1962, 2.

[60]E.g. 'List premiera Czou En-laia do premiera Nehru,' *Trybuna Ludu*, 2 December 1962, 2.

[61]'Poważne ognisko napięcia w Azji,' *Trybuna Ludu*, 20 September 1963, 2. See also Hyer, *The Pragmatic Dragon*.

[62]'A népek érdekében az általános béke nevében,' *Népszabadság*, 26 October 1962, 5; 'Konfliktus a kínai-indiai határon,' *Népszabadság*, 26 October 1962, 5.

[63]Relying mainly on Xinhua news agency press releases, *Népszabadság* printed Chinese governmental statements without mentioning similar Indian declarations. E.g. 'A Kínai Népköztársaság kormányának nyilatkozata a kínai-indiai határincidensekről,' *Népszabadság*, 27 October 1962, 5.

[64]'A tárgyalások utat nyitnak a konfliktus rendezéséhez,' *Népszabadság*, 6 November 1962, 4.

[65]Based on a TASS announcement on a meeting between Leonid Brezhnev and the new Indian ambassador to the Soviet Union. 'India és Szovjetunió kapcsolata példa a békés együttélés elveinek megvalósítására,' *Népszabadság*, 6 November 1962, 5.

[66]Stuber-Berries, *East German China Policy*, 84–5.

it was a mistake to print Grotewohl's speech in *Neues Deutschland* making it accessible for the Indian government which followed international media coverage on the conflict carefully.[67] With New Delhi upset about Grotewohl's Beijing speech, East Berlin's attempt to gain diplomatic recognition from India suffered a major setback.[68]

The image of China in the East German press changed significantly in 1962 when, in contrast to 1959, *Neues Deutschland*, following East Berlin's party guidelines, took a tougher anti-Chinese stance. The India correspondent Manfred Stuhlmann cabled back to Berlin that the hands of the East German diplomats and journalists in Beijing were tied in the conflict between an ally and a friend while the Western powers were using this weakness for their own benefit.[69] In contrast to *Népszabadság*, the German paper speculated that the Indians would agree to peace talks, if the Chinese withdrew their troops to their earlier positions.[70] Such statements made the Chinese appear less peaceful than in the Hungarian press.

Neues Deutschland also reprinted major *Pravda* articles – a sign that the East German leadership feared the repercussions of voicing strong opinions as in 1959.[71] Unlike the Polish and Hungarian papers, however, *Neues Deutschland* was the only tabloid to place the *Pravda* articles on their front page. *Neues Deutschland* reported on the new offer of peace talks made by the PRC in early November and mentioned that Beijing was ready to withdraw its forces to the pre-war positions.[72] Nevertheless, the Berlin newspaper feared that West Germany, the United States and other 'western imperialists' might possibly exploit the situation, installing eventually a new Indian government that would leave the path of neutrality and align itself with the capitalist powers.[73]

Beyond the headlines of the Sino-Indian border clashes, there was something more that had changed in the East European press. Prior to the dispute, both China and India had been portrayed as friends and their relationship as being peaceful. What changed in 1962 was that the newspapers dedicated more attention to India than to China. In fact, from that point on, India was to assume – at least in part – the role of the 'Asian friend' formerly held by China. After 1962, China barely featured in the party papers beyond the political news. Particularly in *Trybuna Ludu*, friendship associations, positive developments in bilateral trade and political dialogue between Warsaw and New Delhi at ministerial level gained considerable attention.[74] Though this was a common trend in East European media, the Polish press was in the vanguard of enthusiasm for India.

A party directive on future reporting on China in the East German press, drafted in spring and summer 1961, suggests that East Berlin hoped to restore harmony with Beijing after the Markkleeberg incident and after the Sino-Soviet conflict went public. All versions of the document were urging for closer ties with Beijing. The press was instructed to contribute to

---

[67]'Wir marschieren gemeinsam zum Sozialismus,' Neues Deutschland, 29 September 1959, 3. On the seriousness with which the Indian government followed the Eastern bloc's press, see 'Sino-Indian border incidents – Attitude of countries of East Europe,' National Archives of India, New Delhi (NAI), List No. 258 S. No. 314 3/96/Eur.E/59.

[68]Johannes H. Voigt, *Die Indienpolitik der DDR: Von den Anfängen bis zur Anerkennung* (Köln: Böhlau, 2008) 293–6.

[69]'Informationsbericht des ADN-/ND-Korrespondenten in Neu Delhi zum Besuch Lübkes,' 30 November 1962, Barch, DY/30/IV 2/2.028/84.

[70]By placing the news on page seven, *Neues Deutschland's* editors seemed at first to downplay the conflict: 'Heftige Kämpfe im Grenzgebiet,' Neues Deutschland, 21 October 1962, 7. 'Erklärung Volkschina,' Neues Deutschland, 25 October 1962, 5.

[71]'Im Interesse der Völker, im Namen des Weltfriedens,' Neues Deutschland, 26 October 1962, 1.

[72]'Neues Verhandlungsangebot Volkschinas an Indien,' Neues Deutschland, 8 November 1962, 7.

[73]'Verdächtige Betriebsamkeit,' Neues Deutschland, 10 November 1962, 5.

[74]Sometimes as part of more comprehensive coverage, e.g. 'Ogólnopolski Zjazd Towarzystwa Przyjaźni Polsko-Indyjskiej,' *Trybuna Ludu*, 22 January 1962, 2.

a more positive image of mutual relations while any reporting on China should not violate the spirit of the Moscow Declaration of November 1960 that formed a truce between the Soviets and Chinese. Future reports on China were to focus on the successes of the Chinese people and party leadership to build socialism, overcome backwardness, and fight natural disasters. East German officials were aware that they had to increase quality and quantity of reporting, if they wanted to warm Sino-East German relations. This strategy included avoiding difficult issues with potential repercussions throughout the bloc, such as the people's communes or the Great Leap Forward and called for a close collaboration between the East German embassy personnel and correspondents.

The East German leadership was well aware that the Chinese were reading the East German newspaper closely. The 1961 press directive therefore called it a mistake when *Neues Deutschland* failed to print condolence telegrams like the one issued by Zhou Enlai after the death of the trade minister Heinrich Rau in March 1961.[75] Printing Zhou's telegram would not have alleviated the grievances of ordinary East German workers while it may have been regarded as a sign of good will in Beijing. Ulbricht needed Mao's support in Moscow to push for a radical solution on the porous inner-German border. Without informing Moscow he sent a delegation to Beijing in January 1961 hoping to find in Mao an ally.[76] The media strategy formulated in early 1961 has to be seen in this light. It is an example of the perceived room to manoeuvre of the leaders of the Eastern European state socialist countries and the role the press could play in such endeavours. Ulbricht eventually got his way, in August 1961, when the Berlin Wall was built. Mao's support against Khrushchev was no longer needed.

A point of no return: the Cultural Revolution

The political leadership in Budapest, Warsaw and East Berlin had a fairly accurate view of the economic, political and social realities of communist China thanks to advisers and diplomats filing numerous reports back to their capitals. Yet with the future of the bloc still unclear, confusion and tentativeness prevailed in the East European party press in the early 1960s, until the onset of the Cultural Revolution made any sympathy for Beijing impossible.

This attitude is evident in state propaganda, as journalists still adhered to the previous line on the alliance and 'friendship.' Though firsthand-accounts and features on China had already been missing for some years, *Trybuna Ludu* still commemorated the anniversary of Sino-Soviet friendship every year in February on its international news page. By and large, those articles paraphrased *Pravda* articles thereby mirroring Moscow's official perception of the climatic change between the two communist giants. As of 1964, after the Sino-Soviet polemic had gone public between February and July 1963, these reports no longer underlined the positive image of the amicable relationship: 'Unfortunately the Soviet-Chinese relations have been experiencing – through no fault of our own – a rapid downturn ... in all areas of cooperation since 1960. But the Soviet people are ready to provide continued comprehensive assistance and support to the Chinese people in their task of building

---

[75]Politisches Archiv des Auswärtigen Amtes (PA AA), A6763, 'Vorschläge zur künftigen Gestaltung der Berichterstattung über Probleme der Volksrepublik China in der DDR-Presse,' 15 May 1961.

[76]Wentker, *Außenpolitik in engen Grenzen*, 168–9.

socialism.'[77] With such an unmistakable shift in language, this report heralded the demise of this annual ritual, which would make its final appearance in 1966.[78]

The tendency in the annual reports about the National Day of the PRC is similar. In general, they featured more prominently in *Trybuna Ludu*. In 1963, once the heated verbal exchange between Beijing and Moscow had gone public, this came with a warning voice against the 'malicious public polemic' by the leadership in Beijing.[79] By reading the papers, everyone would have been able to notice that the radicalisation of Beijing's policies toward Moscow and its allies had widened the gap between the Soviet Union and China. Over the years, articles became shorter, their number grew smaller and the way in which they were arranged on the newspaper pages clearly signalled that Beijing had fallen into disgrace in the Soviet universe.[80] After Red Guards flocked around the Soviet embassy in Beijing in August 1966 and attacked the embassy compound in January 1967, *Trybuna Ludu* completely omitted the founding anniversary of the PRC for the first time in October that year.

Just as in the Polish paper, the tone towards China turned frosty in *Népszabadság* in 1963 and 1964. The Hungarian tabloid copied Soviet articles and reprinted TASS announcements and *Pravda* and *Izvestiia* articles. One of the early examples of negative reporting was a reprint from *Pravda* on Khrushchev's New Year speech in 1964, in which the Soviet leader expressed his desire for peace in the Chinese press. The author claimed that Chinese newspapers were stating incorrect things about the speech and claiming that Khrushchev wanted to hinder the anti-imperialist fight.[81] Nevertheless, the Soviet reports celebrating the anniversary of the Sino-Soviet-treaty continued to be mirrored on the front page of *Népszabadság*.[82]

By 1964, it is obvious that the Hungarian paper was prepared to take a tougher public stance than before. During a joint meeting of János Kádár and Antonín Novotný, the Czechoslovak president urged for a united position of the socialist bloc against China – a position that was reprinted in the Hungarian press.[83] Loyal readers of *Népszabadság* might have got the impression that the leaders in Budapest, Warsaw and East Berlin wanted to show their unwavering loyalty to the Soviet Union by being tough and mocking the Chinese leadership in their propaganda. Novotný's hint that in the past communists had always settled their scores with deviators must have sounded like a neo-Stalinist threat against China. This was not a sensible gesture like the ones the Soviet leadership still made via its statements of friendship, but simply confrontational, probably intentionally so. It made the Kremlin's position appear softer, at least in the more or less undeclared media war taking place in the public sphere of socialist transnationalism.

The people involved in this ideological battle for socialist unity were – in contrast to the political elites in the West – not mere politicians or government officials, but members of an international movement interested in the actions of their peers abroad and in achieving doctrinal purity. Key figures like Kádár, Mao and Ulbricht had, for much of their lifetimes, lived

---

[77]'Artykuł "Prawdy" w 14 rocznicę układu o przyjaźni z ChRL,' *Trybuna Ludu*, 16 February 1964, 2.

[78]In a similarly negative tone: 'W 16 rocznicę podpisania układu o przyjaźni między ZSSR i ChRL,' *Trybuna Ludu*, 15 February 1966, 2.

[79]E.g. 'Święto narodu chińskiego,' *Trybuna Ludu*, 1 October 1963, 4 (quotation); 'Święto narodu chińskiego,' *Trybuna Ludu*, 1 October 1964, 2.

[80]In 1966 the Polish party newspaper ran a *Pravda* story with an unequivocal criticism of the Chinese leadership. 'Dziennik "Prawda" o 17 rocznicy ChRL,' *Trybuna Ludu*, 2 October 1966, 2.

[81]'Minek félrevezetni az embereket?,' *Népszabadság*, 31 January 1964, 8.

[82]'Moszkvai lapok a szovjet-kínai szerződés évfordulójáról,' *Népszabadság*, 15 February 1964, 1.

[83]'Antonin Novotny elvtárs beszéde,' *Népszabadság*, 3 October 1964, 3–4.

BEYOND THE KREMLIN'S REACH? 69

in the hostile environments of their native countries. They had relied on their parties and taken a personal interest in the success of communism at home and abroad. Such personal backgrounds help to explain the volatile atmosphere within the media exchanges, which left fundamental principles of diplomatic etiquette by the wayside. Despite the geographical distance, the communist leaders of the GDR, Hungary, Poland and China shared a common post-war history that came with a highly personal touch, since the old *nomenklatura* was still more or less in place in the 1960s. However much personal contacts had helped to boost relations between Eastern Europe and China in the 1950s, such ties rebounded on them like a boomerang in the 1960s.

In retrospect, the time between the Sino-Soviet polemic in 1963 and the beginning of the Cultural Revolution in 1966 appears to be a phase of particularly ambiguous reporting on China in the Polish, East German, and Hungarian press. It was with anticipatory obedience that *Trybuna Ludu* followed Moscow's line when it came to reporting on China; the Soviet leadership was, of course, horrified by the prospect of a schism. The Warsaw-based party newspaper published the vigorous debate over the leadership and general line of the International Communist Movement. Subscribers were able to read in full the exchange of blows between Moscow and Beijing that took place between February and July 1963. Filling five pages, about half the issue published on 15 July 1963, the ideological debate was impossible to ignore for the Polish, as well as for the Hungarian and East German reader.[84]

Nevertheless, Hungarian reporting remained somewhat bipolar. In contrast to the Polish party paper, *Népszabadság* reported on the anniversary of the founding of the PRC every single year during the 1960s, oscillating between hope, strict neutrality, and anger.[85] Even in 1969, the editorial published next to the telegram sounds rather hopeful, celebrating two decades of history of the PRC and Soviet assistance in building a socialist state.[86] Although intrinsically unrealistic, its wording expressed deep-rooted Hungarian feelings and hopes nurtured by fond memories of the late 1950s.

In East Germany, as in Poland and Hungary, the ideological battle between the Soviet and Chinese leadership in 1963 marked a turning point in favour of Moscow.[87] The Kremlin achieved this loyalty not by means of force.[88] Unlike the Hungarian leadership, the East German political elite did not need a personal briefing in the Kremlin. Since economic relations had already cooled down significantly by 1963, there was not much to be gained by supporting China, even if Ulbricht did not feel any sympathy for Khrushchev. This new stance towards Mao's China was publicly announced on 31 July 1963 after a session of the

---

[84]'Wymiana listów między KC KPZR i KC KP Chin,' *Trybuna Ludu*, 14 March 1963, 2. A Soviet response, the CC CPSU letter of 30 March followed suit. 'List KC KPZR do KC KP Chin', *Trybuna Ludu*, 3 April 1963, 4–5. 'List otwarty KC KPZR do organizacji partyjnych i do wszystkich komunistów w ZSRR,' *Trybuna Ludu*, 15 July 1963, 2–5; 'List KC KP Chin z dnia 14 czerwca 1963 r.,' *Trybuna Ludu*, 15 July 1963, 5–6. Although Beijing's position had not been concealed from the Polish public, it was always put into context of the Soviets reacting to shape and formulate the public's perception in the desired direction. *Népszabadság* saw especially intense reporting on the Sino-Soviet dispute in July 1963 and was clearly in favour of the Soviet Union. E.g. 'Testvérpártok az SZKP nyílt leveléről,' *Népszabadság*, 21 July 1963, 2; and 'Különös módszerek,' *Népszabadság*, 21 July 1963, 4.

[85]'Magyar államférfiak üdvözlő távirata kínai vezetőkhöz,' *Népszabadság*, 1 October 1965, 5; 'Dobi István üdvözlő távirata a kínai nemzeti ünnep alkalmából,' *Népszabadság*, 1 October 1966, 3; 'Üdvözlő táviratak a kínai nemzeti ünnep alkalmából,' *Népszabadság*, 1 October 1967, 3; 'Üdvözlő távirat a kínai nemzeti ünnep alkalmából,' *Népszabadság*, 1 October 1968, 2.

[86]'A kormány távirata a Kínai Népköztársaság Államtanácsához,' *Népszabadság*, 1 October 1969, 3.

[87]Beda Erlinghagen, 'Anfänge und Hintergründe des Konflikts zwischen der DDR und der Volksrepublik China: Kritische Anmerkungen zu einer ungeklärten Frage,' *Beiträge zur Geschichte der Arbeiterbewegung* 49, No. 3 (2007) 118.

[88]Stuber-Berries, *East German China policy*. See also Erlinghagen, 'Anfänge und Hintergründe,' 115.

central committee of the SED. Placed onto the front page, the communiqué condemned the course the Chinese leadership had taken:

> The general line of the communist world movement jointly agreed on by the communist and workers' parties in their Moscow consultations in 1957 and 1960, i.e. also with the agreement of the CP of China, has proven itself completely right and successful ... Therefore we condemn the attempt of the leaders of the CP of China to achieve a revision of this general line. ... To take over the sectarian policy of the leaders of the CP of China would mean impeding the fight against imperialism.[89]

Ulbricht was not caught unawares by the deterioration in Sino-Soviet relations. After the incident in Markkleeberg in June 1960, the first secretary of the Socialist Unity Party had had several quarrels with the Chinese that made him write unpleasant letters to Mao even before July 1963.[90] Ulbricht was also kept abreast about the quantity and quality of reports on the GDR in the Chinese press.[91] Kádár, by contrast, was surprised when he learned personally about the background of the Sino-Soviet differences in Moscow in July 1963. He even lamented in a Politburo meeting in late August 1963: 'What has happened to the Chinese?'[92] Nevertheless, Ulbricht – a cunning strategist – sent his foreign minister, Lothar Bölz, to meet with Zhou in 1964. Subsequently, mutual trade with China increased in 1965 to its greatest level since 1959.[93]

Despite a certain degree of harmonisation in the media, there is strong archival evidence that, even in 1963, the coordination between the Soviet press and the press in Eastern Europe was only rudimentary at best. This holds true for the editorial offices in Berlin, Budapest and Warsaw as well as for the journalists in Beijing. Although guidelines and directives issued by the state propaganda department of their communist regimes closely bound the socialist correspondents, they still enjoyed some limited leverage. One example of this is a basketball match between Albania and the Soviet Union in Beijing on 27 August 1963. East German, Polish and Soviet news agencies correspondents were invited to watch the highly symbolical match, but security personnel refused them access to the stadium. While the Soviet correspondents went home straight away, the others successfully insisted on getting permission to enter the arena. The Soviet correspondents – unaware of this – immediately cabled back to Moscow about this incident. Their report was printed in *Pravda* and *Neues Deutschland*.[94] Enraged, the Chinese Foreign Ministry summoned the Polish and East German correspondents and issued them a warning not to report lies about China. Only then did the East German and Polish correspondents realise that their Soviet colleagues had published an article about the incident without informing them. To avoid similar misunderstandings in the future, correspondents of the socialist bloc states

---

[89]'Kommuniqué der 3. Tagung des Zentralkomitees der Sozialistischen Einheitspartei Deutschlands,' *Neues Deutschland*, 31 July 1963, 1.

[90]E.g. after the World Peace Council meeting in Stockholm in December 1961 or the VI SED Party Congress in January 1963. Cf. 'Protokoll Nr. 1/62 der Sitzung des Politbüros der SED, Anhang 4, Auftreten der chinesischen Delegation auf der Tagung des Weltfriedensrates,' Barch, DY/30/J IV 2/2/808; 'Schreiben des Ersten Sekretärs des ZK der SED, Walter Ulbricht, an den Vorsitzenden der KP Chinas, Mao Zedong, zum Auftreten der chinesischen Parteitagsdelegation auf dem VI. Parteitag der SED,' 12 February 1963, Barch, DY/30/3607.

[91]See e.g. Letter to Walter Ulbricht on a report by ADN chief editor Pötschke, 28 April 1964, Barch, DY/30/IV A 2/2.028/70.

[92]Vámos, 'Mi történt a kínaikkal?,' 14–6.

[93]Wentker, *Außenpolitik in engen Grenzen*, 273.

[94]'Zutritt zum Pekinger Sportsaal verwehrt,' *Neues Deutschland*, 29 August 1963, 8.

held a joint conference at the Czechoslovak embassy in Beijing without prior consultation of their respective party heads at home.[95]

Coordination procedures for a united position on China in the media got increasingly sophisticated. They included embassy meetings in Moscow and Beijing. In the early 1960s the Kremlin occasionally briefed socialist ambassadors in Moscow on Sino-Soviet relations and the diplomats forwarded the information to the party leaders at home.[96] Of similar importance had been gatherings in the socialist embassies in Beijing, with the Soviet one not necessarily the most important venue of exchange.[97] Occasionally the arrival of a new correspondent also served as an opportunity to organise a party where the journalists of the other socialist countries discussed their research methods and shared their expertise.[98]

The working conditions of foreign correspondents in Beijing did not improve during the years to come. The next visible step towards an open Sino-Soviet confrontation in the Eastern bloc press was the beginning of the Great Proletarian Cultural Revolution in China in 1966, when Beijing's image in the Polish, East German and Hungarian press changed from bad to worse. As a consequence, news coverage on China significantly increased in *Trybuna Ludu*, and to a lesser extent in *Neues Deutschland* and *Népszabadság*. In the Polish party paper, reports on the turmoil in China appeared almost weekly between the announcement of the start of the Cultural Revolution in May 1966 and the dissolution of the Red Guards in August 1968. Most of the stories were accounts of the contradictions, violence, hysteria, and anti-Soviet spirit of this socio-political movement from Beijing and the provinces. With such a comprehensive picture of the events, China was back in the Polish news again, this time, however, as part of a gloomy portrayal of a country in decay.[99]

The East German coverage of the Cultural Revolution was less extensive than in Poland and usually hidden on the latter pages of *Neues Deutschland*. Reports on changes in the political hierarchy or reprints from *Pravda* prevailed and German journalists rarely expressed a strong opinion. It appears that the East German leadership did not want to take any risks by adopting a stance towards Mao's China that might differ from the Soviet position.[100] Much as in Poland and East Germany, the tone expressed in *Népszabadság* generally took a more negative turn from 1966 onwards. Reports on the Cultural Revolution and Red Guards did not figure prominently.[101] Longer articles strongly and openly followed Soviet declarations.[102] This made it clear to the readers that no gap could emerge between the Hungarian and the Soviet leadership. In the light of events in China, coordination inside the bloc was eventually institutionalised in 1967.

---

[95]'Informationsbericht des ADN-Korrespondenten in Peking [Gerda Lindner],' 3 September 1963, Barch, DY/30/IV A 2/2.028/70.

[96]See 'Vermerk über ein Gespräch mit dem Leiter der Fernöstlichen Abteilung im Ministerium für Auswärtige Angelegenheiten der UdSSR, Genossen Tugarinow am 8.3.1962,' 10 March 1962, PA AA, G-A315.

[97]On such exchanges, e.g. PA AA, G-A 317, G-A 338, G-A 339.

[98]'Vermerk über Gespräche auf einer Cocktail-Party zu Ehren des neuen Korrespondenten der ungarischen Telegraphenagentur am 15.9.1961 in der ungarischen Botschaft,' 16 September 1961, PA AA, A6744.

[99]E.g. 'Dalsze wystąpienia "czerwonogwardzistów" w Pekine,' *Trybuna Ludu*, 15 October 1966, 2.

[100]Summer and fall 1966 were the heyday of reporting on the Cultural Revolution in the East German party paper. In September 1966 alone, *Neues Deutschland* published 23 articles on this topic, compared with just two to three per month between June and August.

[101]'Újabb felszólítás a "vörösgardisták" Pekingből való távozására,' *Népszabadság*, 4 November 1966, 2.

[102]'A Szovjetunió Kommunista Pártja Központi Bizottságának közleménye a Kínában folyó szovjetellenes kampányról, a kommunista mozgalom egységének kérdéseiről,' *Népszabadság*, 1 September 1966, 1.

Conclusion

Since the end of the Cold War, historians of Eastern Europe, the Soviet Union and China have based their conclusions mainly upon documents from newly-opened archives in Moscow, Budapest, Warsaw, Berlin and beyond. There are good reasons for the decline in popularity of newspapers in such circles: what the party press was producing until the late 1980s could rightfully be called propaganda. Editorial staff were not meant to publish objective news, neither on their country, nor on the Soviet Union or China, but rather their task was to disseminate the official line of the party and the state. Such limitations notwithstanding, historians should not ignore newspapers as a source. Reading socialist newspapers can actually be quite illuminating, if done from a certain angle: while archival sources reflect policy-making issues and the power struggles of a bureaucratic elite, the value of newspapers lies in their function as an information channel between the state leadership and their respective citizens at home and abroad. Being state-run and thus a one-sided means of exchange, newspapers reveal much about what the people were allowed and expected to know at a particular moment in time, shedding light on the diverging official attitudes towards Beijing in Warsaw, Budapest and East Berlin. Such differences not only show that Moscow never gained full control over the Eastern bloc media, but also that party newspaper foreign correspondents like Gerda Lindner maintained informal networks which were often beyond the reach of the editors at home.

Moreover, the official party newspapers fulfilled a role that went beyond the usual function of a newspaper in the West. Because state-run and controlled, party newspapers in Eastern Europe and the Soviet Union were part of a border-crossing network through which the diverging official positions on China could be communicated between Moscow and the leadership of the client states, thus making them particularly valuable for studying inter-party and inter-state relations. When evaluated as source of the images on China, differences are particularly obvious between 1957 and 1962 in the eastern bloc press. This shows that small 'satellites' like Hungary, the GDR, or Poland tried to use the opportunities that arose from the precarious nature of Sino-Soviet relations during that period. The fact that not one of them was able to ignore either China or the Soviet Union meant that they were also forced to act, even if they would have preferred to stay on the sidelines. It was precisely during such moments of reorientation, with old and supposedly eternal policies uncertain but not yet replaced by new ones and with Moscow as the centre of the transnational socialist web of communication hesitant, that different attitudes towards Beijing were able to be voiced via the press. One such moment was the Sino-Indian conflict. Unlike Budapest or Warsaw, East Berlin for quite long remained in favour of Beijing's position in the dispute. With the release of Grotewohl's Beijing speech in East Germany's major newspaper, this position became clearly visible to everyone – including the Indian government. Such differences in reporting between Moscow, Budapest, Warsaw and Berlin slowly dissipated again when the public polemic between Moscow and Beijing in the first half of 1963 forced editors and propaganda officials in Budapest, Berlin and Warsaw to find a common language that was once again in line with Moscow.

Disclosure statement

No potential conflict of interest was reported by the authors.

China as a role model? The 'Economic Leap' campaign in Bulgaria (1958–1960)

Jan Zofka

ABSTRACT
The article examines the transnational dimensions of the industrialisation drive in Bulgaria in the late 1950s and poses the question of how extensively this campaign was influenced by the contemporary 'Great Leap Forward' in China. Although there is no evidence of comprehensive adoption of a Chinese model, there was widespread enthusiasm for China, and technologies were transferred in connection with the Chinese acceleration policies. These transfers did not have a geopolitical implication, as Western Cold War historians had supposed, but rather happened in a context of widespread technological exchange and hint at multi-centrality in the socialist camp before the Sino-Soviet split.

Introduction

Upon returning from a trip to China in October 1958, Sofia's First Party Secretary, Georgi Kostov, told an audience of local militants:

> Probably most of you are impatient to hear what I have to tell about China. I do not object. About China one could talk the whole day. The experience of the Chinese people is very great, great is the heroism and the diligence of the Chinese people. . . . But allow me this time to stick to our own problems, the great tasks set by the Central Committee of our party in its decisions of its October plenum.[1]

However, in outlining the tasks of the Bulgarian communists Kostov constantly referred to what he had seen in China, promoting it as an example for Bulgaria. He expressed fascination for the greatness of Chinese achievements in certain fields of technology and social engineering – above all irrigation and mobilisation of unpaid labour – and his speech culminated in the statement: 'They have shown us the way to do it [to irrigate]'.[2]

---

[1]Protocol of the Assembly of the BCP City Committee with Bureaus of Primary Party Organisations from Agricultural Cooperatives in Sofia District, 4 November 1958, SGDA, f. 1B, op. 25, a.e. 20, l. 228.
[2]Ibid., l. 234.

BEYOND THE KREMLIN'S REACH?

Nowadays, Western scholarship and media present China's 'Great Leap Forward' as an exotic, insane, and of course, tragic and deathly campaign.[3] At the time, before the catastrophic outcome of the campaign was clear, many party officials and members of the technical intelligentsia in East (Central) European states had a different perspective on it.[4] In autumn and winter 1958, political circles in Sofia and throughout Bulgaria were fascinated by the Great Leap Forward and the economic progress they perceived in the People's Republic of China (PRC). More generally, they were enthusiastic about the fact that the country with the world's largest population was part of the socialist camp. The press was full of articles praising the achievements of socialism in China. At the same time, the Bulgarian Party leadership itself called for an 'economic leap' (*ikonomicheski skok*) and fulfilment of the Third Five-Year Plan in 'three to four years'. The Economic Leap campaign in Bulgaria was carried out from 1958 to 1960, when relations between the Soviet Union and the PRC were starting to cool-down and Moscow abandoned Stalinist ideas of economic development through shock policies and fantastical plan goals.[5] Against this backdrop, at the time, some Western scholars of political science and history interpreted the Bulgarian leadership's policy as an adoption of the Chinese campaign and a political provocation of the leadership of the Communist Party of the Soviet Union (CPSU).[6] Starting from this debate, this article poses the following questions: To what extent was this Economic Leap policy in Bulgaria based on transfers of ideas and techniques from China? What do these transfers reveal about the international power relations in the socialist camp and the transnational dimension of state socialism?

The evidence available with today's broader access to archival documentation points to a significant exchange of technology, of knowledge on technical processes, and of ideas on the mobilisation of workforce and the administration of economic structures between China and Bulgaria, and a curious enthusiasm about Chinese socialism in the southeast European country in the late 1950s.[7] By no means, however, did this enthusiasm imply that

---

[3]For media reports see, e.g. '"Der Wahn des Tyrannen". Der Große Sprung nach vorn 1958–1961,' *GEO Epoche* 51, (September 2011). For dedicated scholarly accounts see Frank Dikötter, *Mao's Great Famine: The History of China's Most Devastating Catastrophe, 1958–1962* (New York: Walker & Co., 2010); Yang Jisheng, *Tombstone: The Great Chinese Famine, 1958–1962* (New York: Farrar, Straus and Giroux, 2012). Research has estimated fatalities at between 15 and 45 million, but as this wide range of numbers indicates, the statistical evidence for exact quantification is very fragile. Dikötter, *Mao's Great Famine*, 324–34; Felix Wemheuer and Manning Kimberley, introduction to *Eating Bitterness: New Perspectives on China's Great Leap Forward and Famine* (Vancouver: UBC Press, 2011), 22. The causality of the famine is also debated, as is whether the Great Leap Forward, accompanied by local state violence, was the main cause of the mass starvation or just one among other factors such as foreign trade pressures and bad weather conditions during the 1959–1961 harvests.

[4]Reports about the famine and the economic disaster were already circulating in the Soviet bloc in early 1961. Austin Jersild, *Sino-Soviet Alliance: An International History* (Chapel Hill: North Carolina University Press, 2012), 139; Internal Note of SED Department for Foreign Affairs, 9 January 1961, Stiftung Archiv der Parteien und Massenorganisationen der DDR im Bundesarchiv [SAPMO-BArch], DY 30 – IV 2 /20/123, doc. 23–5.

[5]Lorenz M. Lüthi, *The Sino-Soviet Split: Cold War in the Communist World* (Princeton: Princeton University Press, 2008), 46–51, 80–104.

[6]Jordan Baev, *Drugata studena voĭna. Săvetsko-Kitaĭskiyat konflikt i Iztočna Evropa* (Sofia: Voenno Izdatelstvo, 2012); Liliana Brisby, 'Leaping Forward Without Communes,' *Chinese Quarterly* 1, No. 3 (1960): 80–4; James F. Brown, *Bulgaria Under Communist Rule* (London: Pall Mall Press, 1970).

[7]This article is based on an analysis of internal documents of Bulgarian party organs and state institutions ranging from the Politburo to selected local branches, with a special focus on ministries and party departments that participated in delegations to China at the time. I have also examined periodicals of the agriculture ministry and magazines that reflect the theoretical debate of economists and agronomists (e.g. *Kooperativno Selo* [Cooperative Village], *Novo Vreme* [New Time], *Ikonomicheski Misăl* [Economic Thought]). Most of the research has been undertaken in the framework of an employment at the Leipzig Centre for History and Culture of East Central Europe (GWZO) from 2014 to 2016 and during a fellowship at the Centre for Advanced Studies Sofia in spring 2016.

the Bulgarian leadership questioned Soviet predominance in the socialist camp. Many of the measures in the framework of the Economic Leap campaign could also be interpreted as Khrushchev-style reforms, and contemporary media reports on China were outnumbered by articles praising the achievements of socialism in the Soviet Union and other socialist countries.[8]

The Chinese-Bulgarian relations at the time, the Chinese-style labels of some reform measures and the Bulgarian interest in the developments in China did not have the dramatic world-political character ascribed to them by Western observers in the 1960s. Nonetheless, the Bulgarian Economic Leap campaign still offers interesting insights into Chinese-Eastern European relations as well as into the functioning of twentieth-century state socialism and its transnational dimensions.[9] Bulgaria's government, agriculture specialists and local party officials obviously drew inspiration from their comrades' actions in the PRC. They adopted new techniques in soil cultivation and forestry and embraced the general idea of motivating labour through political mobilisation instead of material incentives. These features of the Great Leap Forward seemed to be appropriate to the Bulgarian planners, as they appeared to be conducive to rapid industrialisation under conditions of scarce capital and abundant rural labour resources. Thus, actors in the socialist camp who sought models of development and technological progress were not oriented exclusively towards Moscow. I will argue in this article that the campaign, far from having been a confrontational move towards Moscow on the part of the Bulgarian leadership, reveals instead that the power centre was not omnipotent and that economic policymakers, planners and specialists in the socialist camp had room to manoeuvre. It also hints at the significance of periphery-periphery relations that bypassed direct Soviet control.

The echo of the PRC's Great Leap Forward in the socialist camp

When Mao Zedong proclaimed the Great Leap Forward in early 1958, the socialist camp was in turmoil. Khrushchev had initiated reforms, decentralised the Soviet economic administration, and tried to enhance agriculture in a way unseen under Stalin. The new Soviet leader's proclamation of de-Stalinisation was breeding conflict inside the Communist parties, and popular unrest in Poland and Hungary put pressure on the governing bureaucracies and governments. These developments changed the power relations between the Soviet Union and its 'satellites'. Under these circumstances the Chinese leadership, no longer willing to accept the role of mere disciple of the Soviet Union, tried to gain a more active role in socialist camp relations. Temporarily, a formula in which the Soviet Union *and* the PRC led the socialist world became popular.[10] Mao's initial claims that China would overtake

---

[8]This is a conclusion of an examination of the main Bulgarian newspapers of the years 1957–1960 (Rabotnichesko Delo, Otechestven Front, Narodna Mladezh, Zemdedelsko Zname).

[9]Research and scholarly debate on the Chinese influence on the Bulgarian Leap are rather fragmented. The economist Kiril Tochkov of Texas Christian University has conducted a research project on the Bulgarian and the Chinese leaps in comparison at the Centre for Advanced Studies in Sofia, and a doctoral study by the historian Ma Li is under way at the Shanghai Cold War International History Studies Centre. For Bulgarian studies highlighting the Chinese influence, see Baev, *Drugata studena voĭna*, 81–9; Vladimir Migev, 'Otrazhenieto v Bǎlgariya na politikata na Kitaĭskata komunisticheska partiya za "Golemiya skok", 1958–1960 g.,' *Minalo* 19, No. 1 (2012): 75–9. For a clear stance rejecting the idea of a significant Chinese influence, see Evgeni Kandilarov, *Iztochna Aziya i Bǎlgariya* (Sofia: Iztok-Zapad, 2016), 153–62 and Iliyana Marcheva, *Todor Živkov: Pǎtyat kǎm vlastta. politika i ikonomika v Bǎlgariya, 1953–1964 g.* (Sofia: Institut po istoriya – BAN, 2001), 189–216.

[10]E.g. Péter Vámos, 'Sino-Hungarian Relations and the 1956 Revolution,' Cold War International History Project Working Paper, Woodrow Wilson Centre, Washington D. C., November 2006, https://www.wilsoncenter.org/sites/default/files/WP54_Final2.pdf, 33–5.

Britain in steel production in a few years had been an approving, albeit competing response, to Khrushchev's 'overtake-the-West' rhetoric.[11]

However, China's ambitions contributed to a cool-down in Sino-Soviet relations. The two powers' differences became evident in the economic policy of the Chinese leadership behind the Great Leap Forward. The Soviet government under Khrushchev's leadership had condemned the rapid industrialisation and collectivisation of the 1930s as erroneous and favoured a more balanced socialist development model, yet Chinese policymakers opted for a return to 'revolutionary Stalinism' as opposed to post-Second World War 'bureaucratic Stalinism'. The Great Leap Forward was thus one of the crucial controversial subjects that paved the way for the Sino-Soviet rift. In 1960, the Soviets further escalated the split by withdrawing their technical experts and advisers from China, leaving projects unfinished and contracts unfulfilled.[12] This decision had far-reaching effects, not just for the Chinese, whose industrialisation project was based on Soviet assistance, but also for the Soviet economy, as China had become the Soviets' main trading partner with an impressive share of 20%.[13]

The shift in Chinese economic policy did not incite political conflict in the beginning. Early on, Soviet specialists complained about the acceleration campaign's harmful consequences for their technical work, but the Soviet leadership forbore to judge the Great Leap Forward right away.[14] The Soviet press was complaisant in its reporting during the first year of the campaign. The sensitive topic of the people's communes was simply omitted, as the line propagated by the Soviet leadership was to avoid interfering in Chinese domestic affairs and thus to refrain from sharp criticism.[15]

In other socialist countries, Moscow's disinclination to publicly position itself against the Chinese experiment opened up space for autonomous interpretation of China's policy. In East Central Europe, sympathetic attitudes towards the Chinese project prevailed at first. In the German Democratic Republic (GDR), for example, officials and observers looked at the Great Leap Forward and the people's communes in China with great interest.[16] Their sympathetic statements went so far that Western observers even thought they had discovered a 'Peking-Pankow axis'.[17] Documents and reports suggest the existence of a faction of GDR officials sympathetic to the PRC, and a presentation on people's communes at an

---

[11]Lüthi, *Sino-Soviet Split*, 84.

[12]Lüthi, *Sino-Soviet Split*, 174–80; Sergey Radchenko, *Two Suns in the Heavens: The Sino-Soviet Struggle for Supremacy, 1962–1967* (Stanford, CA: Stanford University Press, 2009), 14.

[13]By 1950 China had become the Soviet Union's most important trading partner, succeeding Czechoslovakia, Poland and the USA, which had held this position in the immediate after-war years. In 1960, against the backdrop of the quickly deteriorating Sino-Soviet trade, East Germany became the USSR's most important trading partner. *Vneshnaya Torgovlya SSSR. Statisticheski sbornik (1918–1966)* (Moscow: Izdatelstvo Mezhdunarodnye otnosheniya, 1967), 70–1, 206–13. For the significance of Soviet assistance, see Jersild, *Sino-Soviet Alliance*, 15; Deborah Kaple, 'Agents of Change: Soviet Advisers and High Stalinist Management in China, 1949–1960', *Journal of Cold War Studies* 18, No. 1 (2016): 5–30; Shen Zhihua, *Sovetskie spetsialisty v Kitae, 1948–1960* (Moscow: Nauka – Vostochnaya Literatura, 2015), 6–9, 21–2.

[14]Lüthi, *Sino-Soviet Split*, 90.

[15]Shen Zhihua and Xia Yafeng, 'The Great Leap Forward, the People's Commune and the Sino-Soviet Split', *Journal of Contemporary China* 20, No. 72 (2011): 861–80.

[16]Photographer Wolfgang G. Schröter in 1959 portrayed the new China (Deutsche Fotothek, www.deutschefotothek. de; search Schröter/China), documentary films depicted People's Communes in China (DEFA-Film 'Wir berichten aus Pan Yü,' Berlin 1959), and a leading member of the GDR government and Politburo published a treatise on the Great Leap Forward (Horst Sindermann, *Chinas grosser Sprung* (Berlin: Dietz-Verlag, 1959).

[17]Hemen Ray, 'Die ideologische Achse Peking-Pankow,' *Außenpolitik* 12 (1960): 819–25; Martin J. Esslin, 'East Germany: Peking-Pankow Axis?' *China Quarterly* 1 (1960): 85–8; Harald Möller, *DDR und VR China. Unterstützung der VRCh auf politischem, ökonomischem und militärischem Gebiet (1949–1964): eine Dokumentation* (Berlin: Köster, 2003).

BEYOND THE KREMLIN'S REACH? 77

agricultural trade fair near Leipzig sparked domestic turmoil in 1960.[18] China's Great Leap Forward had similar repercussions for other European socialist countries. In the ČSSR, for instance, the economist Michal Falt'lan promoted a partial adoption of the model.[19] Meanwhile, research on Romania and Poland has devoted very little attention to references to the Chinese campaign in these countries, and different researchers have produced contradictory evaluations of the few existing sources.[20] In Bulgaria, high-ranking delegations returning from China praised the Great Leap Forward, and newspapers printed favourable reports about China's achievements. But, did the Chinese campaign resonate beyond these public declarations of sympathy?

A Chinese Great Leap Forward in Bulgaria? The research debate

In late summer and autumn 1958, Bulgarian communists were discussing the directives of the seventh party congress of the Bulgarian Communist Party (BCP). This lengthy succession of media reports and work-collective meetings was typical of the state-socialist process of interpreting and implementing the vague political resolutions put out by the Party leadership. The general line, however, was very clear: the industrialisation of predominantly agrarian Bulgaria was to be accelerated. Thus, in October, the party leaders and the press called on Bulgaria's workers and farmers to 'fulfil the five-year plan in three to four years'. A comprehensive campaign was launched to scour Bulgarian farms, enterprises, land and people for hidden reserves and put the unused resources to use. Newspapers printed experience reports by collective farmers who had tested or even invented new working methods. At the same time, to put pressure on farm managements and workers, the press ran articles about enterprises that permitted failures. Besides these measures for mobilising the workforce (in agriculture), the state invested in huge industrial projects.

Some authors, noting the backdrop of worsening Sino-Soviet-relations, have interpreted this campaign as an adoption of the Chinese Great Leap Forward.[21] What arguments support the notion of Chinese influence in the Bulgarian Economic Leap? First, to some extent the Bulgarian policies were *similar* to the Chinese ones. The core of the campaign in both countries was to mobilise labour for agriculture and infrastructure projects via propaganda and pressure instead of financial incentives. As in China, in Bulgaria the recently collectivised farms were merged into far greater units. The Chinese mobilisation policy

---

[18]Beda Erlinghagen, 'Anfänge und Hintergründe des Konflikts zwischen der DDR und der Volksrepublik China. Kritische Anmerkungen zu einer ungeklärten Frage', Beiträge zur Geschichte der Arbeiterbewegung 49 (2007): 111–40; Letter of Foreign Ministry to the SED Central Committee (CC) Foreign Department, SAPMO-BArch, DY 30, IV-2/20/120; Doc. 116–7.

[19]Martin Slobodník, 'Východný vietor prevláda? Čínsky Veľký skok vpred v Československu', in Martina Bucková and Gabriel Pirický, *Podoby globalizácie v Oriente*, (Bratislava: *Slovenská orientalistická spoločnosť' pri Slovenskij akadémii vied*, 2015), 9–30.

[20]Shen Zhihua and Xia Yafeng opine that Mao received full support for the leap in North Korea, Vietnam, the GDR, Poland, Czechoslovakia, Mongolia, Albania, and Bulgaria, albeit not for the communes in the latter three. Shen and Xia, 'Great Leap Forward,' 876. Lüthi sees Bulgaria and the GDR as having had a special role in endorsing the Leap. Lorenz Lüthi, 'China and East Europe, 1956–1960,' *Modern China Studies* 22, No. 1 (2015), 248, 252–6. Studies on Sino-Romanian relations do not mention any allusions the Romanian leadership may have made to the Great Leap. Mihai Croitor, *România şi conflictului Sovieto-Chinez, 1956–1971* (Cluj-Napoca: Editura Mega, 2009), 123–208; Liu Yong, *Sino-Romanian Relations: 1950's–1960's* (Bucharest: Institutul Naţional pentru Studiul Totalitarismului, 2006). Studies on the COMECON claim without further explanation that the Great Leap had an influence in Romania. Michael Kaser, *COMECON. Integration Problems of the Planned Economies* (London: Oxford University Press, 1965), 77; Gospodinka Nikova, *Săvetăt za Ikonomicheska Vzaimopomosht i Bălgariya, 1949–1960* (Sofia: Izdatelstvo na BAN, 1989), 237.

[21]Baev, *Drugata studena voǐna*; Brisby, 'Leaping Forward,' 80–4; Brown, *Bulgaria Under Communist Rule*.

intrigued Bulgarian officials and engineers because they and their Chinese counterparts faced the same problems: insufficient investment funds and an overabundance of labour. Radio Free Europe counted 350,000 unemployed labourers in Bulgaria at the time, many of them pushed from rural areas to the cities in the aftermath of collectivisation.[22] The British historian Liliana Brisby argues that 'the Chinese drive to substitute a maximum use of labour power for limited capital was what impressed the Bulgarian Communist leaders most'.[23]

Second, some authors take *leadership rhetoric* as the main evidence that the leap policies in Bulgaria were 'Chinese'. At the Central Committee plenary session in November 1958, party leader Todor Zhivkov stated that 'the understanding, that our movement towards communism will be fulfilled only gradually and not also in great leaps, is flawed'.[24] At the same meeting, the BCP Central Committee decided explicitly to shift the slogan from 'speeded-up plan fulfilment' to 'leap in our economic development'.[25] The contemporary British-American historian and Radio Free Europe investigator James Brown is convinced that 'the name itself . . . was borrowed from China, as was the spirit and fervour of the campaign'.[26] However, the Bulgarian leadership and press, rather than use the whole term Great Leap Forward, called the campaign an 'Economic Leap' or a 'leap in the development of the country', or else used 'Great Leap' for developments on a local level.[27] The more official title of the campaign remained the 'All-People's Movement to Fulfil the Third Five-Year Plan in an Abridged Time Frame'.[28] At the mentioned Central Committee plenary sessions in November 1958 and January 1959, the leap terminology often came combined with a rhetoric of the 'Chinese experience'.[29] This connection also is reflected in the autobiographies of leading protagonists, which have drawn a lot of attention from scholars. Todor Zhivkov admits in a short paragraph of his memoirs that he was intrigued by the Chinese experiment in the beginning, before decisively coming out against it. He describes his predecessor, Vălko Chervenkov, who still was a member of government at the time, as the main protagonist who promoted the Chinese model.[30] Chervenkov's non-published memoirs and utterances of Zhivkov's assistant, Niko Jahiel, also are often cited as evidence for a short-lived but definitive adoption of a Chinese model in Bulgaria from autumn 1958 to January 1959, when Khrushchev supposedly called the Bulgarian leadership to order at the XXI party congress of the CPSU.[31] Indeed, the CPSU leader dedicates several pages of his memoirs to the spreading of the Great Leap Forward in the Soviet dominion. Interestingly enough, he acknowledges to have been most worried by tendencies in the Soviet Far east of praising and adopting the Chinese campaign, but he also accounts that the Soviet leadership became concerned 'when we learned that the Chinese propaganda was beginning to have an effect in Bulgaria. ... They [the Bulgarians] started enlarging their collective farms to

---

[22]Brown, *Bulgaria under Communist Rule*, 85.

[23]Brisby, 'Leaping Forward', 81.

[24]Protocol of the enlarged meeting of the BCP Central Committee, 11 November 1958, Bulgarian Central State Archive (CDA), f. 1B, op. 5, a.e. 356, l. 4, http://politburo.archives.bg/bg/2013-04-24-11-09-24/1950-1959/2773--------11--1958--].

[25]Ibid., l. 140.

[26]Brown, *Bulgaria Under Communist Rule*, 87.

[27]See, e.g. *Zemedelsko Zname*, 15 November 1958, 1; 9 December 1958, 1; January 1, 1959, 4; January 21, 1959, 1; also 'Za golemiya skok v Burgaski okrăg,' *Kooperativno Selo*, January 30, 1959, 2.

[28]E.g. *Rabotnichesko Delo*, 17 October 1958, 1. ('vsenarodnoto dvizhenie za izpălnenie na tretata petiletka v săkrateni srokove').

[29]Protocol BCP CC, 11 November 1958, CDA, f. 1B, op. 5, a.e. 356, l. 4, http://politburo.archives.bg/bg/2013-04-24-11-09-24/1950-1959/2773--------11--1958--], l. 13, 46, 47, 86, 118.

[30]Baev, *Drugata studena voĭna*, 82; Todor Zhivkov, *Memoari* (Sofia: IK Trud i pravo, 2006), 468–9.

[31]Baev, *Drugata studena voĭna*, 82.

ridiculous sizes, and they overinvested in heavy industry. (…) We felt compelled to talk things over with the Bulgarian comrades and give them an opportunity to hear our point of view'. At the following meeting in Moscow, Krushchev remembers saying to the Bulgarian leaders that 'we feel that the Chinese experience is not applicable to European conditions, and that if you persist in your efforts to imitate China's Great Leap Forward it may result in serious complications'. The main concern in Khrushchev's talk to his Bulgarian comrades, however, seems to have been money and not ideology: 'We've received information that you've been forced to place large orders [for industrial equipment] with the capitalist world. You're incurring debts which you might not be able to repay. We're afraid you'll have to ask us for money and we won't be able to help you'.[32] According to Khrushchev, the Bulgarian government changed some of its directives and reduced the size of the largest farms, but the problems of large investments in heavy industry persisted. In general, the leap rhetoric itself and the campaign-style measures went on in 1959 before they were stopped in the following year.

A third major issue in the debate about China's influence on Bulgarian policy was the role of *Bulgarian delegations* to China in autumn 1958. A high-ranking parliamentary delegation, led by the mentioned former party leader Vălko Chervenkov, visited factories, steelworks and farms and was obviously fascinated by the Chinese economic experiment. After returning to Bulgaria, Chervenkov praised the Chinese model publicly, for example, in several newspaper articles and in a speech in front of the parliament.[33]

Fourth, authors tried to identify *factions* inside the Bulgarian leadership that promoted a Chinese way. Chervenkov is seen as the central figure in this network. He could not enforce his ideas, but he found followers among officials of the national nomenklatura and local politicians. The historian James Brown suggests that conservative Stalinists who opposed Khrushchev's reform policies gathered around Chervenkov.[34] Research has not yet clarified how significant this faction was, how it might have functioned, or how far it was pro-Chinese, beyond being Stalinist die-hards.

Fifth, some authors have argued, the concept of people's communes was in some cases adopted *locally*. These researchers thought they detected the most spectacular example of following a 'Chinese' role model in the municipality of Botevgrad near Sofia: local leaders announced that the entire district had been unified into a 'giant cooperative' (*kooperativ-gigant*) and even dared to call the project the Botevgrad Commune (*Botevgradska komuna*).[35,36]

In opposition to all these arguments, other scholars dispute the idea of a 'Chinese' Great Leap in Bulgaria, insisting that the Bulgarian industrialisation drive of 1958/1959 was essentially 'Soviet'.[37] They argue that the basic goals of the major industrial projects undertaken in the Third Five-Year Plan (1958–1962) had been approved by the party

---

[32]*Khrushchev Remembers. The Last Testament*, ed. Strobe Talbott (Boston: Little, Brown and Company: Boston, Toronto, 1974), 275–78.

[33]Baev, *Drugata studena voĭna*, 82.

[34]Brown, *Bulgaria under Communist Rule*, 88–9. There were pro-Chinese factions or splinter groups in other Soviet-bloc countries as well. See Margaret Gnoinska's chapter in this issue about the 'Mijal group' in Poland.

[35]I. Nikolchovski, 'V Botevgradska okoliya sega ima samo edin kooperativ-gigant', *Rabotnichesko Delo*, 7 December 1958, 1; Brown, *Bulgaria under Communist Rule*, 88; Brisby, 'Leaping Forward', 81. However, an investigation of local and national archives did not show any indications of a (geo-)political scandal, which the founding of this enterprise supposedly produced. See below section 'People's Communes'.

[36]See below section 'People's Communes'.

[37]John R. Lampe, *The Bulgarian Economy in the Twentieth Century* (London: Croom Helm, 1986); Marcheva, *Todor Zhivkov*, 194–5.

leadership in 1956, long before the Chinese Communist Party launched its Great Leap Forward campaign.[38] They also point out that Bulgarian policies during the campaign were more imitative of Khrushchev's reforms than akin to China's Great Leap Forward. Moreover, the Leap terminology and the goal of implementing the Five-Year Plan in four years could also be seen as a throwback to the Soviet discourses of the Stalinist industrialisation campaign of the 1930s.[39]

Drawing, in addition to the literature cited above, on archival material of Bulgarian state institutions this article argues that there is no substantial evidence that the Bulgarian leadership or a faction of it wished to confront Moscow or question the Soviet Union's leadership in the socialist camp. Ultimately, there was no attempt of a comprehensive adoption of the Chinese Great Leap Forward. Nonetheless, and apart from the question of whether the Bulgarian Economic Leap campaign was 'Chinese' or 'Soviet', the Chinese Great Leap Forward had repercussions on developments, policies and society in Bulgaria. The delegates who had travelled to China brought home a variety of techniques for improving agricultural production as well as methods of mobilising labour that were discussed and partially implemented in the Bulgarian Economic Leap campaign.

Transfers from China to Bulgaria

Mobilisation of Unpaid Labour

The Great Leap policy for mobilising unpaid labour in China attracted great interest from Bulgarian planners and politicians, who were eager to make use of unused land, labour, machines and other resources. The search for 'hidden reserves' generally was crucial to the Economic Leap campaign. Party officials suggested, for example, that there was no reason farmers should sit idle in winter; instead, they could prepare the soil for sowing and dig ditches and pits.[40] As the overall aim of the campaign was to increase yields with little capital investment, it is hardly surprising that the prospect of getting people to work without pay was highly attractive to the campaigners. Thus, party officials, town council clerks, teachers and other intellectual workers were called on to take part in 'physical labour', and farmers and workers were required to work additional days in agriculture and on huge construction sites. The unpaid labourers helped to dig canals, construct dams and supported agricultural work, not only during harvests but also in the winter campaigns for amelioration works, land terracing or silo pit construction.[41]

The idea of mobilising unpaid workforce beyond particular professions was explicitly inspired by the policies of the Chinese Great Leap Forward. In the speech mentioned at the beginning of this article, Sofia's Party Secretary Georgi Kostov openly expressed enthusiasm about the use of unpaid labour in the PRC:

---

[38]Lampe, *Bulgarian Economy*, 149; Ulf Brunnbauer, *'Sozialistische Lebensweise'. Ideologie, Gesellschaft, Familie und Politik in Bulgarien, 1944–1989* (Vienna: Böhlau, 2007), 176.

[39]Ronald Grigor Suny, *The Soviet Experiment: Russia, the USSR, and the Successor States* (New York: Oxford University Press, 1998), 234.

[40]'Prez zimnite dni,' *Zemedelsko Zname*, 16 January 1959, 1.

[41]Migev, 'Otrazhenieto', 77.

And I will tell you, the great dam near Beijing that we saw; workers and farmers built it in 160 days. If we had done it the way we do projects, the planning organizations would have planned the project for three years, and then we would have spent five years building it with machines, and we would have spent hundreds of millions if not billions of Leva. And they – [they built it] in 160 days.[42]

Accordingly, he demanded a change in mentality: Bulgarians should not continue requesting state money for everything, but instead take the initiative themselves. He concluded unambiguously that the Bulgarian economy needed unpaid labour, too.

The hours of unpaid labour exacted by the campaign cannot be quantified, and it is even more difficult to measure what economic gain came of them. Much of the work done was of dubious benefit and many of the projects were met with opposition from experts or workers on the ground. In the end, the practice of using unpaid labour on construction sites was stopped in 1960 because of its economic inefficiency.[43] Albeit unsuccessful in result, the initial reasoning behind the mobilisation campaign had been an economic one: tasked with increasing productivity without improved machinery, the campaigners settled on the idea of squeezing as much as possible out of the labour force. The Chinese policy was an explicit example, but it did not preclude the simultaneous application of Soviet models for the same purpose. The ministry of heavy industry, for example, conducted a campaign for the 'method Mamaĭ' and called its workers to emulate the Soviet coal miner's record-setting shift.[44]

Agricultural Techniques

The Bulgarian leadership's unambiguous fascination with the Chinese campaign extended beyond labour mobilisation to a second sphere: agricultural techniques. Successes with wheat and cotton farming, ways of constructing terraced fields, means of fighting erosion and creation of irrigation infrastructure were the top issues in reports by the specialists who had travelled to China, and these issues were publicly discussed with reference to China's campaign.[45]

Soil cultivation and planting techniques were of special interest to Bulgarian planners and agronomists.[46] Detailed reports addressed features of the Chinese campaign like deep ploughing and close planting, which had also been part of the Lysenkoist agenda for increasing agricultural yields with little investment. Remnants of Lysenko's ideas, which lost their hegemony in the biology and agronomy of the Soviet Union and China as of 1952 and 1955, respectively, still wandered through the socialist camp and were perpetuated in the Bulgarian Economic Leap campaign, via the example of China.[47] However, the Bulgarian

---

[42] Protocol of the Assembly of the BCP City Committee BCP with Bureaus of Primary Party Organisations from Agricultural Cooperatives in Sofia District, 4 November 1958, Sofia Municipal and District Archive (SGODA), f. 1B, op. 25, a. e. 20, l. 238.

[43] Migev, 'Otrazhenieto', 77.

[44] 'Decision of the Ministry for Heavy Industry and the Trade Union on the Introduction of the Methods of the Noted Soviet Miner Nikolaĭ Mamaĭ as a New Form of Competition between Workers,' CDA, f. 414, op. 1, a.e. 38.

[45] 'Taka Kitaĭskite kooperatori poluchavat rekordni dobivi,' *Kooperativno Zemedelie* 1959, No. 5, 42–3; Report of the Agricultural Delegation to the PRC and North Korea to the BCP CC, 8 December 1958, CDA, f. 1B, op. 18, a.e. 217, l. 21–7.

[46] 'Iz opita,' *Kooperativno Zemedelie* 1959, No. 5, 42–3; Report of the Agricultural Delegation to the PRC and North Korea to the BCP CC, 8 December 1958, CDA, f. 1B, op. 18, a.e. 217, l. 21–7.

[47] For the significance of Lysenkoism, aka Michurinism, in China, see Lüthi, *Sino-Soviet Split*, 52–3, 88; Laurence Schneider, 'Lysenkoism and the Suppression of Genetics in the PRC, 1949–1956,' in *China Learns from the Soviet Union, 1949–Present*, ed. Thomas P. Bernstein and Hua-yu Li (Lanham, MD: Lexington Books, 2010), 327–58.

emulation of these 'Chinese' methods did not have geopolitical implications. Party officials and agronomists were convinced of the usefulness of deep ploughing in late summer, and had tested the technique in previous years.[48] Thus, deep ploughing can be understood as part of the 1950s extensivist modernisation of agriculture rather than a Soviet satellite's geopolitical move against Moscow. Furthermore, the campaigners of the agricultural ministry did not impose their idea indiscriminately on all farms but conceded that 'it is above all necessary to start from the local conditions and experience'.[49]

Another field of interest for Bulgarian agricultural specialists comprised forms of *experimenting* in the framework of China's Great Leap Forward. A databased approach to detailed analysis of cultivation methods held the most promise for fast modernisation and planning in agriculture. The expert delegation to China was fascinated by the test fields of the Chinese agronomists, who presented the records of their yields without reservation.[50] After party leader Todor Zhivkov highlighted Chinese experiences with experimenting on the BCP's Central Committee plenum,[51] agricultural state farms set up new test fields in the Bulgarian countryside. The press reported that several state farms were experimenting in test fields 'following the example of the Chinese villagers'.[52]

In the Bulgarian specialists' review of Chinese agriculture, cotton farming was one of the most important topics. Upon returning home from China, the agricultural delegation informed the Central Committee of the BCP that China had become the world's biggest cotton producer. Minister of Agriculture Ivan Prămov proclaimed that Bulgarian cotton farms stood to benefit from 'experiences from other countries – Korea and China'.[53] Prămov promised that his ministry would take all measures necessary to introduce the methods the delegation had presented as the basis for the proliferation of record-breaking yields in China and Korea, including the infamous deep ploughing, the use of large amounts of fertiliser, and the use of seedlings raised in greenhouses. The ministry issued a directive recommending the seedling method, edited an information brochure, and dispatched two Korean specialists to travel through Bulgaria helping farmers apply the new methods.[54] That the campaign's results were a complete success is dubious: officials reported to the ministry that the assigned farms had failed to realise a substantial part of the planned planting of cotton according to the new method.[55] Still, the enthusiasm for China in the higher echelons of party and government had touched the everyday life of Bulgarian villagers.

---

[48] An agricultural journal quotes Todor Zhivkov: 'Deep ploughing is our greatest water reservoir!' [Dălbokata oran e naj-golemiyat naš yazovir!] 'Na dălboka oran!' *Kooperativno Zemedelie* 1959, No. 7, 1–2. For earlier campaigning for, and testing of, deep ploughing, see also 'Na vsichki ploshti za proletnicite – dălboka oran,' *Kooperativno Zemedelie* 1958, No. 6, 1.

[49] 'Na vsichki ploshti za proletnicite – dălboka oran,' *Kooperativno Zemedelie* 1958, No. 6, 1 (author's translation).

[50] Report of the Agricultural Delegation to PRC and North Korea, 8 December 1958, CDA, f. 1, op. 18, a.e. 217, l. 27–37.

[51] Zhivkov's speech according to the protocol of the BCP CC plenum, 11 November 1958, CDA, f. 1B, op. 5, a. e. 356, l. 15, http://politburo.archives.bg/bg/2013-04-24-11-09-24/1950-1959/2773--------11--1958-.

[52] 'Vsenaroden pochod za săkrashtavane srokovete na petiletkata,' *Zemedelsko Zname*, 12 November 1958, 1.

[53] Protocol BCP CC, 11 November 1958, CDA, f. 1B, op. 5, a. e. 356, l. 118, http://politburo.archives.bg/bg/2013-04-24-11-09-24/1950-1959/2773--------11--1958--.

[54] 'Ukazaniya na Ministerstvoto na zemedelieto … za razsadno zasazhdane na pamuka,' *Zemedelsko Zname*, 3 December 1958, 2; Dimităr Yurukov, 'Zasazhdane na pamuka chrez razsad v Kitaĭskata Narodna Republika i v Korejskata N-d Republika,' *Kooperativno Selo*, 3 December 1958, 2; Sava Kănev, 'Meropriyatiya za izpălnenieto na tretiya petgodishen plan za pamuka,' *Kooperativno Zemedelie*, No. 9 (1959): 20–1.

[55] Instructive Report on Preparations for Planting Cotton, Vegetables, and Tobacco, and Material Supply of TKZS, CDA, f. 89, op. 61, a. e. 138, l. 22.

Without judging the methods, one can say that the goal of this campaign-style transfer of cotton-growing techniques from China was to increase yields of a cash crop that was a crucial raw material for the expanding textile industry. Bulgaria's cotton-growing offensive was not at all a geopolitical move to follow China and turn against the Soviet Union. On the contrary, cotton farming was fully in line with the Soviet leadership's intention to extend the cultivation of cotton in Uzbekistan and Turkmenistan.[56] The copying of Chinese agricultural techniques was not due to blind enthusiasm; rather, it was based on an economic rationale.

People's Communes in Bulgaria?

A further sphere of transfer concerned the governance and size of agricultural enterprises. The Bulgarian leadership instructed cooperatives to unify into much bigger farms comprising several villages in the winter of 1958/1959. The enlargement of the single enterprises reduced their number from 3700 to 850.[57] Whether and how the Chinese concept of the people's commune influenced this reform was a bone of contention in practice as well as in research at the time. Western authors claimed to have identified a people's commune founded by local officials, Chinese brochures happily reported that Bulgaria was experimenting with the model of the commune, and Soviet politicians warned their comrades from Sofia to abstain from this kind of experiment.[58] Khrushchev himself criticised the Bulgarians for their 'excessively large collective farms', but at the same time admitted that 'in our country too we failed to avoid "gigantomania"'.[59]

In fact, the achievements of the people's communes were praised by the Bulgarian press, by the delegations to China, and prominently discussed by the former party leader Vălko Chervenkov.[60] Certainly, China's project of people's communes contributed somehow to Bulgarian policymakers' idea to enlarge agricultural enterprises. The agricultural delegation sent to China in autumn 1958 reported in detail on the governance structure in the Chinese communes, issuing a recommendation to examine it further at virtually the moment the Bulgarian leadership announced the enlargement campaign.[61]

However, the attempt to measure Chinese influence according to the size of agricultural entities in Bulgaria stands on shaky ground. Whether the size of the enterprises reached the dimensions promoted in China's agricultural policy or remained in the framework favoured by the Soviet Union was not decided by a single policy-making institution that had made

---

[56] Julia Obertreis, *Imperial Desert Dreams: Cotton Growing and Irrigation in Uzbekistan and Turkmenistan, 1860s–1991* (forthcoming); Julia Obertreis, 'Infrastrukturen im Sozialismus. Das Beispiel der Bewässerungssysteme im sowjetischen Zentralasien', *Saeculum* 58, No. 1 (2007): 157.

[57] Migev, 'Otrazhenieto', 77.

[58] Baev, *Drugata Studena Voĭna*, 81–3; Brown, *Bulgaria under Communist Rule*, 88; *Newsletter on the Communist Parties in the World*, Beijing, No. 211, 20 December 1958, 4.

[59] *Memoirs of Nikita Khrushchev*, vol. 2, *Statesman (1953–1964)*, (ed.) Sergei Khrushchev, (University Park, PA: Pennsylvania State University Press, 2007), 449. In the USSR the number of *kolkhoz* enterprises dropped from 236,900 in 1940 to 93,300 in 1953 and 37,600 in 1964; see Manfred Hildermeier, *Geschichte der Sowjetunion 1917–1991. Entstehung und Niedergang des ersten sozialistischen Staates* (Munich: Oldenbourg, 2007), 696, 796.

[60] Ivan Grigorov, 'Golemiyat skok', *Narodna Mladezh*, 5 July 1958, 1; 'Narodnite komuni – delo na milionite kitaĭski selyani', *Kooperativno Selo*, 1 October 1958, 1; Vălko Chervenkov, 'Narodnite Komuni v Kitaĭ', *Rabotnichesko Delo*, January 15, 1959, 1; 'Informaciya ot răkovoditelya na delegaciya v KNR Vălko Chervenkov', *Kooperativno Selo*, 3 February 1959, 3.

[61] Report of the Agricultural Delegation to PRC and North Korea, 8 December 1958, CDA, f. 1, op. 18, a.e. 217, l. 4–20, 84–5.

84 BEYOND THE KREMLIN'S REACH?

a basic decision to follow either the Great Leap Forward or Khrushchev's reform policies. Rather, the Central Committee of the BCP pushed for a vague unification of cooperatives. It was the local and regional nomenklatura members that hammered out the final composition of the 'united agricultural cooperatives'. Officials from different provincial towns and villages quarrelled over the size and structure of the new enterprises. Local power, posts and property had to be redistributed. Diverging interests led to open conflict about which villages were to be included and what place would become the new centre of the united farm.[62] The Bulgarian government and party leadership was not in overall control of this process. Thus, conditions were ripe for an occurrence like the establishment of a people's commune by local zealots in contravention of the leadership's policy line, as James Brown and Liliana Brisby thought they had detected in the founding of a giant cooperative in the provincial town of Botevgrad near Sofia. They suggest that local elites had taken the Bulgarian leadership's Economic Leap policies too far without understanding the wider ideological implications and that this local experiment of a *Botevgradska Komuna* was quickly terminated by an intervention from above. In this particular case, however, that just does not seem to be what happened.

The founding of the 'Unified Agricultural Cooperative "Botevgradska Komuna"' was indeed accompanied by many conflicts and a power struggle among local elites. Cadres were shuffled, and the size of the enterprise and municipality was changed several times. Soon after having become the biggest cooperative in Bulgaria, it was split into two. However, the main resultant cooperative kept the name *Botevgradska Komuna*, which remained in use until the privatisation of the enterprise in the early 1990s. The name, which probably helped to inspire the story of a Chinese inspiration of the founding of the enterprise, was anything but alien to the Bulgarian socialist nomenklatura: it was a reference to the Socialist Party's historical victories and local governments in the 1910s and 1920s in several Bulgarian municipalities, like Samokov, Sliven and Botevgrad, which had been called 'Commune' in the tradition of the famous Parisian example. The socialist regime in Bulgaria later made these 'Communes' part of its national narrative with municipalities organising anniversaries and local newspapers as well as several cooperatives being named after them.[63] Furthermore, the local files examined for this study contain no indication that a China–Soviet Union dichotomy was used as rhetorical strategy in any of the local elite's disputes, nor any mention that the cadres expressed a conviction that the Chinese People's Communes were the example the district of Botevgrad should follow. Neither did an investigation of the Botevgrad district archive unearth documents revealing a decisive political intervention from above that would have ended a 'Commune' experiment.[64] The *Botevgradska Komuna* was not a scandal in a geopolitical contradiction between Bulgaria and the Soviet Union but just one (albeit a special one) of many newly formed merged cooperatives.

---

[62]See examples among letters from local party officials to the BCP CC in CDA, Fond 1B, op. 18, a. e. 219; l. 6–15; 35–42.

[63]For example, the town's newspaper and the agricultural cooperative of Samokov were called 'Samokovska Komuna'. For the regime discourse on the Bulgarian Communes, see, e.g. Stoianka Pobornikova, 'Slivenskata Komuna prez 1915–1923 godina', *Izvestija na Instituta po Istorija na BKP* 12 (1964), 405–55.

[64]Protocols of the Sessions of the BCP Primary Organisation at the Botevgrad District Council (SGODA, f. 195, op. 10, a. e. 25; f. 457, op. 1, several files), at the Botevgrad Town Council (f. 185, op. 25, a. e. 5; f. 299, op. 2 and 3, several files), at the Sofia District Council (f. 698, op. 1, a. e. 3), and of the District Council's Department for Agriculture (f. 614, op. 9; op. 6; several files). A town history volume treats the enlargement in a few technical sentences without even mentioning the renaming. Simeonka Vlaĭkova, *Botevgrad prez godinite*, vol. 2 (Sofia: Zvezdan, 2003), 39.

Thus, although the drive to enlarge the agricultural enterprises to some degree has received inspiration from the Chinese campaign, it was not intended to provoke Moscow by following a 'Chinese' path. The Bulgarian leadership often reiterated this point once Khrushchev had more clearly spoken out against the people's communes.[65] Meanwhile, the idea of enlarging the Bulgarian agricultural enterprises persisted. The 1970s saw the formation of 'agro-industrial complexes' of sizes exceeding those of the unified agricultural cooperatives of the late 1950s. In the eyes of the Bulgarian leadership, enlargement of the country's agricultural enterprises had always been an economic necessity.[66]

Goals and results of the Bulgarian Economic Leap

The Bulgarian Economic Leap campaign was neither an enthusiastic adoption of the Chinese example nor a mere emulation of Khrushchev's economic policy in the Soviet Union. The Bulgarian leadership was committed to the goal of industrialisation, especially to a programme of setting up heavy industry. The moderate bias towards strengthening consumption and agriculture promoted by Soviet economic policies at the time did not seem fully appropriate, nor was it attractive to accept Bulgaria's assigned role in COMECON as a vegetable and fruit supplier. Khrushchev and the CPSU urged the poorer countries in COMECON to concentrate on what they were doing best (agriculture) and supply the socialist market with the resulting goods in exchange for machinery from the more industrialised countries. Thus, the Bulgarians tried to revise their role in the socialist international division of labour. The Bulgarian government was not the only one that acted reluctantly or even opposed Khrushchev's suggestions for deepening the division of labour in COMECON. Even industrialised countries, which supported the general idea, tried to preserve those parts of their industries that did not fit into the specialisation scheme. The most prominent opposition came from the Romanian leadership, which obstructed many projects and measures for a deepened cooperation in the early 1960s.[67]

In the Bulgarian case, a letter of 1955 from Khrushchev to the Central Committee of the BCP stated that the building up of a steel industry in Bulgaria was 'a fantasy', and that the only viable path of economic development was the Soviet-assisted mechanisation of agriculture.[68] Industrialisation in Bulgaria, he suggested, should not go beyond bicycle production and eventually, at a later stage, assembly of cars from prefabricated components produced in other COMECON states.[69] The Central Committee sent a very thankful reply expressing full agreement to Moscow's stance, but in fact, the committee's debate revealed divergent opinions on the topic.[70] In further negotiations on Bulgaria's role in COMECON, the Bulgarian side managed to obtain from the Soviet Union – in clear contradiction to Khrushchev's initial reasoning – considerable credits and support for building up steel and

---

[65]Baev, *Drugata Studena Voĭna*, 82–4.

[66]Lampe, *Bulgarian Economy*, 152–3.

[67]Lee Kendall Metcalf, *The Council of Mutual Economic Assistance. The Failure of Reform* (New York: Columbia University Press, 1997, 57–65; Kaser, *COMECON*, 83–84; André Steiner, 'The Council of Mutual Economic Assistance – An Example of Failed Economic Integration?' *Geschichte und Gesellschaft* 39 (2013), 240–58.

[68]Letter from Khrushchev to Praesidium of CC CPSU [which, after approval, was sent to the CC BCP], 27 October 1955, f. 1B, op. 5, a.e. 189, l. 3–9, see l. 6 [http://politburo.archives.bg/bg/2013-04-24-11-09-24/1950-1959/2876-------6-7—1955-].

[69]Ibid., l. 7.

[70]Daniel Vachkov and Martin Ivanov, *Bălgarskiyat vănshen dălg 1944–1989. Bankrutăt na komunisticheskata ikonomika* (Sofia: Institut za izuchavane na blizkoto minalo, 2008), 94–102; Protocol of CC BCP Plenary Session, 6–7 December 1955, CDA, f. 1B; op. 5; a.e. 187, http://politburo.archives.bg/bg/2013-04-24-11-09-24/1950-1959/2877-------6-7--1955---.

machine-construction industry complexes.[71] The most prominent of these projects was the giant steel mill in Kremikovci, which indeed was of doubtful use economically, just as Khrushchev had predicted in his 1955 letter.[72]

Although the Kremikovci steel mill was not the only investment that proved to be inefficient, the results of the Bulgarian campaign were not at all as catastrophic as the outcome of the Chinese Great Leap Forward. No one starved to death, and neither agricultural nor industrial production was substantially diminished. Rather, growth was stable. In view of the ambitious goals, which had been formulated in autumn 1958, this was a disappointing outcome. When announcing the successful completion of the Economic Leap in 1960, the Bulgarian leadership had to cheat. Zhivkov and the State Plan Commission announced happily that *growth rates* had doubled while they originally had promised that the *amount of production* would rise by that factor.[73] In general, though, the Bulgarian industrialisation process remained on track. Unemployment was down, and several factories had been modernised and new ones erected. The share of industry in the net material product rose from 23 to 48% from 1948 to 1960, and industrial employment grew by 11.5% annually between 1955 and 1960.[74]

With the rapid industrialisation process the Bulgarian leadership aimed to escape the bad terms of international trade for agricultural products with Western countries and the COMECON states alike.[75] The long- and short-term goals in the process of transforming Bulgaria from a backward, agricultural country into a developed, industrialised one could not be attained without capital. Technology and raw materials had to be bought on world markets. Yet Bulgaria lacked the capital to do so. To remedy the mismatch between goals and available resources, the Bulgarian economic politicians adopted a double strategy. The means to develop heavy industry had to be borrowed, mainly from the Soviet Union. The other side of the double strategy was a strict policy of cost reduction – a state-socialist form of austerity. For this second part of the development strategy, Bulgarian planners and politicians found inspiring examples in the Great Leap Forward in China.

However, the first line of the double strategy thwarted the second. The erection of Kremikovci and the renovation of other industrial facilities exceeded the financial capacities of the Bulgarian government, because the cost of importing machinery from socialist and Western countries exceeded by far the gains made from exports, mostly of agricultural products. Bulgaria was entering a debt crisis that began to escalate in 1959 as a direct consequence of the industrial investments in the course of the Economic Leap.[76]

---

[71]Brown, *Bulgaria under Communist Rule*, 86–7; Brunnbauer, *Sozialistische Lebensweise*, 172–3; Vachkov and Ivanov, *Bălgarskiyat vănshen dălg*, 94–102; Nikova, *Săvetăt za Ikonomicheska Vzaimopomosht*, 209–10, 224. Letter from Khrushchev to CC CPSU/CC BCP, 27 October 1955, CDA f. 1B, op. 5, a.e. 189, http://politburo.archives.bg/bg/2013-04-24-11-09-24/1950-1959/2876-------6-7--1955-.

[72]Michael Palairet, "'Lenin" and "Brezhnev": Steel Making and the Bulgarian Economy, 1956–90,' *Europe Asia Studies* 47, No. 3 (1995), 493–505; Brunnbauer, *Sozialistische Lebensweise*, 184–206. As the exploitation of natural mineral deposits near Kremikovci proved non-viable and inefficient, iron ore and coking coal had to be imported from the Danube and the Black Sea to the steel factory near Sofia. The weak Bulgarian industry was not able to absorb the steel mill's produce and it had to be dumped on the world market at prices lower than production costs, going primarily to Japan.

[73]Brown, *Bulgaria under Communist Rule*, 85, 93.

[74]Lampe, *Bulgarian Economy*, 153; Brunnbauer, *Sozialistische Lebensweise*, 179.

[75]For the unfavourable terms of trade for Bulgaria see Vachkov and Ivanov, *Bălgarskiyat vănshen dălg*, 100–5.

[76]Rumen Avramov, *Pari i de/stabilizaciya v Bălgariya, 1948–1989* (Sofia: Institut za izuchavane na blizkoto minalo, 2007), 123–4. Between 1958 and 1962 the foreign debt to capitalist countries grew eightfold. In 1959 alone it rose from slightly more than $20 million to $115 million.

Bulgaria's debt problem and the various actors' attempts to mitigate it reveal the extent to which economic processes in the seemingly isolated Soviet bloc were part of the global circulation of capital. In 1959 and 1960, the Bulgarian National Bank had to renegotiate and restructure its debts several times to avoid bankruptcy. As the bank did not possess the means to exercise control over imports (i.e. hard currency outflow) or over the realisation of the export plan (i.e. currency inflow), there was no remedy but recourse to new loans or extension of loan periods. The Bulgarian National Bank had to seek help from Soviet-owned banks in the West – the Moscow Narodny Bank in London and the Banque commercial pour l'Europe de Nord in Paris.[77] These banks were in a peculiar position between the Soviet government's political interests and the regulations and conventions of the countries and financial markets they acted in. Because of being part of the international banking system, it was crucial for these banks to preserve their prestige as 'good debtors'. However, they also had the task to support the socialist partners in covering their debt, because the Soviet prestige depended not least on the reliability of the whole bloc. In 1959, their share in Bulgaria's foreign convertible currency debt amounted to 66%, temporarily putting them – or the Soviet state bank, as their owner – in the position of a lender of last resort for the crisis-ridden brother country.[78] Thus, these banks, because of their intrinsic interest in preventing payment default on the part of the Bulgarian National Bank, displayed a will to impose a strict policy of saving hard currency on the Bulgarian government. 'In a certain sense', writes the Bulgarian economic historian Rumen Avramov, 'they played the same role the IMF would be playing decades later'.[79]

National and supranational institutions in the West were startled by the potential of default on the debts Bulgaria owed to the western-based Soviet banks and, to a limited extent, directly to western banks.[80] Bulgarian negotiators had to travel to Paris and London (not to Moscow) several times to meet with personnel from the Gosbank-owned banks as well as representatives of the French government and Western banks. The Bank for International Settlements in Basel issued credits for debt restructuring, too. A temporary solution was found in resorting to the Bulgarian gold reserves. With the decision to let the Moscow Narodny Bank sell part of the Bulgarian National Bank's gold reserve on London markets, a taboo was broken. In the following years, the gold reserves were used as an active asset by deposing them in London or Basel as a security for further loans. Until the middle of the 1960s, Bulgaria lost the bulk of its gold reserves but in concurrence with generous trade agreements with the Soviet government, the foreign debt could be reduced to a manageable amount.[81]

The debt crisis became the stepping stone for the reforms of the 1960s. Simultaneously with the debt restructuring measures, the National Bank urged the government to

---

[77]Central Intelligence Agency, 'Soviet-Owned Banks in the West', Intelligence Report, October 1969, available online in CIA Library, https://www.cia.gov/library/readingroom/docs/DOC_0000233857.pdf. These two banks had been Soviet-controlled since the 1920s and gained fame for their early involvement in Eurodollar business in the 1950s.

[78]Avramov, *Pari i De/stabilizaciya*, 135–40, 166.

[79]Ibid., 185 (author's translation).

[80]Vachkov and Ivanov, *Bălgarskiyat vănshen dălg*, 110. In March 1960 the Bulgarian debt in short-term credits in convertible currency was $129.4 million, of which $90 million was owed to socialist banks – including $76 million to the Soviet-owned banks in London and Paris – and $39.4 million to Western banks and enterprises, mainly in West Germany and Italy.

[81]Avramov, *Pari i De/stabilizaciya*, 196–9; Vachkov and Ivanov, *Bălgarskiyat vănšen dălg*, 104–20. See also: Report of the Ministry for Foreign Trade and the Bulgarian National Bank to the Committee for Currency Questions and Trade Balance, 4 March 1966, CDA, f. 259, op. 28, a.e. 3, l. 1–3.

curtail import, meaning also to temper growth and domestic consumption, and push exports to liquidate the structural deficit.[82] Ending its leap policies, the Bulgarian leadership substantially lowered the plan goals for 1961.[83] In general, the political leadership recurred to a more intensive growth model. This turn from creating growth through greater inputs to a policy of increasing productivity was in line with the reform debates in the other COMECON countries at the time. The crucial questions were at what level decisions on investment and resource allocation should be made, how the outcome of production processes was to be measured and how prices should be determined. In the Bulgarian reforms, to a certain extent, decision-making competences were shifted from the ministerial level to a lower level of enlarged entities of production (above the enterprise level). The fate of the reforms was, not only in Bulgaria, coined by the contradiction of the party and economic bureaucracy's goal to raise efficiency on the one hand and to keep control over the whole process on the other. In a certain sense, the Bulgarian leadership was successful in restructuring the industry and opening it up to new branches during the following decades. Bulgaria was able to, additionally to its role as supplier of fruit, vegetables and forklift trucks, make itself the specialist for computers and data processing devices in the COMECON.[84] However, the chronic trade balance deficit, which rooted in the bad terms of trade on the world market, in the long run could not be liquidated by these steps, and in the 1980s the socialist regime ran into its next – final – debt crisis.[85]

Conclusion

The Economic Leap campaign in Bulgaria from 1958 to 1960 was not a comprehensive adoption of China's Great Leap Forward. Far from leading to a coherent Chinese-style economic policy, the Chinese campaign's reverberations in Bulgaria were limited to some fragmented inspirations, a curious enthusiasm in certain echelons of the bureaucracy, and transfers of agricultural technologies and methods of temporary labour mobilisation.

Bulgarian planners, economists, politicians and technical experts did see promise in the Chinese Great Leap Forward, but not in the sense of an original Chinese way to be emulated. Rather, they viewed China's leap as a model for cost reduction in a late Stalinist-style industrialisation drive. The parallels between the two countries' industrialisation projects, undertaken in circumstances of prevailingly rural structures, lack of investment resources and abundant labour, made the Great Leap Forward an interesting example to the Bulgarian leadership. The rationale guiding the Economic Leap campaign and the transfers of techniques and technologies from China was primarily economic in nature.

---

[82] Avramov, *Pari i De/stabilizaciya*, 180.

[83] Brown, *Bulgaria under Communist Rule*, 143. The planned growth for industry was lowered from 27.8% for 1960 to 7.8% for 1961.

[84] Brown, *Bulgaria under Communist Rule*, 160–72; Lampe, *Bulgarian Economy*, 199–204; Martin Ivanov, *Reformatorstvo bez reformi. Politicheskata ikonomiya na bălgarskiya komunizăm 1963–1989* (Sofia: Inst. za Izučavane na Blizkoto Minalo, 2008). Victor Petrov is researching the temporarily successful Bulgarian attempts to build up a computer and chip industry in a doctoral project at Columbia University ('A Cyber-Socialism at Home and Abroad: Bulgarian Modernisation, Computers, and the World 1967–1989').

[85] Avramov, *Pari i De/stabilizaciya*, 200–11.

The goal of national industrialisation indeed conflicted with the strategy of division of labour envisaged by the Soviet leadership, though not in the geopolitical sense of a 'Chinese' deviation on Bulgaria's part. Bulgarian planners and politicians sought add-ons to capital-intensive industrialisation on the one hand, and alternatives to Bulgaria's role as a fruit, vegetable and tobacco supplier to COMECON and world markets on the other. The history of the Bulgarian Economic Leap shows that the campaign was not an example of a potential geopolitical breach in the bloc, but evidence that Soviet power was not unlimited in such economic questions. To be sure, Moscow did have a huge influence on Sofia's policies, but it still had to negotiate. It could not simply impose its will. This was all the more so because the socialist states were dependent on the capitalist West's offer of the most modern machinery, certain materials and the convertible 'hard' currency, which was necessary to purchase these.

Instead of having a geopolitical intra-bloc implication, the technological transfers observed here happened in a context of political promotion and extensive realisation of exchanges of technologies, knowledge and ideas. The Bulgarian Economic Leap campaign and the technical transfers from China thus were facilitated by the socialist context. Transfers of technology and models for economic policies did not necessarily have to originate in Moscow and to a certain extent were not controlled and sanctioned by the Soviet leadership.

In the specific case of exchanges between Bulgaria and China, relations changed once Soviet political decisions made the PRC a politically unacceptable outcast in the socialist camp. However, that China would become a sort of internal enemy in the socialist camp was not yet clear at the end of the 1950s. Furthermore it should be noted that Bulgarian foreign trade officials continued attempting to persuade their Chinese business partners to increase trade again after 1960. Trade between the two countries never stopped totally, as was also the case with other Soviet bloc countries. Bulgaria's Economic Leap policy was not a provocation against Soviet leadership, and Bulgaria was not on the brink of becoming a second (or rather first) Albania. It is the Cold War perspective that presents the Bulgarian industrialisation drive of the late 1950s as either Soviet or Chinese, and assigns geopolitical meaning to measures of economic development. The interpretations in Western research from the 1960s and 1970s tend to exaggerate the politicisation of interactions while minimising mercantilist rationales in the state socialist economic and foreign policies.

Acknowledgements

I would like to thank Sören Urbansky and Péter Vámos for very helpful commentaries on my manuscript and Rumen Avramov, Ge Jun, Ma Li, Stefan Troebst and the participants of the conference 'Beyond the Kremlin's Reach? Transfers and Entanglements between Eastern Europe and China during the Cold War Era', at the GWZO Leipzig for further recommendations on sources and arguments.

Disclosure statement

No potential conflict of interest was reported by the author.

Promoting the 'China Way' of communism in Poland and beyond during the Sino-Soviet Split: the case of Kazimierz Mijal

Margaret K. Gnoinska

ABSTRACT

Kazimierz Mijal – a promoter of the "China Way" in Polish communism during the Sino-Soviet split – was not only a nuisance to Warsaw's leadership domestically but had a certain effect on international politics within the communist world. He was used as a political tool by both Albania and China, and complicated Poland's delicate diplomacy with both Beijing and Moscow. His long biographical and personal journey – forced but also intentional, grounded in belief and shaped by geopolitics – embodies contradictions and paradoxes of the international communist movement which often spread beyond the reach and control of the Kremlin during the cold war.

Introduction

In late 1966, at the height of the Sino-Soviet split and the Great Proletarian Cultural Revolution in China, Chairman Mao gave a warm welcome in Beijing to Kazimierz Mijal – once a high-ranking official in Stalinist Poland and now the self-proclaimed First Secretary of the Communist Party of Poland (KPP). The KPP was illegal in Poland and Mijal had been forced to flee the country and eventually settled in Albania under the auspices of Enver Hoxha. Clearly energised by his own revolution, Mao Zedong urged Mijal to rally the Polish people in the anti-imperialist and anti-revisionist revolution, as well as seizing an opportunity to use zealous comrades like Mijal to reduce Moscow's influence and discredit Soviet revisionism of Marxist-Leninist thought in Poland.

While there have been efforts to examine the effects of Maoist thought during the Cold War globally, the case of Poland has not yet been given due attention.[1] This article seeks to fill this gap by shedding light on the varieties of 'believers' within Communism like Mijal who were open promoters of a 'China way' within Polish Communism. In fact, Mijal became

---

[1]See especially Alexander C. Cook, ed. *Mao's Little Red Book: A Global History* (Cambridge: Cambridge University Press, 2014). The volume devotes chapters to East Germany, Albania, and Yugoslavia, as well as Western European, Asian, and African countries.

the Polish embodiment of anti-revisionism within the international communist movement; he defended Stalin and his legacy and joined those communists who rejected a pro-Soviet orientation, thereby aligning himself with China and Albania. The article also shows that Poland's engagement with China at its highest levels of leadership offers a nuanced and complex picture of a communist leadership that publicly sided with Moscow in the Sino-Soviet split but behind the scenes continued to make efforts to unite the fragmented communist world while pursuing Poland's interests. This article argues that Mijal's actions, clearly a nuisance for the leadership of the Polish United Workers' Party (PUWP) domestically, had a certain effect on international politics within the communist world by complicating, especially, Władysław Gomułka's delicate diplomacy with both Beijing and Moscow.

To be sure, Mijal did not manage to garner support among the workers in Poland and thus did not further Beijing's ambitions of fomenting a radical revolution in the Soviet bloc. His efforts were eventually silenced by the Polish security services on instructions from the party. At the same time, the case of Mijal demonstrates that Maoist thought did resonate to some degree with the younger generation of Polish communists who also saw it as a means of challenging the Kremlin's control of Eastern Europe. Mijal and his group were able to test the authority of the PUWP, albeit for a short period of time, by trying to awaken the consciousness of a nation heavily influenced by Soviet style communism. And, even though, following the Sino-Albanian split and China's choice to embark on a path of economic modernisation in the 1970s, Mijal eventually became a useless political tool for both Tirana and Beijing, he did leave a mark on the international communist movement. Therefore, the article also highlights that the Sino-Soviet split emerges as a kind of folding of international Communism in on itself, creating room for people like Mijal whose agency derived from the Sino-Soviet split and who was used by Mao and Hoxha to pursue their own agendas. The article pieces together a story of the creation of some agency – small and limited, and contradictory, but agency nonetheless – that was shaped by ideology and geopolitics.

Despite his long and interesting life – a journey of one man from Poland to Stalinist Albania to Mao's China and back to Poland after Deng Xiaoping's ascent to power – Mijal did not leave memoirs, diaries, or a full biography. What we do have available and accessible are some of his writings, interviews conducted by historians and journalists in post-communist Poland, his 1946 official autobiography in the party archives, governmental and party documents, and references to Mijal in other primary and secondary sources. Clearly, such materials should be carefully used and evaluated, as each one is a genre with its own conventions and context. For example, there is no doubt that Mijal, in his official autobiography, placed emphasis on his humble beginnings, obstacles to obtaining education, and his communist consciousness in early adulthood – all of which served to solidify his correct political background in the eyes of communist authorities in post-WWII Poland. At the same time, what is remarkable about Mijal and his commitment to Marxist-Leninist ideology is that he was neither willing to whitewash it nor was he ashamed of it. If anything, he was steadfast in his beliefs and convictions regarding the superiority of the Marxism-Leninism of Stalin and Mao over the capitalist system that he witnessed being implemented in the early 1990s in Eastern Europe.

Also, though Mijal may have exaggerated his sole contribution in mobilising the Poles for a revolution, as well as his close relationship to leaders such as Hoxha and Mao in his days of exile from Poland, other sources corroborate that he was the driving force of promoting the 'China way' while still in Poland and then in exile. To be sure, both of these leaders used Mijal for their own political purposes, and it is doubtful that they permitted the level of friendship that Mijal attributes in his later interviews. Still, either unavailable or inaccessible at the moment are documents depicting in more detail his relationship with Hoxha and Mao, as well as Moscow's actual perception of Mijal. Nevertheless, the available sources not only shed much light on his persona and ideology, but provide a unique and valuable window into one long biographical and personal journey – forced but also intentional, grounded in belief and shaped by geopolitics. Mijal's life embodied the contradictions and paradoxes of the international communist and workers' movement that was often beyond the reach and control of the Kremlin during the most crucial periods in the Cold War that involved the gradual disintegration of the communist world.

Mijal as a Polish force – a brilliant ascent and a gradual fall from power

Kazimierz Mijal lived to be almost 100 years old. He was born on 15 September 1910 in central Poland outside of Warsaw into a peasant family.[2] His parents had 18 children in total, including those from their previous marriages, and Mijal was the youngest. According to Mijal, he owed much to his mother, who pushed him to get an education against all odds. In 1926, he began to study economics at the State Trade School in Warsaw while delivering coal and tutoring.[3] He then became the head accountant and manager of a Warsaw pub called *Polonia,* and later served in the army, where he was injured and received disability. Subsequently, he served as the head of the Organisational and Control Section of the Accounting Department at the Warsaw Branch of the Municipal Savings Bank and audited classes in the Department of Finance and Economics at the School of Political Studies.[4] The outbreak of World War II and the German occupation of Poland, however, prevented him from obtaining a diploma. Mijal claims that he remained unemployed until June 1942, frequenting the Public Library in Warsaw and 'extensively reading on economics, philosophy, and history.'[5] While we may never fully determine his actual whereabouts during this time, it was during wartime that he became involved in communist activities.

Despite the emphasis in his party autobiography that his humble peasant background and work with white-collar labour unions 'decisively shaped his class consciousness,' Mijal began his communist political career very late as compared to many pre-WWII Polish communists. Unlike Bolesław Bierut, Gomułka, and many others, who spent the interwar years in and out of Polish prisons Mijal was never a member of the illegal Polish Communist Party (KPP) that was dissolved by Stalin during the Great Terror of the 1930s. Many of the pre-WWII KPP members were executed at the orders of Stalin, and the ones who did survive, ironically, were serving their prison sentences in Poland at the time.[6] It was not until 1941

---

[2]Biuletyn Informacji Publicznej, Instytut Pamięci Narodowej [The Institute of National Remembrance, hereafter: IPN]. https://katalog.bip.ipn.gov.pl (Accessed 19 February 2017).

[3]Kazimierz Mijal, Autobiography, November 1946, Archiwum Akt Nowych [Archives of Modern Records in Warsaw, hereafter AAN], Akta Osobowe [Personal Files] 3985 [hereafter: Mijal, Autobiography], 1–2.

[4]Ibid., 4.

[5]Ibid., 6.

[6]M. K. Dziewanowski, *The Communist Party of Poland: An Outline of History* (Cambridge, MA: Harvard University Press, 1976) and Gabriele Simoncini, *Ethnic and Social Diversity in the Communist Party of Poland, 1918 – 1938* (Hoover Institution, Stanford University Press, 1992).

BEYOND THE KREMLIN'S REACH? 93

that Mijal co-founded the short-lived group *Proletariusz* and joined the newly formed Polish Workers' Party (PPR).[7] He soon became useful to the party by helping mastermind one of the largest bank robberies of the Wehrmacht's accounts in Warsaw, attributing its success to his connections with the Municipal Savings Bank.[8] Subsequently, he became one of the most trusted and best-informed men in Bierut's entourage. Having served as the secretary of the PPR district in Krakow and the Central Committee (CC) of the PPR in Warsaw, he became the secretary and treasurer of the State National Council (KRN), which constituted the nucleus of Poland's post-WWII communist government.[9]

As long as Poland adhered to Stalinism and the communist camp remained united, for the most part, bolstered by the Sino-Soviet partnership, Mijal's political career continued brilliantly and his faith in the progression of Marxism-Leninism in his native Poland, the Soviet bloc, the Soviet Union, and faraway East Asia seemed unquestioned.[10] He never became a member of the Politburo of the PUWP, but served on its Central Committee and held high level governmental positions, including the presidency of the City of Łódź, Chief of the Bureau of the Council of Ministers, member of the Parliament, and the Chief of the Office of the Council of Ministers – the most prestigious post of his career.

Khrushchev's Secret Speech in February 1956 at the 20th Communist Party of the Soviet Union (CPSU) Congress and the upheaval that followed in both Poland and Hungary proved detrimental to Mijal's political and personal life. A member of the 'Natolin' faction within the Polish party, Mijal was horrified when Gomułka – the newly reinstated CC PUWP First Secretary at the now legendary VIII Plenum in October 1956 – began to embrace and promote de-Stalinisation. Mijal had been a vehement opponent of Gomułka in the past and was particularly vocal in contributing to his removal from power in 1948.[11] In 1956, the 'Natolinians' lost to the 'Puławian' clique who generally came from the intelligentsia and advocated the liberalisation of the socialist system. Mijal opposed such changes, seeing them as a 'great turn to the right in socialism' that would restore capitalism.[12]

By the late 1950s, the 'Natolin' group was no longer influential in Poland's political life.[13] In early 1957, Mijal was stripped of his position as the Chief of the Office of the Council of Ministers and offered the position of the Director of the National Investment Bank. His political career experienced a major blow in 1959 when he was not re-elected to the Central Committee at the Third PUWP Congress, mainly due to his criticisms of Gomułka's

---

[7]Mijal, Autobiography, 5–6; Władysław Gomułka (Andrzej Werblan, ed.), *Pamiętniki, tom II* (Warszawa: Polska Oficyna Wydawnicza 'BGW', 1994), 259.

[8]Mijal, Autobiography, 13–16; Ibid., 343; 368. On the formation of the communist rule in Poland after WWII, see: Piotr Gontarczyk, *Polska Partia Robotnicza: Droga do władzy, 1941–1944* (Warszawa: Fronda, 2006); Krystyna Kersten, *The Establishment of Communist rule in Poland, 1943–1948* (Berkeley, CA: University of California Press, 1991); Andrzej Paczkowski, *Zdobycie Władzy 1945–1947* (Warszawa: Wydawnictwo Szkolne i Pedagogiczne, 1993); Anita Prażmowska, *Civil War in Poland, 1942–1948* (New York, NY: Palgrave Macmillan, 2004).

[10]See especially, Shen Zhihua and Yafeng Xia, *Mao and the Sino-Soviet Partnership, 1945–1959: A New History* (Harvard Cold War Studies) (Lanham, MD: Lexington Books, 2015).

[11]Andrzej Paczkowski, *Spring Will Be Ours: Poland and the Poles from Occupation to Freedom* (University Park, PA: The Pennsylvania State University, 2003), 205.

[12]'Ostatni Towarzysz,' Robert Mazurek, Interview conducted with Kazimierz Mijal in 2001. This was the last major interview given by Mijal. https://tj1111.wordpress.com (Accessed on 11 November 2015). [Hereafter: Mazurek, Interview with Mijal, 2001].

[13]Mieczysław F. Rakowski, *Dzienniki Polityczne, 1958–1962* (Warszawa: ISKRY, 1998), 88.

policies.[14] According to Andrzej Werblan, a historian and a former Politburo member, stripping Mijal of the Central Committee membership was more Khrushchev's decision than Gomułka's.[15] Regardless of who made the final decision, the fact remains that Mijal was removed from political life. Nevertheless, he continued to question the aims of de-Stalinisation, seeing it as dangerous to the construction of socialism according to Marxism-Leninism. Even after decades, he continued to claim that Gomułka's policies of the 1950s, especially his abandonment of collectivisation of the countryside and a more relaxed policy towards the Catholic Church, were harmful to Polish communism.[16] It was in this context that, gradually, Mijal's political ideas began to align with those of the Chinese leadership, which viewed de-Stalinisation as erroneous, revisionist, and detrimental to Marxist-Leninist thought.

Mijal as a Bridge to China: 'Grupka Mijalowska'

In the early 1960s, the Sino-Soviet split rocked the international communist and workers' movement, causing smaller nations within the communist world, as well as communist parties elsewhere, to choose sides in what came to be a deeply ideological and geopolitical dispute with far-reaching consequences for the Cold War.[17] With the clear exception of Albania (and to a lesser degree Romania), all leaders of the Warsaw Pact nations followed Moscow in the Sino-Soviet dispute.[18] The Soviet leadership, however, was keenly aware, and in fact anxious, about the levels of loyalty and allegiance of its Eastern European allies. The Kremlin's concern was no doubt, and unsurprisingly, brought about by Mao's ambitions 'to be the standard bearer for the world's socialist countries in catching up with and overtaking capitalism and imperialism, and to make China a leading example in the international communist movement.'[19] To ensure tighter coordination, the International Department of the Central Committee of the Communist Party of the Soviet Union (CC CPSU), especially Oleg B. Rakhmanin and Mikhail S. Kapitsa, created multilateral platforms such as the 'Interkit.' This institution gathered China experts from the USSR, Eastern Europe, and other

---

[14]Antoni Marek, 'Kazimierz Mijal – Dogmatic Diehard or Political Adventurer,' 6 June 1967. https://www.osaarchivum.org/files/holdings/300/8/3/text/42-3-217.shtml (Accessed May 13, 2011); Piotr Gontarczyk, et al., eds. *Marzec 1968 w dokumentach MSW Tom I, Niepokorni* (Warszawa: IPN, 2008), 699.

[15]Grzegorz Sołtysiak, 'Żołnierze Partii.' *Gazeta Wyborcza*, 11 December 1993; Robert Skobelski, *PRL wobec państw socjalistycznych w latach 1956–1970: współpraca-napięcia-konflikty* (Poznań: Wydawnictwo Poznańskie, 2010), 40–41.

[16]Mazurek, Interview with Mijal in 2001.

[17]Li Danhui and Xia Yafeng, *Mao and the Sino-Soviet Split, 1960–1973: A New History* (forthcoming 2017); Jeremy Friedman, *Shadow Cold War: the Sino-Soviet Competition for the Third World* (Chapel Hill, NC: University of North Carolina Press, 2015); Austin Jersild, *The Sino-Soviet Alliance: An International History* (Chapel Hill, NC: University of North Carolina Press, 2014); David Tompkins, 'The East is Red? Images of China in East Germany and Poland through the Sino-Soviet Split' in *Zeitschrift für Ostmitteleuropa-Forschung* 62/3 (2013): 393–424; Shen Zhihua and Li Danhui, *After Leaning to One Side: China and Its Allies in the Cold War* (Washington D.C.: Woodrow Wilson Centre, 2011); Sergey Radchenko, *Two Suns in the Heavens: The Sino-Soviet Struggle for Supremacy, 1962–1967* (Washington D.C.: Woodrow Wilson Centre, 2009); and Lorenz M. Lüthi, *The Sino-Soviet Split: Cold War in the Communist World* (Princeton, NJ: Princeton University Press, 2008); Odd Arne Westad, Brothers in Arms: The Rise and Fall of the Sino-Soviet Alliance, 1945–1963 (Stanford, CA: Stanford University Press, 1998).

[18]Elidor Mëhilli, 'Mao and the Albanians,' in *Mao's Little Red Book,* 165–184; Elidor Mëhilli, 'Defying De-Stalinisation: Albania's 1956,' *Journal of Cold War Studies* 13, No. 4 (2011): 4–56 and Mircea Munteanu, 'When the Levee Breaks: The Impact of the Sino-Soviet Split and the Invasion of Czechoslovakia on Romanian-Soviet Relations, 1967–1970,' *Journal of Cold War Studies* 12, No. 1 (2010): 43–61; Larry L. Watts, 'A Romanian INTERKIT? Soviet Active Measures and the Warsaw Pact "Maverick" 1965–1989,' Working Paper No. 65 (Washington D.C.: Woodrow Wilson Centre, December 2012).

[19]Shen and Li, *After Leaning to One Side, 165.*

Moscow allies with the goal of controlling Eastern European countries' China policies to make them fall in line with those of Moscow.[20] However, despite the many constraints and limitations placed upon them, Eastern European leaders still managed to challenge and/or test Moscow on its anti-China policy.

Poland seems to have occupied a special place in Mao's policy among the Soviet bloc nations. The Sino-Polish relationship had a solid foundation developed in the early days of the PRC and was further strengthened by Warsaw's perception of China's opposition to the Soviet use of force against Poland during the October 1956 crisis. Also, Warsaw was the site of Sino-American ambassadorial talks, Poland was a member of international peace commissions in Indochina and the Korean Peninsula, and the Sino-Polish Joint Shipping Venture (*Chipolbrok*) helped China circumvent the US embargo in the 1950s when the young PRC was making its debut on the international stage.[21,] The Chinese believed that the Poles wanted to maintain relative independence from the Soviet Union, and they were not too far from the truth. Their analysis of Polish-Soviet relations was generally accurate, highlighting the intricacies of Gomułka's often trying relationship with the Soviet leadership, his desire to 'maintain some level of independence' from Moscow, and Poland's 'hopes to improve its relations with China, so as to strengthen its position in the partnership with Russia.'[22] This and other considerations indicated that Chairman Mao decided to leave some room for manoeuvre in his dealings with Poland.[23]

Gomułka sought to challenge the Sino-Soviet split and mend fences between Moscow and Beijing because he believed that a reconciliation between the two communist giants would strengthen Poland's national security and advance its economic interests. In doing so, he tested the patience of the Soviet leadership (albeit not to the same degree as did the Romanian and Albanian leaders) and so complicated the dynamics of the communist world.[24] Gomułka's willingness to question Soviet policies on China made him useful to Beijing's leadership in its competition with Moscow. Poland was receptive, to some degree and at various points in time, to Mao's differentiation policy, which began in the latter half of the 1950s and which fit within the larger framework of his radical vision of continuous

---

[20]'Secret, Note from the CC CPSU re: recent Sino-Soviet relations,' AAN, KC PZPR: XIA/86, p. 332–345; Confidential, „Soviet Comrades and the current policy of the Chinese leadership (Internal Summary of the informational-instructional material received from the Soviet embassy in Berlin, 22 March 1972), Archiwum Ministerstwa Spraw Zagranicznych [Archive of the Ministry of Foreign Affairs in Warsaw, hereafter AMSZ] Dept. II, Chiny, z-24/76, w-2; James Hershberg, Sergey Radchenko, Peter Vamos, and David Wolff, 'The Interkit Story: A Window into the Final Decades of the Sino-Soviet Relationship,' CWIHP Working Paper No. 63, Woodrow Wilson Centre, Washington, D.C., April 2011.

[21]Margaret K. Gnoinska, 'Czechoslovakia and Poland: Supervising Peace on the Korean Peninsula, 1953–1955,' *Journal for the History of Central, Eastern and Southeastern Europe* (Slovansky Prehled), 98 (2012): 293–320; Margaret K. Gnoinska, 'Poland, Intra-Communist Dynamics, and the Second Geneva Conference on Laos, 1961–1962' in *L'échec de la paix. The Failure of Peace in Indochina (1954–1962)*, ed. Christopher E. Goscha and Karine Laplante (Paris: Les Indes Savantes, 2010), 305–325; and Margaret K. Gnoinska, 'Poland and the Cold War in East and Southeast Asia, 1949–1965,' (PhD diss., The George Washington University, 2010), 167–260; 452–517; and 643–703 and Shu Guang Zhang, Economic Cold War: America's Embargo against China and the Sino-Soviet Alliance, 1949–1963 (Washington, D.C.: Woodrow Wilson Centre Press, 2001), 165; Gnoinska, 'Poland and the Cold War in East and Southeast Asia,' 39–102.

[22]Cable from the Chinese Embassy in Poland, 'Polish Celebration of Our National Day, the Polish Communist Party's Attitude toward China, and Our Views,' 17 October 1961, PRC FMA 109–02311–01, 13–16, accessible at https://digitalarchive. wilsoncenter.org/document/119518.

[23]Li Danhui, 'Guanyu 1960 Niandai Zhongguo Yu Dongou Wuguo Guanji Deruogan Wenti Laizi Zhongguo Dangan Wenxian De Xin Zhengju,' *Eluosi Yanjiu*. 2011 No. 4, 105–129 [Li Danhui, 'Several Issues in China's Relations with Five East European Countries in the 1960s – New Evidence from Chinese Archives,' *Russian Studies* No. 4 (2011): 105–129].

[24]'Dealing with China in the 1960s and the 1970s: Two Different Approaches by Władysław Gomułka and Edward Gierek' in Enrico Fardella, Charles Kramer, and Christian Ostermann, eds. *Same Dreams, Different Beds: Sino-European Relations and the Transformation of the Cold War* (Stanford University Press/Woodrow Wilson Centre, forthcoming 2017).

revolution.[25] Beijing sought to differentiate the Soviet bloc states by the closeness of their relationship with the Kremlin. The policy was aimed at challenging Soviet hegemony in the region, undermining the CPSU's prestige, and creating a new centre of the workers' movement that encompassed various parties and groups supportive of the Chinese line.[26] Such 'differentiation' also allowed Chinese leaders to further erode bipolar conformism, and Poland was complicit in this process.

The Sino-Soviet divergences, combined with Mao's differentiation policy towards Eastern Europe, and the tightening of the screws by Moscow on its allies to coordinate their policies, facilitated a brief resurgence of the proponents of China's version of communism, which Mijal adhered to. The ideas of continuous revolution, the cult of personality, and non-compromise with the West all resonated with veteran 'Natolinians' like Mijal who were once supporters of Stalinism and who now saw an opportunity to return from the sidelines to the centre of political and party life in Poland. Though removed from party life and working in the National Investment Bank, Mijal continued to criticise Gomułka's economic policies, including his Five Year Plan (1961–1965), and became more involved politically.[27] His activism attracted and inspired members of a younger generation of Polish communists who also opposed the stagnant and technocratic version of Soviet communism and took it upon themselves to disseminate more radical Maoist ideas in Poland. The group soon became known as 'Mijal's group' *(grupka Mijalowska)* and began to challenge the authority of the communist party and test Moscow's patience.

Initially, the main nucleus of the group, in addition to Mijal, consisted of Lech Opieliński and Stanisław Sienkiewicz. Both were editors of a monthly publication called *Chiny*. Subsequently, the two most vocal proponents of Maoism in Poland were Józef Śnieciński, a journalist and an employee of the Ministry of Finance, and Krzysztof Jarzębski, an economist in the Ministry of Justice. They often met in secrecy at the headquarters of the Sino-Polish Friendship Association in Warsaw, where they made copies of CCP propaganda materials. Since the Chinese embassy and consulate employees were under constant surveillance by the Polish security services, the main contact between China and Mijals' group was handled by the Albanian embassy, as Tirana by then had broken off relations with the Soviet Union. 'The group received a significant amount of money from the Chinese to cover copy costs,' recalled Gomułka's secretary Walery Namiotkiewicz.[28] Just like Mijal, these activists were disappointed with Khrushchev's speech and the changes that were taking place in the communist world.[29] 'The role of the Soviet Union in the international communist movement began to wane with Stalin's death,' Jarzębski explained in the early 1990s. 'His successors like Khrushchev were not able to fill Stalin's shoes and were simply eclipsed by Mao.'[30] According to Śnieciński, 'Gomułka was not able to fulfil our expectations, so we preferred to form our own group […] We wanted to make a breakthrough in the Polish consciousness.'[31] These young individuals, supported and guided by Mijal, were attracted to the ideas

---

[25]See especially, Chen Jian, *Mao's China and the Cold War* (Chapel Hill: University of North Carolina Press, 2001).

[26]Political Report of the Polish Embassy in Beijing, 62.11.01–63.09.20, AMSZ, z-32/66, w-3, pp. 44–63; Top Secret Cable, Polish Embassy in Beijing, Ambassador Jerzy Knothe to Zenon Kliszko and Foreign Minister Adam Rapacki, 29 October 1963, AMSZ, z-6/77, w-105, t-614.

[27]Mazurek, Interview with Mijal, 2001.

[28]Walery Namiotkiewicz, *Byłem Sekretarzem Gomułki* (Warszawa: Wydawnictwo Comandor, 2002), 43.

[29]Józef Śnieciński in *Gazeta Wyborcza*, 13 May 1996. https://wyborcza.pl/1,75248,138749.html (Accessed 22 June 2015).

[30]Ibid.

[31]Sołtysiak, 'Żołnierze Partii,' 1993.

of a revolutionary change that would galvanise the proletariat instead of the stagnation that was emanating from both Warsaw and Moscow at the time. They were taken by the cult of personality and 'pure' ideology of Marxism-Leninism implemented in the cities, factories, and cooperatives in Albania.[32] Śnieciński, in particular, was an energetic young man, and apparently a prolific writer, who became the leader of the group and wanted to act.[33]

Therefore, in December 1963, following the publication of the main theses of the Fourth PUWP Congress – which aimed to glorify the twentieth anniversary of the foundation of post-WWII Poland – Mijal's group took it upon itself to write a piece that became quite controversial and caused concern among the party leadership.[34] The pamphlet, entitled *W walce zwycięstwo! Bierność i milczenie to zguba!* (*Struggle Brings Victory! Indifference and Silence Only Bring Defeat!*), was disseminated to the party apparatus in 10,000 copies (a significant number at the time) with the help of the Albanian embassy. The tone was clearly radical, calling on the working class to 'eliminate the revisionist vermin and bring about the resurrection of the revolutionary party based on the principles of Marxism-Leninism.'[35] The pamphlet directly accused Gomułka of 'purging the old and experienced party leaders devoted to the communist cause.'[36] This pamphlet was, of course, illegal, and the activities of the group were under constant surveillance by the Ministry of Internal Affairs. Although the state security apparatus knew everything about these oppositional activities, it allowed the group to function for some time. The reason for this inaction lies most likely in the intentions and plans of Minister of Internal Affairs Mieczysław Moczar, who wanted to gain more power within the communist party. The existence of 'Mijal's group' appeared convenient because it distracted Gomułka's attention from Moczar and his supporters' own ambitions.[37] Overall, however, it must be mentioned that even though Polish security services continued surveillance of CCP propaganda, they were more lenient than, for example, the Stasi in the GDR.[38,]This can most likely be attributed to the less authoritarian system in Poland as compared to East Germany, as well as to Gomułka's policy of minimising confrontations with the Chinese.

However, on the morning of 6 April 1964, arrests of 'Mijal's group' began in full.[39] In all, the security services apprehended around 100 people and some 1,000 were stripped of their party membership. Deputy Minister of Internal Affairs Franciszek Szlachcic interrogated some of the arrested members of the group, indicating the gravity of the matter. Although the authorities did interrogate Mijal, he was eventually released and never put on trial.[40] The trial of the younger members of the group, including Śnieciński and Jarzębski, began later

---

[32]Ibid.

[33]'Józef Śnieciński Collection' obtained in 2013 by the Hoover Institution Archives of Stanford University, Stanford, CA, USA. https://pdf.oac.cdlib.org/pdf/hoover/2013C29.pdf.

[34]The actual authorship has been disputed by Mijal and Śnieciński, both claiming credit.

[35]Sołtysiak, 'Żołnierze Partii', 1993.

[36]IPN BU 0365/99 t. 1., Biuro Udostępniania i Archiwizacji Dokumentów, IPN; Sołtysiak, 'Żołnierze Partii', 1993.

[37]Andrzej L. Sowa, *Historia Polityczna Polski, 1944–1991* (Krakow: Wydawnictwo Literackie, 2011), 304.

[38]See, for example, Information 1/70/63 re: propagating and publishing materials of the embassies of the PRC and Albania, as well as some anti-party tendencies and activities of reactionary elements which are using [Sino-Soviet] divergences for harmful purposes], IPN, 0296–61 t.1, Tajne, Dept. III, 12 November 1963, MSW, p. 58 and See, for example, Quinn Slobodian, 'Badge Books and Brand Books: the Mao Bible in East and West Germany,' in Alexander C. Cook, *Mao's Little Red Book*, 206–224. Comments by Dr. Bernd Schaefer at an International Conference, *China and the World in Mao's Last Decade, 1966–1976*, The University of Hong Kong, 9–10 January 2009.

[39]Sowa, *Historia Polityczna Polski, 1944–1991*, 303.

[40]Mazurek, Interview with Mijal, 2001.

that year. Unlike Mijal, these members simply did not have his stature and clout and were sentenced to prison.[41] Śnieciński was sentenced to two and a half years and was conditionally released in 1966, after which he served as deputy editor-in-chief of *Horyzonty Techniki*. He was kept under surveillance, along with other former members of 'Mijal's group,' during the tense months of March 1968.[42]

Mijal's name was nowhere to be found in the trial transcripts. As Namiotkiewicz explained years later, Mijal was not sentenced because he was 'very careful' in his dealings with the Chinese, unlike the younger members of the group who 'were taking money from foreign embassies for their activities' and attempting to foment the working class to 'organise strikes,' thereby 'engaging in illegal activity.'[43] It is also plausible that a high-profile trial would have political ramifications within the party, as suggested by Mieczysław Rakowski – a candidate member of the CC PUWP and editor-in-chief of *Polityka* (and subsequently the last First Secretary of communist Poland).[44] Such a trial could give Mijal too much publicity and attract the attention of the working class, which in collusion with intelligentsia could pose a more serious threat to the party.

China's support for Mijal's activities seems to have further complicated Poland's relations with the Soviet Union. The timing of the interrogations and arrests of the 'Mijal group' was certainly not a coincidence. They all took place a little over a week prior to Gomułka's high-level talks with Khrushchev on 13–15 April 1964 in Moscow. The Polish leader had to prove to the Kremlin that he would not tolerate Chinese propaganda, which was clearly resonating with some members of the Polish society at the time. He must have thus been proud, and certainly relieved, to report to his superiors in the Kremlin that the Chinese influence on the party was now 'irrelevant,' even though there were still some illegal groups which copied propaganda pamphlets printed in Albania. 'We have already made arrests of some of these members,' Gomułka reassured his Soviet counterpart. 'There are no workers in these groups, only intelligentsia and party members who had "dogmatic" tendencies and were able to influence the party in the past, and who now only criticise our party, the Soviet Union, and propagate the China line.'[45] The fact that Gomułka emphasised that there were 'no workers' in 'Mijal's group' indicates that the Polish leader, just like many others in the Soviet bloc, was terrified of the idea of an alliance between intellectuals and workers, as had happened in 1956 and which was to occur again in the 1970s and the early 1980s. Khrushchev was particularly interested in knowing what aspects of political life the so-called Polish Maoists were able to influence. Gomułka was quick to point out that they 'attacked' Poland's economic policy, as well as criticised unemployment, low wages, and the loss of revolutionary fervour. Eager to close the topic and move on to other matters, Gomułka concluded,

---

[41]Zofia Strug, 'Za Wielkim Sternikiem,' [With the Great Helmsman], *Nowy Robotnik*, No. 3, 2002.

[42]Franciszek Dąbrowski, Piotr Gontarczyk, and Paweł Tomasik, eds. *Marzec 1968 w Dokumentach MSW: Tom 2 Kronika Wydarzeń, Część I* (Warszawa: IPN, 2009), 353; 431.

[43]Namiotkiewicz, *Byłem Sekretarzem Gomułki*, 45.

[44]'Telegram from the Embassy in Poland to the Department of State,' Warsaw, 19 November 1964, Foreign Relations of the United States, 1964–1968, Volume VVII, Eastern Europe.

[45]Document No. 19, 'Transcript of Polish-Soviet Talks in Moscow, 13–15 April 1964, Secret of Special Significance,' in Andrzej Paczkowski, *Tajne Dokumenty Biura Politycznego PRL-ZSRR, 1956–1970* (London: Aneks, 1998), 220.

The activities of these groups are not a problem for our party, but I am afraid that they are being taken advantage of and used by reactionary elements, revisionists, and enemies of socialism, adding fuel to the fire and undermining the very nature of socialism.[46]

Here, the Polish leader was clearly referring not just to Poland, but the unity of the communist world and how further divergences would be detrimental to the communist side in its competition with the West on the chessboard of the Cold War.

Certainly, Mao's support for groups like that of Mijal may have fit in Beijing's differentiation framework, but this was not the way to coax the Polish leadership to the Chinese side when the Poles were trying to carefully navigate the slippery trails of Sino-Soviet interactions, propping up some vestige of communist unity, and keeping itself in power at home. Prior to the open and radical activities of the members of 'Mijal's group' in the early 1960s, Gomułka did not think that political opposition based on Maoism had any chance of emerging in Poland. After it surfaced, however, and its members were able to play on anti-Soviet slogans and take advantage of the dissatisfaction among intellectuals, party members, and some of the working class in various factories, Gomułka decided to take matters into his own hands.[47] This included not only the quelling of opposition at home for domestic purposes, as presented above, but also a more decisive stance against the PRC at the Fourth PUWP Congress in June 1964.

The meetings held at the Fourth PUWP Congress, which took place on 15–20 June 1964, were rampant with anti-Chinese speeches, some of which honed in on the activities of Mijal's group. In his speech, Zenon Kliszko, a close associate of Gomułka, made references to the group, which he blamed for trying to '"Polonize" the Chinese CP ideological platform and set this "Polish" version of "Sinofied Marxism" against the policies and ideology of our Party…and which violated the Party statutes and the law, by conspiratorially distributing political calumnies against the Party, its policies and its leaders.'[48] This new stance of the Polish leadership towards China was most likely used for domestic purposes to strengthen the authority and unity of the party, as well as to appease the Kremlin by proving that the Polish leadership was capable of dealing with domestic Maoists. Clearly, Gomułka's regime was not going to let activities that would question its own rule go unnoticed amid heated Sino-Soviet debates and tensions. It was one thing to have the PRC embassy disseminate its own propaganda materials. It was quite another to have Polish communists such as Mijal and other young men frustrated with Gomułka's government get directly involved with making pamphlets and distributing them through Albanian connections. After all, Albania had broken off relations with the Soviet Union by siding with China and had sought to erode the prestige and legitimacy of the CPSU in Poland and other Eastern European countries. This, in turn, would incite anti-Soviet slogans that the Polish leader wanted to avoid at all costs, remembering the events of 1956. Thus, although Gomułka may have been initially 'amused' by Mijal's criticism of his 'revisionism' in the 1950s, he was not going to tolerate the possibility of Maoism infiltrating deeper into Polish society, nor surely any dissent within the party.[49]

---

[46]Ibid., 220.

[47]Namiotkiewicz, *Byłem Sekretarzem Gomułki,* 45.

[48]'Poland's "Chinese" Faction,' Radio Free Europe (Munich) June 20, 1964, https://www.marxists.org/history/erol/poland/poland-chinese.pdf (Accessed 4 March 2017).

[49]Namiotkiewicz, *Byłem Sekretarzem Gomułki,* 43.

According to Deputy Minister Szlachcic, 'The leadership of the party was always indignant about pamphlets that were generated from within the party; the leadership was more tolerant of the opposition coming from the right than the left.'[50] This indicates that the Polish communist party was clearly concerned about more radical critics from within the party than by those who advocated political pluralism and freedom of expression, as was the case in March 1964 with writers protesting the tightening of press censorship (such demands were silenced by the party leadership, which declared that there should be no place for works of art whose ideology was directed against socialism).[51] This shows that people like Mijal were threatening to the party because they were promoting a more revolutionary approach that could mobilise the workers who were stifled by the technocracy and bureaucracy of a party which had forgotten about its role as the vanguard of the proletariat.[52] The paradox, however, is that while Mijal called on the Poles to exercise their right to workers' democracy via his revolutionary pamphlets, his illegal party called for a return to Stalinism - collectivisation of the countryside, rapid industrialization of the country, socialist work competition, glorification of the Stalinist era in Poland, and eulogising Stalin personally.[53] Gomułka was opposed to Stalinist policies, as they did not reflect the national conditions of Poland and would clearly not tolerate that line.

In addition, the Gomułka of 1964 was different from the Gomułka of 1956, when he encouraged liberalisation in political life. Now, the Polish leader retreated from the 'October Thaw' and tightened the screws on his population (although to a much lesser degree than his Eastern European counterparts such as Hoxha, Ceausescu or Honecker). It is noteworthy that only a few years later, Gomułka carried out an anti-Zionist and anti-Semitic campaign to keep his political position, which was threatened in yet another power struggle in March 1968, and that he contributed Poland's armed forces to quell the Prague Spring in Czechoslovakia for fear of spillover.[54] Therefore, his treatment of 'Mijal's group' should be understood within both the domestic and foreign relations context of Gomułka's policies. Eliminating the threat to his own authority from people like Mijal, however, would further complicate the already difficult relationship between Warsaw and Beijing, as well as add more quirks to the already delicate and unequal relationship between Warsaw and Moscow.

Having been released from interrogations in 1964, Mijal went on criticising Gomułka and his government on their deviations from Marxism-Leninism. He was surely emboldened by Mao's new policies which stressed open attacks on revisionism.[55] Although the Maoist group was fractured by the arrests, interrogations, and sentences, in December 1965, Mijal took it upon himself to found the Communist Party of Poland (KPP) in Warsaw, which was meant to serve as an opposition faction within the PUWP. He considered the

---

[50]Strug, 'Za Wielkim Sternikiem,' 2002.

[51]Paczkowski, *Spring Will be Ours*, 295.

[52]Ibid., 298.

[53]'The Programme of the Communist Party of Poland,' Radio Free Europe (Munich), January 16, 1967 https://www.marxists.org/history/erol/poland/cpp-programmeprogram.pdf (Accessed 4 March 2017).

[54]See especially, Jerzy Eisler, 'March 1968 in Poland,' in Carole Fink, Phillip Gassert, and Detlef Junker, *1968, The World Transformed* (Cambridge: Cambridge University Press, 1998); Dariusz Stola, *Kampania antysyjonistyczna w Polsce, 1967–1968* (Warszawa: IPN, 2000); Piotr Gontarczyk, et al., eds. *Marzec 1968 w dokumentach MSW Tom I: Niepokorni* (Warszawa: IPN, 2008); and Bożena Szaynok, *Z historią i Moskwą w tle. Polska a Izrael 1944–1968* (Warszawa: IPN, 2007).

[55]Enrico Fardella, Charles Kramer, and Christian Ostermann, eds. *Sino-European Relations During the Cold War and the Rise of the Multipolar World: A Critical Oral History* (Washington, D.C.: Woodrow Wilson Centre, 2015), 12–13; 71–72.

BEYOND THE KREMLIN'S REACH? 101

party to be 'the only rightful headquarters of the communist struggle.'[56] Other prominent members were Władysław Dworakowski and Hilary Chełchowski, who were members of the CC PUWP and even the Politburo in the 1950s. Interestingly, the choice of the name for the party is actually quite paradoxical, as it referred to the pre-war KPP, which Stalin brutally decimated and dissolved in 1938. Mijal had never been a member of that KPP. At the same time, he deemed it 'pure,' 'healthy,' and true to Marxism-Leninism, in contrast to Gomułka's revisionist line.[57] Mijal appointed himself the First Secretary of the Provisional Central Committee of the new KPP. He published *Under the Banner of Marxism-Leninism Toward Socialism*, which was a revolutionary manifesto that challenged the ruling party and its practices, both past and present.[58] Mijal's KPP was illegal in Gomułka's Poland and was under constant surveillance.

To avoid any future arrests and to be able to propagate his cause, Mijal decided to escape to Albania. Tirana proved a logical choice given its close ties with the PRC and open defiance against the Kremlin at the time. Mijal's actions and his residence in Albania further added to the already high tensions between the Polish and Albanian leaderships, thereby bringing about more fragmentation within the Eastern bloc.[59] The details of Mijal's escape are still not entirely clear, but based on the available evidence the journey was quite an ordeal and logistics were facilitated by the Albanian embassy. 'The Albanians provided me with a diplomatic passport bearing the name of Serwet Mehmetko,' recalls Mijal,

> and on 13 February 1966, I left Warsaw's Central Train Station for Berlin. […] It was very cold and snowing very hard, so I was wearing a padded leather coat, a fur hat, and only carried a small briefcase, no suitcase or other luggage so as not to raise any suspicion.[60]

In East Berlin, the Albanian contact took Mijal to West Berlin, from where he flew to Paris. 'It was very warm when I arrived in Paris, so I looked like I had just come from the North Pole,' said Mijal. 'So, they bought me a light coat which I have to this day.'[61] From Paris, he flew to Rome, from where he travelled by ferry to Albania.

Mijal in exile as the tool of both Chinese and Albanians

Chairman Mao continued to support the so-called 'leftist factions' in Eastern European parties and clearly wanted to take advantage of any differences between them and Moscow. The Chinese leader seems to have understood that Moscow's relations with each of these Soviet bloc nations varied in terms of the levels of loyalty. Therefore, when Mehmet Shehu – Albanian leader Enver Hoxha's right hand man – told Mao that all Eastern European parties were Soviet vassals, the Chairman retorted that the presence of leftist factions, especially in Poland and Bulgaria, suggested otherwise. This is why the Chinese leader continued his support for Mijal after Mijal secretly escaped to Albania.[62]

---

[56]Antoni Marek, 'Kazimierz Mijal – Dogmatic Diehard or Political Adventurer?' 26 June 1967, Radio Free Europe. https://www.marxists.org/history/erol/poland/cpp-diehard.pdf (Accessed 22 August 2016).

[57]*Kazimierz Mijal – marksista bezkompromisowy*, Interview conducted with Przemysław Gasztold-Seń on https://histmag.org/Kazimierz-Mijal-marksista-bezkompromisowy-10590 (Accessed 20 June 2015) [Hereafter: *Marksista Bezkompromisowy*].

[58]Mieczysław F. Rakowski, *Dzienniki Polityczne, 1963–1966* (Warszawa: ISKRY, 1999), 350–357.

[59]Skobelski, *PRL wobec państw socjalistycznych w latach 1956–1970*, 156–161.

[60]Mazurek, Interview with Mijal, 2001.

[61]Ibid.

[62]Li Danhui, 'Several Issues in China's Relations with Five East European Countries,' 105–129; on Bulgaria, see especially, Jordan Baev, 'Bulgaria and the Coordination of the East European Policy Toward China after the Soviet-Chinese Discord (1960–1989), paper prepared for the "Interkit" Workshop organised by FRIAS in Freiburg, Germany, May 12–13, 2011.

Mijal's escape to Albania in early 1966 and China's continued support for his activities contributed to complicating relations between Warsaw and Moscow. Soon after Mijal's escape, Gomułka had to give explanations – this time to the new leader in Moscow, Leonid I. Brezhnev – as to the influence of Maoists on the Polish population. In his comments, as in the past, he was sure to present the situation as non-threatening to the authority of the Polish communist party: 'The "Mijal affair" is in no way a reflection of the moods within expelled the party. This is a very narrow group. We have already imprisoned them. And, we have the Albanian ambassador in Warsaw.'[63] As far as the existence of the KPP, he made it clear that this was 'pure sabotage' and 'not a problem' because in 99 percent of the cases the propaganda materials from abroad were intercepted by the Polish security services.[64] The Polish leader then eagerly turned to economic matters – his priority – which had always occupied a large part of the high-level talks between the Soviets and the Poles. Clearly, he did not want to engage in a detailed discussion on the issue of Mijal. The fact that he did not mention either Albania or China by name, and made no criticism of Chairman Mao in front of the Soviets, also indicates that Gomułka did not want to add more fuel to the fire engulfing Sino-Soviet relations. The actions of communists like Mijal, however, were of concern for the Soviets, especially those in the 'Interkit.'

Indeed, while Mijal's escape to Albania may have reduced his influence, it did not end his efforts to promote the China line to the Poles. This, in turn became a nuisance to Gomułka, who valued economic relations with China, especially given that Soviet-Polish economic relations were marred by tensions and difficulties brought about by his incessant pleas for more import opportunities and economic assistance from the Soviet Union.[65] Therefore, the Polish government attempted to assume as much of a pragmatic attitude toward China as possible by focusing on matters of mutual interest, such as economic and maritime relations. Chinese officials, however, would engage the Poles in ideological polemics, including 'venting' about Soviet revisionism. The Chinese were often taken by surprise when Polish diplomats would not engage in such debates, and instead, after listening to the rants, would focus on discussing bilateral matters over a cup of tea.[66] The Chinese clearly perceived their interactions with the Poles through a more ideological lens fueled by Mao's desire to expand his revolutionary communism and influence in Eastern Europe.

The Chinese leader, however, did not seem to fully grasp the delicate relationship between Moscow and Warsaw. His support for Eastern European communists who were drawn to the Maoist ideology of continuous revolution but whose chances at home to expand it were quite abysmal, in fact, created the opposite of the intended effect. In other words, while Mao may have wanted to help Gomułka gain some kind of a leverage vis-à-vis Moscow, he ended up complicating things for the Polish leader. As demonstrated in numerous exchanges with the Soviets in the early and mid-1960s, and also during the days of the Cultural Revolution in China, Gomułka aimed, albeit behind the scenes, to mend relations between Moscow and Beijing, as he hoped that this would benefit Poland in the long run, not only politically but

---

[63]'Transcript of Soviet-Polish Conversations in Moscow 10–15 October 1966, Secret,' AAN, KC PZPR: XIA/83, pp. 373–474; also in Paczkowski, *Tajne Dokumenty*, 379.

[64]Ibid., 379.

[65]Top Secret Telegram, Piotr Jaroszewicz in Moscow to Władysław Gomułka and Prime Minister Józef Cyrankiewicz in Warsaw, 26 February 1964, AMSZ, z-6/77, w-118, t-683.

[66]Interview by the author with Janusz Lewandowski (the Head of Asia Department within the Polish Foreign Ministry in the 1960s), 25 October 2006, Warsaw.

also economically. Mao's support for people like Mijal only further complicated Gomułka's work in trying to bring the Chinese and Soviets closer to reconciling their differences. Mao's attempts and efforts to prop up any opposition to the authority of the communist parties of the Warsaw Pact nations not only failed to disintegrate the Soviet-East European bloc, but actually encouraged anti-Chinese sentiments in Eastern European countries, including Poland, where the government took unkindly to the CCP secretly supporting the so-called 'healthy elements' that wanted to split from and challenge the communist parties in power.[67]

Like Mao, the Albanian leader – Enver Hoxha – was also interested in using Mijal as a political tool. The Albanian authorities provided Mijal with a villa in Tirana where he had a cook who came every morning. He allegedly had much time to read, take walks, and travel all around Albania while enjoying its warm climate.[68] Mijal asserts that he did not receive any money, since the Albanian party officials would pay for everything. It appears, however, that he held a job at the Sino-Albanian Joint Stock Shipping Company, which allowed him to travel abroad, especially to China.[69] While this description of his life seems quite idyllic, the reality is that Mijal was still living in a highly Stalinist state which made sure that, while being protected, he was also under constant surveillance by the security services so as to not pose any threat to Hoxha's regime. On the premises where Mijal lived, there was a house for a security service employee, and a soldier would also patrol the grounds. In fact, Mijal never left without a bodyguard.[70] While in Albania, Mijal found supporters among other pro-Chinese communists, most notably Belgian Maoists such as Jacques Grippa, who would publish Mijal's writings like *Under the Banner of Marxism-Leninism Toward Socialism* for a wider audience outside of Poland in the pro-Chinese Belgian paper Voix du Peuple.[71]

By offering someone like Mijal a place to reside in Albania for about twelve years, Hoxha was able to demonstrate that Albania offered a safe haven for those in the Soviet bloc who had the courage to openly stand up to the Kremlin and support Beijing in the Sino-Soviet split. Mijal, therefore, seems to have served the purpose for the Albanians of being a useful political and propaganda tool against Moscow. He met on several occasions with Hoxha and was highly active in the Polish section of Radio Tirana, a propaganda arm of the Albanian government which disseminated Maoist thought and anti-Soviet slogans aimed at undermining the legitimacy and the authority of the communist leadership in the Warsaw Pact nations. But, since Mijal was not physically in Poland, the influence of his party, whose membership at its peak was hundreds of sympathisers, began to wane.[72] As Deputy Minister of Interior Szlachcic explained in spring 1967, 'There is no KPP in Poland. There is only Mijal in Albania and a few disgruntled old communists.'[73]

Nevertheless, undeterred, Mijal continued to represent the 'real Polish Marxists' as the First Secretary of the CC KPP and visited Beijing in this capacity toward the end of 1966, where he was received by Chairman Mao.[74] He made the trip on a private plane with the CCP

---

[67]Li Danhui, 'Several Issues in China's Relations with Five East European Countries,' 105–129.

[68]Mazurek, Interview with Mijal, 2001.

[69]*Marksista Bezkompromisowy* (Accessed 12 November 2015).

[70]Ibid.

[71]Chinese Endorsement of pro-Peking CP, 20 September 1968, Radio Free Europe Report. https://www.marxists.org/history/erol/poland/cpp-endorsement.pdf (Accessed 24 August 2016).

[72]Sowa, *Historia Polityczna Polski, 1944–1991*, 304; *Marksista Bezkompromisowy* (Accessed 20 June 2015).

[73]Mieczysław F. Rakowski, *Dzienniki Polityczne, 1967–1968* (Warszawa: ISKRY, 1999), 33.

[74]Mao Zedong met Kazimierz Mijal on December 21, 1966. See Zhonggong zhongyang wenxian yanjiushi, ed., *Mao Zedong nianpu (yijiusijiu-yijiuqiliu)*, vol. 6, 18.

Politburo member Kang Sheng, who was on a visit in Albania. Mao met with Mijal in private at his swimming pool in the CCP's central headquarters, the State Council *Zhongnanhai*. The visit took place at the height of the Great Proletarian Cultural Revolution in China, when revolutionary fervour was fueled by the Red Guards wreaking havoc by propagating Mao's thought in the most radical of ways. Mijal's conversation with the Chairman began with discussion of the philosophy of Aristotle, as well as referencing German philosophers, after which political matters were discussed. Overall, however, the exchange was filled with party jargon evoking much optimism for the world revolution. Mao made sure to emphasise to Mijal that if he saw hope in China, he would see hope all over the world, including Poland and the Soviet Union. Mao was clearly energised by his own revolution and exhorted his Polish comrade to organise the working class to rise up against the bourgeoisie. Mijal, on his part, also seems to have been taken by the revolutionary atmosphere, as well as the Chairman's enthusiasm and support for the communist cause. 'As I depart China,' Mijal said, 'I am more confident about the anti-imperialist and anti-revisionist struggle. China's revolutionary struggle is my greatest support and it is imperative that we all rally around China.'[75] Mijal reminisced in his later interviews that Chairman Mao 'was very kind' to him and his contacts with Zhou Enlai were 'very friendly,' including dinner invitations during his visits to China.[76]

The Chinese press continued to duly report on the visits of Mijal, including his visit in 1969.[77] In addition, it would also reprint KPP manifestos and other writings of Mijal that heavily criticised the policies of the 'Gomułka clique' and exalted the 'theoretical writings of Stalin and Mao Zedong' as 'a real treasure-house of knowledge for every revolutionary,' as well as venerated the alleged positive revolutionary fervour of the Polish people.[78] Despite such support from the centre of the anti-revisionist revolution in Beijing, however, Mijal's efforts to bring about a revolution in Poland did not materialise. His influence began to wane with the solidification of the Sino-Soviet split and with the new leadership in Poland under Edward Gierek pledging its allegiance to Moscow on China policy and focusing on increasing the standard of living.

At the same time, while Mijal may no longer have posed an official threat to the authority of the Polish party in the 1970s, his interactions with the Chinese were duly reported by the Polish embassy in Beijing to the Ministry of Foreign Affairs in Warsaw. These included references to Mijal in the Chinese media and his congratulatory letters as the First Secretary of the Communist Party of Poland to the Chairman.[79] Unlike his predecessor, Gierek did not have the same aspirations of bringing China back to the communist camp, but he also could not ignore the new role of China in the Cold War chessboard brought about by the opening of China after the turbulent days of the Cultural Revolution and after the Sino-American

---

[75]Li Danhui, 'Several Issues in China's Relations with Five East European Countries,' 105–129.

[76]Mazurek, Interview with Mijal, 2001.

[77]'Delegation of Communist Party of Poland Concludes Visit in China,' Peking Review, No. 47, 21 November 1969. https://www.marxists.org/history/erol/poland/cpp-delegation.pdf (Accessed 4 March 2017).

[78]'The Communist Party of Poland is a Working-Class Party,' released by the Communist Party of Poland and reprinted in The Beijing Review, 30 August 1968. https://www.marxists.org/history/erol/poland/cpp-working-class.pdf (Accessed 25 August 2016) and 'Magnificent Victory of China's Great Cultural Revolution Inspires Polish Working Class,' Beijing Review, 18 October 1968. https://www.marxists.org/history/erol/poland/cpp-cr.pdf (Accessed 4 March 2017).

[79]See, for example, 'Mijal's Communist Party of Poland in the Chinese Media' prepared by Dr. Jan Rowiński, Warsaw, 21 January 1976, AMSZ, Dept. II, Chiny, 22–1-75.

reconciliation.[80] This is why the Polish government wanted to maintain a good relationship with Beijing, especially for economic gain. Mijal's illegal party and its activities, albeit no longer threatening, continued to be a nuisance in Sino-Polish bilateral relations, especially since they also included anti-Soviet tones which were unwelcome to people like Gierek who pledged loyalty to Moscow.[81]

Mijal managed to be useful to Hoxha as a political tool in propagating the China line in the rest of the Soviet bloc only as long as the relations between Tirana and Beijing were close and united against a common enemy – the Soviet Union, of course. In 1978, however, the Sino-Albanian split influenced Mijal's political life. Naturally, he would now be deemed a *persona non grata* in the Albanian capital since he continued to champion Maoist thought and supported China. 'They increased their patrol on the street outside of my house and also cut off my phone,' recalled Mijal on his relations with the Albanians in an interview with Norwegian communists at the time.[82] Indeed, the relationship between Mijal and Enver Hoxha went sour. In fact, in his memoirs, the Albanian leader accuses him of betrayal and ingratitude and calls him a 'charlatan advocate of the rotten Chinese line.'[83] Allegedly, Mijal had 'enormous problems' leaving Albania, but eventually reached Beijing via Bucharest thanks to the political asylum granted by the PRC government. While in China, he lived in a villa district of Beijing, where the Chinese 'were very hospitable.'[84] However, by this time all of his original patrons, including Chairman Mao, Zhou Enlai, and Kang Sheng, were no longer alive. The post-Maoist leadership in China, too, was no longer interested in challenging Moscow's influence in Eastern Europe as eagerly as it had under Chairman Mao. This, in turn rendered Mijal's services useless in the new China which was embracing elements of capitalism and opening up to the world. Eventually, Mijal himself became disillusioned with Deng Xiaoping's economic reforms.

Therefore, in 1983, after 18 years of exile, Mijal returned illegally to Poland via Paris with the help of other European communists whose names he would not reveal. There is no evidence as of now that would suggest that he was in some kind of danger in China; on the contrary, the Chinese sought his advice on how to reform China and even arranged a meeting between him and Włodzimierz Brus (a Polish economist who emigrated to England in 1972 and who authored *The General Problems of the Functioning of the Socialist Economy*). Mijal was also received by Hua Guofeng to discuss economic investment policies in a socialist economy.[85] After a year and a half living in Poland, he was arrested in November 1984, imprisoned for three months, and interrogated as to his activities outside of Poland. But, by then, the Polish authorities must have concluded that a seventy-four year old man did not pose any threat to the system. Besides, he was no longer of any use to either Albania or China.

---

[80]Secret, Urgent Note of the Conversation between [Foreign Minister Stefan Jędrychowski] and the newly nominated PRC ambassador to Poland – Comrade Yao Guang on September 4, 1970], AMSZ, Chiny 1970, 46/75, w-1, pp. 1–5 and "Urgent Note Regarding 'the Visit' of K. Mijal in Beijing," January 31, 1975, Historyand Public Policy Programme Digital Archive. https://digitalarchive.wilsoncenter.org/document/117847 (Accessed 18 August 2016).

[81]'Poland's Communists Will Defeat Revisionist Rule – An Interview with Kazimierz Mijal, Chairman of the Communist Party of Poland,' *Class Struggle*, No. 7, 1977, 113–119; 'Theory of Three Worlds – Excerpts from an Article by Kazimierz Mijal,' Beijng Review No. 51, 16 December 1977. https://www.marxists.org/history/erol/poland/3-worlds.pdf (Accessed 4 March 2017).

[82]'They Condemned me to Passivity and Silence,' an Interview with Kazimierz Mijal *Revolution* Vol 4. No.2 January 1980, https://www.marxists.org/history/erol/poland/cpp-interview.pdf (Accessed 4 March 2017).

[83]Enver Hoxha, *Reflections on China II 1973–1977* (Tirana, Albania: «8 NENTORI» PUBLISHING HOUSE,1979), 443–456.

[84]Mazurek, Interview with Mijal, 2001

[85]Ibid.

Conclusion

Following the Sino-Soviet split, Polish leaders like Gomułka and Gierek wanted to keep Maoism out of Poland. They continued to build socialism based on Marxism-Leninism in line with the Soviet leadership, which advocated de-Stalinisation. At the same time, Gomułka, in particular, believed that Poland would best thrive within a unified communist camp that included China, which he viewed as indispensable in the global competition with the capitalist West.

Mijal's absence would not have necessarily implied better Sino-Polish relations, as factors such as Poland's place in the Soviet sphere and Mao's post 1964 policies of openly attacking the revisionism of the Soviet Union played a major role in this respect. However, Mijal's activities promoting the 'China way' in communism in Poland and beyond created a nuisance for the Polish communist party, added yet another layer of tensions between Warsaw and Beijing, and contributed to complicating Poland's already delicate and uneven relationship with the leadership in Moscow. In addition, Mijal's activism advocating Maoist China's revolutionary radicalism contributed to tightening the screws on Polish society. Mijal's agency, derived from the presence of the Sino-Soviet split, is also an example of the cracks in state socialism which intensified the disunity within Polish communism and revealed that the intricate dynamics of the communist bloc often spread beyond the reach and control of the Kremlin.

In the end, Mijal was not successful in realising his goal of galvanising the intellectuals and working class in Poland to carry out an anti-imperialist and anti-revisionist world revolution. However, his story pieced together here, that is, the journey of one man – from Poland to Albania to China and back to Poland – depicts paradoxes of the international communist and workers' movement through one fascinating life during key moments in the Cold War.

Disclosure statement

No potential conflict of interest was reported by the author.

A Hungarian model for China? Sino-Hungarian relations in the era of economic reforms, 1979–89

Péter Vámos

ABSTRACT
In the wake of the introduction of the Chinese reform and opening up policy in 1978, the Beijing leadership paid special attention to the Hungarian experience with its reform of the economic management system. This article argues that although it is hard to identify single measures within the complex system of Chinese economic reforms that can be labelled as Hungarian in their origins, reference to a reform community proved to be an effective tool for Beijing's leaders to emerge from isolation in the socialist bloc, rally international support, and strengthen domestic legitimacy for their reform agendas throughout the 1980s.

Introduction

In the wake of the 1989 people's movement in China and the systemic change in Hungary, the study of the transformation of state socialism was a hot topic among political scientists and economists, both Western and Chinese. A series of comparative studies investigated the relationship between economic and political reform, whether political transformation had to precede economic transformation or economic transformation had to come first, which might or might not be followed by political transformation and to what extent the socialist system could reform itself.[1] During the 1980s, the Chinese leaders were keen on studying the economic and social reforms undertaken in Eastern Europe, especially Hungary, but for different reasons. The prime motive behind this new interest was that both China and Hungary were working on reforming their economies, which had been following the Soviet model since the 1950s. As the general direction of economic reforms, establishing a socialist market economy by incorporating market elements into the socialist system and harmonising plan and market was similar, Chinese economists and politicians were keen to

---

[1]See e.g. Peter Van Ness, ed., *Market Reforms in Socialist Societies: Comparing China and Hungary* (Boulder: Lynne Rienner Publishers, 1989); Keith Crane and K. C. Yeh, *Economic Reform and the Military in Poland, Hungary and China* (Santa Monica: RAND, 1990); Andrew G. Walder, ed., *The Waning of the Communist State: Economic Origins of Political Decline in China and Hungary* (Berkeley: University of California Press, 1995); Yanqi Tong, *Transitions from State Socialism: Economic and Political Change in Hungary and China* (Lanham: Rowman and Littlefield, 1997); Mária Csanádi, *Self-Consuming Evolutions: A Model on the Structure, Self-Reproduction, Self-Destruction and Transformation of Party-State Systems Tested in Romania, Hungary and China* (Budapest, Akadémiai Kiadó, 2006).

learn from the Hungarian reform experience. Although Chinese authors writing about the reform of economic management often referred to a 'Hungarian model' (*Xiongyali moshi*), it is hard to identify single measures within the complex system of Chinese economic reforms that can be labelled as 'Hungarian' in their origins. Moreover, although Hungarian reforms started a decade before Deng Xiaoping launched the new policy of reform and opening up in 1978, the initial momentum of reform in Hungary had been lost by 1972, not least as a result of direct Soviet pressure. For Western observers in the late 1980s, therefore, Chinese and Hungarian reforms seemed to be similar not only in their direction but also in the fact that, as a result of the resistance by the bureaucratic establishment at various levels, in both countries they had stalled out within a decade.[2]

This article explores the considerations behind the Chinese interest in the Hungarian reform experience, and the Hungarian openness toward Chinese overtures during the last decade of the Cold War. Based on documentary evidence from Hungarian archives and Chinese publications from the period, I show that both Chinese and Hungarian leaders were keen to establish mutual relations based on an imagined reform community, sometimes even despite open Soviet criticism. I argue that reference to a reform community proved to be an effective tool for both leaderships to rally support and strengthen domestic legitimacy for their reform agendas throughout the 1980s. The article therefore focusses more on the political and ideological aspects of the story and attempts to analyse the Chinese practice of making use of references to the Hungarian experience against the backdrop of slowly improving Sino-Soviet relations. China used the relatively weak Eastern European Soviet client states for its domestic and foreign policy objectives. Creating a broad range of low level ties with Eastern Europe was useful for the Beijing leadership in domestic terms, as China utilised the Soviet satellites as a means to affirm its socialist identity and to legitimise the Party's new policies. In terms of foreign policy, through broadening Sino-East European relations, Beijing could exert pressure on the Moscow leadership and test Soviet tolerance and willingness to improve bilateral relations.

The Chinese interest in Hungarian economic reforms

By the late 1970s, Hungary could look back on a decade of experience with reforms: the New Economic Mechanism had been launched on 1 January 1968. China, at the time, was just embarking on its reform path. Similar to Hungary, China's leaders took on the task of transforming a command-planned, highly centralised system under public ownership into a market-oriented, decentralised, mixed ownership system, improving incentive systems in order to increase production and establishing an interrelated legal framework in order to reduce the absolute dominance of the state over economic activity. Also similar to Hungary, reforms in China lacked a clear goal model and a guiding theory. Beijing proceeded with reforms without a concrete plan – in the words of Deng Xiaoping, 'crossing the river by feeling for stones' (*mozhe shitou guo he*). To remain with the stone metaphor, the Hungarian experience was considered as 'one of the stones from the other hill,' which, according to a Chinese proverb, 'is good for working jade' (*ta shan zhi shi, ke yi gong yu*).[3]

---

[2]Nicholas R. Lardy, *Foreign Trade and Economic Reform in China, 1978–1990* (Cambridge: Cambridge University Press, 1992), 3; Peter Van Ness, ed. *Market Reforms in Socialist Societies: Comparing China and Hungary* (Boulder: Lynne Rienner Publishers, 1989).

[3]Su Shaozhi, 'Xiongyali jingji tizhi gaige zhong de ruogan lilun wenti' [Some theoretical problems of the system of economic reform in Hungary], *Jingji wenti tansuo* [Inquiry into economic issues] 2 (1980): 1–9.

In the wake of the Sino-Soviet split, Maoist China was proud to rely on its own resources in their pursuit to reach communism. When Deng Xiaoping took over command by 1978, self-reliance and revolutionary radicalism were substituted by pragmatic moderation and the corresponding shift from the primacy of politics to that of economics. In pursuit of improved economic performance, Deng launched the modernisation of agriculture, industry, national defence, and science and technology at the 3rd Plenum of the 11th Chinese Communist Party (CCP) Central Committee (CC) in December 1978. The following April, Feng Yujiu, the new Chinese ambassador to Budapest, during his introductory visits to Hungarian state leaders, explained that China wanted to develop the country on the basis of the four modernisations, and although the basic principle was self-reliance, 'that was only one half of the solution,' and had to be supplemented by learning from more developed countries. The Chinese ambassador praised Hungary for having achieved outstanding results in certain fields within a relatively short period of time.[4] The Chinese willingness to learn from Hungary came as a pleasant surprise for the Hungarians, as, since the Sino-Soviet split, Beijing's leaders had not recognised the Eastern European Soviet client states as socialist and labelled the ruling parties of the Soviet bloc as revisionist.

In the summer of 1979, the Chinese authorities made inquiries about the Hungarian willingness to host a delegation of economists from the Chinese Academy of Social Sciences (CASS) – a research organisation under close State Council and Party supervision – and received a positive response from their Hungarian counterparts.[5] However, because of existing Sino-Soviet tensions, the Chinese side exercised caution not to offend Soviet sensitivities and at first sent a delegation of representatives of Xinhua News Agency in August 1979. As by the mid-1960s bilateral relations were frozen, and during the Cultural Revolution (1966–76) no personal contacts were conducted. The visit of the Xinhua delegation was considered a major breakthrough.

The real purpose of the visit soon became clear for the Hungarian hosts. The MTI News Agency reported to the Hungarian Ministry of Foreign Affairs, the state organ that was in charge of coordinating China-related activities in Hungary, that the Chinese guests were interested 'primarily in the reform and modernization of our economic management system ... rather than in news agency work or technical development.' The head of the Chinese delegation made no secret of the purpose of their visit and stressed that 'China appreciated and closely followed the Hungarian system of economic management,' which they considered to be an attempt to reform the rigid Soviet-type economy.[6] The Chinese visitors enquired about the motives behind the introduction of the New Economic Mechanism and about the causes of its subsequent revisions. They raised questions about recent developments in Hungary, including the new price reform, which was instituted in June 1979, only a few weeks before the delegation's arrival. In the summer of 1979, Hungary introduced a three-tier price system that divided prices into fixed, fluctuating within limits and freely set. The aim of the price reform was to bring prices nearer to values, to create a closer link between domestic producer prices and world market prices and to establish a uniform

---

[4]Introductory visits by the new Chinese ambassador. Budapest, 12 April 1979. Hungarian National Archives (Magyar Nemzeti Levéltár Országos Levéltára, hereafter: HNA) XIX-J-1-j Kína 78–1 002744/3/1979; Budapest, 17 April 1979. HNA XIX-J-1-j Kína 78–1 002744/4/1979.

[5]Cypher telegrams from the Hungarian Embassy in Beijing to the Hungarian MFA: Chinese enquiries about the Hungarian system of economic management. Beijing, 30 August 1979 – 3 December 1979. HNA XIX-J-1-j Kína 78–5 004792/1–6/1979.

[6]Report of Árpádné Páll, deputy head of MTI International Department: Report on visit of the New China [News Agency] delegation. Budapest, 15 August 1979. HNA XIX-J-1-j Kína 78–8 004830/1979.

exchange rate for the Hungarian currency, which in turn was a precondition of joining the International Monetary Fund. The Chinese took notice of the new policy immediately. An article on the reform of the economic system in Hungary, published in the *Guowai jingyan pingjia* (Assessment of foreign experiences) section of the journal *Jingji guanli* (Economic Management) in June 1979, only days after its introduction, introduced the price system and the tax system, though with little comment.[7] In the same section of the same journal, an article devoted entirely to the Hungarian price system was published in November 1979.[8]

In August, the Chinese proposed that a delegation of four economists would visit Hungary for three weeks in November. The Hungarian Ministry of Foreign Affairs supported the idea but stressed that the organisation and programme of the visit should be in line with the Hungarian Socialist Workers' Party (HSWP) Politburo resolution passed in March.[9] The resolution, which defined the framework and direction of Hungarian China policies for the next three years, identified hegemonism and anti-Sovietism as 'key elements' of China's policy. Echoing the official Soviet evaluation, the document concluded, 'It is becoming increasingly clear … that the Chinese leadership, during its struggle against the Soviet Union, the socialist countries, and the forces of socialism and progress in general, has actually become an ally of imperialism.' Nevertheless, in the field of inter-state cooperation, the HSWP resolution showed more pragmatism, as it called for a need 'to maintain correct relations, with a strict adherence to our principled standpoint … in accordance with our … interests.' The document also stressed the need for close coordination with the Soviet Union and the 'fraternal' socialist countries:

> Taking the international significance and importance of this question into consideration, in the field of conducting relations with China we should continue to coordinate our activity with the cooperating socialist countries. At the appropriate level, we should have consultations about the prospective and topical questions of our relations with China.

In this case, the 'appropriate level' meant the Soviet Embassy in Budapest, which the Hungarians consulted before, during, and after the visit. The decision to receive the Chinese economists was courageous, especially in light of the Politburo resolution, which, again echoing the Soviet views, claimed that Chinese economic development was aimed at the 'fulfilment of China's big-power ambitions and the modernization of its military technology, and to increase the danger of an extreme distortion of the socialist characteristics of China's future development.'[10]

The delegation of Chinese economists left Beijing in mid-October, and after three weeks in Romania and Yugoslavia – two socialist states that at the time kept a distance from Moscow and thus were considered 'friendly' by Beijing – arrived in Budapest on 24 November. It was led by one of Deng Xiaoping's closest associates in the reform process. Yu Guangyuan, vice-president of CASS and director of its Institute of Marxism-Leninism and Mao Zedong Thought. Other members included Su Shaozhi, deputy director of Yu's institute, and Liu Guoguang, deputy director of CASS Institute of Economics, both ardent

---

[7]See: Ji Jing, 'Xiongyali jingji guanli tizhi de gaige' [Reform of the Hungarian economic management system], *Jingji guanli* [Economic Management Journal] 6 (1979): 52–6.

[8]Du Lihui and Wei Yunlang, 'Xiongyali de jiage zhidu he jiage diaozheng' [Hungary's reform of the price system and price adjustment], *Jingji guanli* [Economic Management Journal] 11 (1979): 59, 60–1.

[9]MFA, 4th Territorial Department, László Bulyovszky's report: Chinese enquiry about the Hungarian system of economic management. Budapest, 12 November 1979. HNA XIX-J-1-j Kína 78–5 004792/3/1979.

[10]HSWP CC Resolution, 6 March 1979. HNA M-KS 288. f. 5/767/1979.

advocates of reform, and Huang Hai, a young researcher from the Institute of Economics.[11] The visit was kept low key. The delegation was received as guests of the Chinese embassy in Budapest, a common practice during the first years of renewed contacts, as neither side wanted to inflame Soviet sensitivities.

The guests set a friendly tone by criticising earlier Chinese policies and speaking frankly about what they had gone through during the Cultural Revolution. In return, their Hungarian partners also spoke openly about the domestic and external forces that by 1972 had managed to slow down the reform process in Hungary and warned their Chinese colleagues that they would face similar problems because there were always some supporters of the bureaucratic planned economy within party leaderships.[12] Yu was pleasantly surprised by their first meetings, as they were prepared for more formal negotiations similar to those in Romania and Yugoslavia.[13]

The Chinese economists visited over 30 institutions, including state organs responsible for economic management, economic research institutions under direct government control, research institutes, and several industrial and foreign trade enterprises, state farms, and agricultural cooperatives. They consulted with senior economists and political leaders, including Rezső Nyers, a former HSWP CC secretary and 'father of the Hungarian economic reforms', who in 1974 had been removed from his posts and became director of the Institute of Economics at the Hungarian Academy of Sciences. As Chinese economists knew relatively little about the Hungarian considerations behind recent developments: the topics of discussion included the meaning and extent of commodity production under the socialist system, the division of authorities of the country and its enterprises, the administrative and economic means of production and consumption regulation in the socialist system, and the differences between the socialist market and the capitalist market. Based on their Hungarian experience, the Chinese economists concluded that the nonsocialist forms of ownership 'can play a positive role when treated well.'[14] Originally, the visit was planned for three weeks, but the delegation stayed for an extra week and left Hungary on 22 December. They expressed their satisfaction with the visit and extended an invitation to a Hungarian delegation to visit China in the course of 1980.

But only a few days after the Chinese economists left Hungary, the Soviet Union invaded Afghanistan, which had a detrimental effect on Sino-Soviet relations. In April 1979, the Chinese announced that they intended to let the Sino-Soviet Treaty of Friendship, Alliance and Mutual Assistance, which was signed on 14 February 1950 for a term of 30 years, expire without seeking an extension, but proposed negotiations 'of outstanding issues and the improvement of relations between the two countries.'[15] However, as China's leaders considered the Soviet move as a direct threat to their country's security, in January 1980 they announced that to continue negotiations with the Soviets was not appropriate under

---

[11]As the Hungarians never heard of Huang, they suspected he was from another 'organisation'. Memoirs of Barna Tálas. Manuscript. Courtesy of Barna Tálas.

[12]Ibid.

[13]Ambassador Róbert Ribánszki's cable: Official Chinese enquiry about our experiences of economic management. Beijing, 22 October 1979. HNA XIX-J-1-j Kína 78–5 004792/1/1979.

[14]Yu Guangyuan, 'Suggestions on China's Economic Restructuring', in *Chinese Economists on Economic Reform – Collected Works of Yu Guangyuan*. ed. China Development Research Foundation (London: Routledge, 2014), 30.

[15]*Beijing Review*, 6 April 1979, 3–4, quoted by Jonathan D. Pollack: 'The Opening to America', in *The Cambridge History of China* (General Editors: Denis Twitchett and John K. Fairbank). vol. 15, *The People's Republic*, part 2, 'Revolutions within the Chinese Revolution, 1966–1982', ed. by Roderick MacFarquhar and John K. Fairbank (Cambridge: Cambridge University Press, 1991), 402–72.

the new circumstances. In fact, negotiations did not resume until the autumn of 1982.[16] In this situation, the leadership of the Communist Party of the Soviet Union (CPSU) exerted even stronger political pressure on the 'fraternal' parties and pushed them to refrain from pursuing a policy leading to any kind of détente with China, a country that, in the opinion of the Soviet leadership, was the most ardent advocate of anti-Sovietism.[17] The Soviet intervention in Afghanistan was also detrimental to Hungarian foreign policy, which was committed to cross-European cooperation and to Hungarian intentions to support Chinese reforms, thereby strengthening the international position of Hungarian reforms. Under such circumstances, the visit of the delegation of Hungarian economists had to be postponed.

On their return, the members of the Chinese delegation published widely on their Hungarian experiences and argued that there were several aspects of the Hungarian reform process that could and should be emulated by China. They were particularly impressed by the achievements of the New Economic Mechanism, which had been launched after a three-year preparatory period. Yu Guangyuan summarised the results of the survey as follows: 'The reform of the Hungarian economic management system, in our opinion, should be acknowledged as relatively successful.'[18] The findings of the Chinese investigators were published as a book in August 1981, with a print run of 3700 copies, for domestic distribution only. It recorded the delegation's meetings with Hungarian officials and economists and contained an assessment of the Hungarian economic management system and suggestions for the Chinese leadership by the delegation members.[19] This publication introduced the phrase 'Hungarian economic model' (*Xiongyali de jingji moshi*), which was widely used in Chinese economic literature in the following years.[20]

In the Hungarian MFA's evaluation, 'The rather one-sided, positive introduction of Hungarian experiences mirrors the subjective wish of the reporters to make the idea of the need for reforms more acceptable in China, and to promote the adaptation of the Hungarian model.'[21] Indeed, the Chinese leadership used references to Eastern European reforms as a means to improve their country's position in the socialist community, to further strengthen their relations with Eastern Europe, and as a propaganda tool for domestic purposes. Reference to a 'reform community' and to the common elements of the reforms undertaken in Eastern Europe and China had an important domestic role to play in affirming China's socialist identity and legitimising the Party's new policies. As Tian Zengpei, head of the Foreign Ministry's Soviet and East European Department told the Hungarian

---

[16]On the process of Sino-Soviet normalisation see: Péter Vámos, '"Only a Handshake but no Embrace": Sino-Soviet Normalisation in the 1980s,' in *China Learns from the Soviet Union, 1949 – Present*, ed. Thomas P. Bernstein and Hua-yu Li (Lanham: Lexington Books, 2010), 79–104.

[17]The phrase 'fraternal parties' was used for the ruling parties in Bulgaria, Czechoslovakia, the GDR, Hungary, Poland (and Romania with reservations) in Europe, plus Mongolia, Vietnam, and Cuba. These parties were part of the close coordination mechanism within the Soviet bloc.

[18]Yu Guangyuan, et al., *Xiongyali jingji tizhi kaocha baogao* [Survey report on the Hungarian economic system] (Beijing: Zhongguo shehui kexue chubanshe, 1981), 215.

[19]Yu et al., *Xiongyali jingji tizhi kaocha baogao*. The Hungarians obtained a copy of the book from the Soviet embassy in Beijing. Hungarian ambassador's cable. Beijing, 24 June 1982. HNA XIX-J-1-j-Kína-504 004530/1982.

[20]See, e.g.: Su Shaozhi, 'Shilun Xiongyali jingji tizhi gaige' [On Hungarian economic reforms], *Shijie jingji wenhui* [World economic papers] 1 (1983): 13–24.

[21]Hungarian MFA IV. Territorial Department, China Desk report (reporter: György Újlaki): The introduction and evaluation of the report by the group of Chinese economists who visited Hungary in 1979. Budapest, 6 April 1982. HNA XIX-J-1-j-Kína-51 001232/1/1982.

ambassador in the summer of 1985, in the Chinese view, Eastern European countries had embarked on the modernisation of their economies based on conceptions similar to those developed in Hungary and in China. He expressed his hope that this process could contribute to the building of relations between China and Eastern European socialist countries.[22]

At the beginning of the 1980s, the Chinese press, while primarily serving the leadership's propaganda purposes, tended to emphasise only the successes of other socialist countries' reform efforts. Domestic problems and differences between European socialist states were generally overlooked.[23] This is not surprising, as the main task of media reports, after all, was to support current domestic policies. A Western observer concluded that the lessons drawn from the reforms in Eastern European socialist states 'had a more obvious basis in domestic events than in the experiences of the foreign country' that they analysed.[24] The Chinese goal was to justify Chinese policies and to bring the superiority of socialism into full play. Media reports used the positive images of Eastern European socialisms to strengthen the socialist character of Chinese reforms. In 1985, Deng Xiaoping stressed that:

> Reform is part of the self-perfecting process of the socialist system, and to a certain scope and extent, it is also a revolutionary change. It is a major undertaking that shows we have begun to find a way of building socialism with Chinese characteristics.[25]

Chen Yun's formulation of the essence of the reforms was simpler and more straightforward: 'We are Communists. Our goal is to build socialism.'[26]

One lesson that the Chinese learnt from blindly copying the Soviet experience and practices during the 1950s was that they had to find an economic system that met the requirements of modernisation.[27] Premier Zhao Ziyang, with the support of reform-oriented economists, including Sun Yefang, Yu Guangyuan, Su Shaozhi, and Liu Guoguang, proposed the examination of different economic models with the aim to 'learn foreign things' and 'unify theory and practice' in order to provide experience for the Chinese 'to choose their own road of socialist construction according to their specific conditions.'[28] There was only one requirement, however: adherence to the Marxist-Leninist theoretical basis. As Yu Guangyuan put it:

> As to what kind of an economic reform plan our country should adopt, we can only express opinions on the basis of in-depth research on the Marxist theory of socialism, the reality of China and foreign experience, rather than simply after a survey of the economic reform in a particular country.[29]

As a result, the experiences and practices of Eastern European socialist countries in general and Hungary in particular were not taken as exclusive foreign sources of Chinese reforms. During the early phase of the reform era, the Chinese studied the experiences of more developed countries, regardless of their social and economic systems. In 1980, Hu Yaobang substantiated this approach by quoting from Mao's essay 'On the People's Democratic Dictatorship,' written in 1949, in which Mao called all cadres to 'learn to do

---

[22]The Hungarian ambassador's cable to the Hungarian MFA. Beijing, 23 August 1985. HNA XIX-J-1-j-Kína-50 004238/1985.

[23]Nina Halpern, 'Learning from Abroad: Chinese Views of the East European Economic Experience, January 1977–June 1981,' *Modern China* 11, no. 1 (1985): 77–109.

[24]Ibid., 96–8.

[25]Deng Xiaoping's Speech at the CPC National Conference, Beijing, 18–23 September 1985. *Peking Review*, 39/1985, 30 September 1985, 15.

[26]*Peking Review*, 39/1985, 30 September 1985, 19.

[27]Yu Guangyuan, 'Suggestions on China's Economic Restructuring,' 26.

[28]Tribute to President Tito. *Peking Review* 1980/20, 19 May 1980, 5.

[29]Ibid., 36.

economic work from all who know how, no matter who they are.'[30] Beijing did not adopt one single model, but imported those elements and ideas that could be utilised in the modernisation process. The Chinese set out to build an 'eclectic state', which did not deny its Leninist roots, but drew on the lessons learnt from communist party states and East Asian countries with similar cultural traditions, as well as elements of the reform experiences of states in the authoritarian Middle East, in corporatist Latin America, in social democratic Western and Northern Europe, in federalist North America, and in Australia.[31] Just to mention one example, China's new economic legal system was influenced by the West German legislation on industrial property and by American legislation through American lawyers acting as advisers, legal scholars, and practitioners in China.[32]

Despite structural differences between the Chinese and other socialist economies, Eastern European and Soviet developments were subject to close attention. From 1977 on, the concept of three models of socialism – the Yugoslav 'open socialism', the Hungarian 'restrained socialism', and the Soviet system – was being discussed, and consideration was given to comparative study. At first, the search for a socialist model of economic management system centred on Yugoslavia. In fact, the function of Yugoslavia's presentation as a reformist country was to promote the need for socialist reform. As Hu Qiaomu, one of China's chief ideologists noted, Tito and his comrades were 'the first to recognise that socialism should not be confined to one model.'[33] During his visit to Yugoslavia in November 1979, Hu 'saw with his own eyes that members of academic circles there were doing their best to closely link theory with practice' and 'he was impressed by the fact that their creative work had contributed to Yugoslàvia's socialist construction.'[34] Economist Sun Yefang commented that while the Yugoslavs were 'really practicing socialism', they 'have broken away from the conventional Soviet methods which were formerly considered inviolable.'[35] The interest in the enterprise-based socialist market economy lasted at least until the middle of the 1980s, and in the case of agricultural reforms even until the late 1980s. But as the Chinese leaders were suspicious about Yugoslavia's decentralised political system, it was not taken as a role model for China.

Hungary, which added market mechanisms to the system of economic management and provided limited room for private entrepreneurs, was the second country to spark Chinese interest. For the reform-economists, the Hungarian model, which was principally socialist but quite flexible, represented a happy medium between the inadequately centralised economy of Yugoslavia and the excessively centralised Soviet planned economy.[36] Sociologist Gilbert Rozman observed that from the first half of the 1980s, when a policy of retrenchment of the role of the state replaced unrealisable plans for massive investment to stimulate growth, Hungary was deemed to be a suitable model. As China emerged from its isolation in the socialist bloc, forging closer economic ties with Eastern Europe, Beijing's new preference for the Hungarian model and its refusal to refer to China as a separate socialist

---

[30]'Hu Yaobang's Speech – At the Second National Congress of the Scientific and Technical Association,' *Peking Review*, 1980/15, 14 April 1980, 15.

[31]David Shambaugh, 'Introduction: The Evolving and Eclectic Modern Chinese State,' in *The Modern Chinese State*, ed. David Shambaugh (Cambridge: Cambridge University Press, 2000), 1–14.

[32]S. Messmann: 'Economic Legislation in China,' in *Trends of Economic Development in East Asia*, ed. Wolfgang Klenner (Berlin: Springer, 1989), 435.

[33]*Peking Review* 1980/20, 19 May 1980, 4.

[34]Ibid.

[35]*Peking Review* 1980/20, 19 May 1980, 5.

[36]Ambassador Mátyás Szűrös's cable. Moscow, 19 December 1979. HNA XIX-J-1-j-Kína-5–004792/10–1979.

model also signalled its desire to be accepted into the mainstream of the socialist world.[37] Yu Guangyuan presented Hungary as an example for China, as Hungary 'not only studied theoretical articles on socialist economic systems written by foreign economists, but also sent people to countries such as Yugoslavia and Czechoslovakia to research their economic reform theory and practice' and paid close attention to the movement of economic reform in the Soviet Union and Eastern European countries.[38]

By the early 1980s, reform had become a general phenomenon in European socialist countries. Chinese analysts studied the Czechoslovakian experiences with state-owned enterprises and the salary system of factory workers, paid special attention to Bulgaria's efforts to reform the cadre system and streamline the cadre apparatus and pointed to the possible similarities between the social consequences of price reform in Poland and China.[39] By the end of the decade, the most preferred Eastern European model for China seemed to be the GDR, which appealed to the Chinese 'as a key actor in East-West and intra-Warsaw Pact relations, a Soviet ally with hankerings after diplomatic independence, a strong industrial economy, and (so it seemed) a stable regime under firm and all-pervasive party control.'[40]

The reason why all Eastern European leaderships felt the need for reform was that by the early 1980s the system could not be maintained for long without the introduction of market mechanisms. The East European leaderships hoped that with the introduction of economic reforms the socialist system could be rescued from collapse. In a similar vein, Chinese propaganda described the future prospects of economic reforms in a positive manner.[41] Su Shaozhi, an influential supporter of Hungarian-style reforms, attributed the problems that Hungary had to face primarily to the global economic crisis in the wake of the 1973 oil crisis, which affected especially those countries that were sensitive to foreign trade. He also mentioned domestic factors, including low economic effectivity and productivity rates, which he called a common problem for 'Eastern' countries.[42]

However, the severe economic difficulties in Eastern Europe, which also affected Yugoslavia and Hungary, added to the downgrading of the relevance of their reforms in China. Between 1985 and 1987, Hungary had zero economic growth, an inflation rate of 7–8% per annum, and an adverse trade balance. Yugoslavia had a 200 per cent inflation rate and a foreign debt of US$21 billion. By the mid-1980s, it had become obvious for the Chinese leaders that Eastern European reforms could provide applicable solutions for some Chinese problems, but they could not serve as a standard or a model, as these countries differed from China in size as well as economic development. As to the lessons from Hungary's economic reforms, Su Shaozhi reiterated, 'There is no universal pattern to follow, nor it is possible to copy the models of other countries.'[43]

---

[37]Gilbert Rozman, *The Chinese Debate about Soviet Socialism, 1978–1985* (Princeton University Press, 1987), 60.

[38]Yu Guangyuan, 'Suggestions on China's Economic Restructuring', 33–4.

[39]Cypher telegram 106 by 'Jász'. Beijing, 13 April 1988. Állambiztonsági Szolgálatok Történeti Levéltára (Historical Archives of the Hungarian State Security, hereafter: HAHSS) 1. 11. 4. S – II/2/1988: 35. About the Chinese study of reforms introduced by socialist countries. 28 April 1988. HAHSS 1. 11. 4. S – II/2/1988: 71–69 (Translation from Russian. For the Russian original see: Spravka: Ob izuchenii Kitaem reform, sovershaemykh v socialistyicheskykh stranakh. HAHSS 1. 11. 4. S – II/2/1988: 68–66.

[40]Alyson J. K. Bailes, 'China and Eastern Europe: A Judgment on the "Socialist Community"', *The Pacific Review* 3, no. 3 (1990): 228.

[41]Ambassador László Iván's report (reporter: Sándor Kusai): The Chinese public media on socialist countries (September 1986 – February 1987). Beijing, 20 February 1987. HNA XIX-J-1-k-Kína-8–3067-1987.

[42]Su Shaozhi, 'Xiongyali jingji tizhi gaige zhong de ruogan lilun wenti' [Some theoretical problems of the Hungarian reform of economic management] *Jingji wenti tansuo* [Inquiry into economic problems] 2 (1980): 1–9.

[43]Su Shaozhi, 'A Chinese View on the Reform of the Economic Mechanism in Hungary: A Comment', in Van Ness, *Market Reforms in Socialist Societies*, 208.

Despite Chinese interest in Eastern European reforms, the Soviet experience of the problems of economic modernisation was considered by Chinese leaders as most relevant to the practice-oriented reforms on which the PRC was embarking. Along with lessons drawn from other Western and Asian reform experiences, the only reforms to be taken into account were those in the Soviet Union.[44] As Huan Xiang, vice-chairman of CASS explained to the Czechoslovak ambassador in Beijing, although the Soviet Union belonged to the First World from the theoretical point of view, this did not prevent China from studying issues pertaining to the social system in the Soviet Union, Soviet experiences, achievements, and failures.[45]

The Sino-Hungarian reform community under Moscow's shadow

Presenting Eastern Europe as China's ally in reforming the Soviet-style socialist economy or at least substantiating the reforms by drawing a parallel between China and the Soviet Union's Eastern European allies was part of what Moscow's leaders called China's anti-Soviet policy. In fact, China's long-time ambition was to regain its former greatness and centrality in international affairs. During the first decade of the PRC Mao wanted to achieve this goal by leaning on the Soviet Union's side. However, starting from the late 1950s, Beijing's leaders gradually turned against their former ally and by the late 1960s considered military aggression from the North as the greatest threat to the country's national security. The Beijing leadership identified states as potential friends or enemies based on their relations with the PRC's major opponent, the Soviet Union, and distinguished among the socialist states based on their degree of autonomy from the USSR. Internationally, Beijing's intention was to drive a wedge between the Soviet Union and its closest allies. Meanwhile, Beijing's propagandists wanted to prove for the domestic audience that China was not alone in turning its back to the Soviet Union. The Chinese interest in Yugoslavia and especially Romania, which during the 1980s was not in the forefront of economic reforms, to say the least, should be seen in this context.

During the 1980s, the major tendencies of the development of Sino-East European relations can be characterised by a gradual switch from informal exchanges to formal relations, from peripheral fields of cooperation to central issues, and from small steps to major moves. China did not spare efforts to foster economic and even political ties with Eastern Europe at a time when it refused to continue negotiations with the USSR. It was following the outset of the Sino-Soviet thaw in 1979, and especially after the resumption of political consultations in 1982, that Beijing accelerated efforts to re-establish the system of relations it had had with socialist countries in the 1950s. However, the relationship as it was envisaged by the Beijing leadership had to be based on mutual benefit and the principles of peaceful coexistence instead of proletarian internationalism, which in practice would have meant the acceptance of Soviet superiority.

Nevertheless, bilateral relations between China and Eastern European socialist countries, including Hungary, did not develop at a fast pace. The Hungarians kept themselves to the

---

[44]For a detailed analysis of Chinese writings on the Soviet Union from first years of the reform era see: Rozman, *The Chinese Debate*.

[45]Ambassador Róbert Ribánszki's cable. Beijing, 17 February 1981. HNA XIX-J-1-j-Kína-22 001658/1981.

basic principle drawn up in Moscow, according to which improvement of Sino-Soviet relations was a precondition to significant changes in Sino-East European relations.

Starting from the late 1960s, the Soviets intended to control all spheres of cooperation between their satellites and China, from economic and cultural relations to more sensitive scientific and technological cooperation, not to mention military or party-to-party contacts. Even the annual bilateral trade agreements with detailed lists of export and import goods were subject to Soviet approval. The close coordination of China policies was implemented on different levels, including multilateral and bilateral meetings of the top leaders, consultations of ministers and deputy ministers in Moscow or in other capitals, meetings of 'friendly' ambassadors in Beijing (the 'ambassadors' club'), *Interkit* meetings of Party Central Committee International Department officials, scientific conferences of China specialists from government organisations and research institutes, and consultations of Soviet diplomats with government officials and party workers.[46] Eastern European diplomats were summoned to Moscow for consultations, and one of their main tasks in Beijing was to coordinate their countries' steps with the Soviet Union. In 1982, the first counsellor of the Hungarian embassy in Beijing reported that, as a result of broadening contacts, the tasks of the Embassy were to undergo some changes as well. Whereas previously the activities of the embassy were almost exclusively dominated by reporting, after 1982 more energy had to be devoted to the management of bilateral relations and coordination with other fraternal countries.[47]

The tight Soviet control stemmed from the danger that, in Soviet opinion, China could pose by winning over the Soviet Union's closest, but in several aspects still uneasy, allies. The Soviet grip on Mongolia was strongest, but the 1956 events in Hungary, the 1968 intervention in Czechoslovakia and the Polish events of 1980–1 showed that the threat with the Brezhnev doctrine of limited sovereignty, and the presence of Soviet armed forces, was strong enough to keep the satellites away from maverick activities.

In the early years of the reform era, China made an increasing number of proposals designed to improve bilateral relations in various fields of economic, cultural, and social life. The first exchanges included visits by delegations on tourism, film crews, and the re-establishment of relations between friendship societies. According to a Hungarian evaluation, the process of normalisation was characterised by the fact that 'essentially all initiatives, or for the most part, have been taken by the Chinese. Another feature is the delay in the development of relations with the Soviet Union, which is 1–1.5 steps behind the rest.'[48] The Hungarians carefully examined the initiatives and responded to them in accordance with their Politburo resolution of March 1979.

The atmosphere of Sino-Soviet political relations slightly improved in 1982. The Soviets made the first big step with Brezhnev's March 1982 speech in Tashkent to pave the way

---

[46]The phrase, derived from the Russian word for China ('*Kitai*'), refers to, strictly speaking, a series of meetings on China held interchangeably in the different capitals of the Soviet bloc between 1967 and 1985. Participants were representatives from the party central committee international departments of 'fraternal' parties. But broadly speaking, the phrase also covers the whole coordination process of China policies of the Soviet bloc during the second half of the cold war, including economic and trade relations, at 'economic Interkits', cultural contacts, and China-related research at the meetings of sinologists. See: James G. Hershberg et al., *The Interkit Story. A Window into the Final Decades of the Sino-Soviet Relationship* (Washington, DC: Woodrow Wilson International Centre for Scholars, Cold War International History Project, 2011). Working Paper No. 63. http://www.wilsoncenter.org/publication/the-interkit-story (accessed November 29, 2017).

[47]Report of Tamás G. Gál, Budapest, 24 June 1982. HNA XIX-J-1-j-Kína-I-19 002810/1982.

[48]15 December 1986. (No title) Secret telegram from 'Jász' (Agent's codename in Beijing): On the relations between China and the socialist countries in 1986. Historical Archives of Hungarian State Security (hereafter, HAHSS) 1. 11. 4. S-II/2/86/4.

for the resumption of talks. The Soviet leader called China a socialist country, supported China's position on Taiwan, expressed his willingness to improve relations with China, and proposed consultations between the two sides. The Chinese responded in kind, proposing consultations aiming at the normalisation of political relations. The formal adoption of an independent foreign policy posture at the CCP's 12th Congress and the dropping of 'socialist imperialism' and 'contemporary revisionism' from the 1982 Constitution of the PRC, which signalled to Moscow that China would no longer collaborate with the United States in policies generated explicitly by an anti-Soviet design, was as much a gesture to Moscow as a reflection of the major ideological changes that had taken place since Deng launched his policy of reform and opening up.

Taking advantage of the Sino-Soviet thaw, the East German and the Hungarian MFA initiated political consultations with their Chinese colleagues immediately following the first round of renewed Sino-Soviet vice-foreign ministerial consultations in October 1982. East German-Chinese consultations took place in February 1983, and the first consultation between the Hungarian MFA head of department in charge of Hungarian-Chinese relations Jenő Jakus and his Chinese counterpart Ma Xusheng was held in Beijing a month later, upon initiative from the Hungarian side. During the meeting with his Hungarian colleague, Ma described the atmosphere of improving Sino-Hungarian relations as friendly. Both sides were satisfied with the trade agreement and with scientific and technological exchanges. The Chinese side promised the further development of relations for the year 1983, but stressed that there was no need to hurry or to strive for a single big result. As they said, solid and stable foundations had to be established first, so that future activities could rely on well-established foundations.[49] Nevertheless, Soviet diplomats in Budapest immediately warned their Hungarian partners:

> By continuing political consultations and establishing certain contacts with the Soviet Union, the Chinese leadership, in line with its firm goal, aims to ease the implementation of its differentiated policy. While Beijing takes only small steps toward the Soviet Union, its aim is to make a big step toward other socialist countries, and thereby break the united front in the China issue. Under such circumstances, vigilance and coordination of actions by friendly socialist countries is especially desirable.[50]

Beijing's intention to exert pressure on Moscow by attempting to distance the Soviet Union from its allies is clearly demonstrated in the Chinese argumentation on the similarities between Chinese and Eastern European approaches to reform. Returning the Chinese economists' 1979 visit to Hungary, a delegation of Hungarian social scientists could finally visit China after the resumption of Sino-Soviet political consultations in 1982. During the visit, the Chinese argued that

> [t]he real estrangement and split with the Soviet Union occurred after 1978, when the Chinese leadership decided to break with the rigidly centralised system of social and economic management based on omnipotent party leadership introduced in the 1950s. Former Chinese leaderships had only ideological controversies with the Soviet Union, but now debates focus on the differences between dogmatic and constructive approaches to the socialist social and economic system. They added that it was their conviction that sooner or later almost all socialist countries would distance themselves from the 'Soviet model, even those where reforms have not yet started.'

---

[49]Ambassador László Iván's cable, Beijing, 30 March 1983. HNA XIX-J-1-j-Kína-145 002379/1983.
[50]Head of Department Ferenc Szabó's note: Soviet diplomat on Sino-Soviet consultations. Budapest, 30 May 1983. HNA XIX-J-1-j-Kína-003622/1983.

The Chinese knew that their message would reach Moscow. The final report of the delegation was approved by Gyula Horn, then Secretary of State in the Hungarian MFA, and one copy of the report was provided by the HSWP CC to the Soviet embassy in Budapest.[51]

The Soviets kept stressing the potentially harmful character of seemingly benevolent Chinese political moves even after the Tashkent speech. In the summer of 1982, Oleg B. Rakhmanin, the deputy director of the CPSU CC International Department for Relations with Fraternal Countries who was responsible for the coordination of China policies, told the 'friendlies' that the CPSU did not oppose the gradual development of trade relations and other contacts with China, but warned that the unduly positive opinion of those working on practical issues might encourage the excessive development of relations by the fraternal parties' leaderships. As a result, he continued, the socialist countries could become de facto members of the wide anti-Soviet united front initiated by the Chinese.[52] Furthermore, Rakhmanin repeatedly warned: 'Any kind of competition would harm the unity of socialist countries and the cause of renewing relations with China.'[53]

In October 1982, the Hungarian Party leadership issued new China policy guidelines, which, in theory at least, remained in effect until the systemic change in 1989–90. The resolution described 'the coordinated actions of the countries of the socialist community' as successful, as they 'have produced an essentially moderating effect on Chinese foreign policy.' It stressed, '[t]he normalisation of our relations is … an issue of outstanding international significance,' but also added that its achievement 'requires a firm and principled conduct, political awareness, and concord with the Soviet Union and the other countries of the socialist community.' The resolution mentioned the system of policy coordination as an 'established framework' and emphasised the need for a comprehensively studied standpoint, a common principled line, and coordinated activity at three levels: (a) in relation to China's growing activity in the international organisations; (b) in bilateral relations and in China's relations with the socialist community as a whole; and (c) within Hungary, where the Ministry of Foreign Affairs was in charge of coordination of the activities of all Hungarian organs and institutions which maintained contacts with their Chinese counterparts.[54]

Although the Soviets warned their allies not to be misled by the Chinese and not to fall victim to the anti-Soviet considerations of Beijing (as they put it: 'The Chinese see anti-Sovietism as a currency with which they pay for Western political and economic help'), it became more obvious for the Eastern European leaderships that China's search for partners no longer had direct anti-Soviet implications.[55] In the summer of 1983, a Chinese diplomat from the MFA Hungarian Desk told his Hungarian partner that

> China had long given up turning Hungary against the Soviet Union, or to make it similar to Yugoslavia or Romania. He said that both sides must be practical, as there were many opportunities for the development of relations, even if we do not agree on certain political issues.[56]

Nevertheless, the CPSU continued its fight against Maoism well into the 1980s. Rakhmanin made increasingly desperate and futile efforts to retain the CPSU's total control over its

---

[51]Report of the delegation of Hungarian social scientists to China. Budapest, 2 July 1982. HNA XIX-J-1-j-Kína-51–002291/6/1982.

[52]Ambassador Mátyás Szűrös's cable, Moscow, 7 July 1982. HNA XIX-J-1-j-Kína-103 004774/1982.

[53]Ambassador Mátyás Szűrös's cable. Moscow, 25 May 1982. HNA XIX-J-1-j-Kína-103 0024/7/1982.

[54]Resolution of the HSWP CC, Budapest, 26 October 1982. HNA M-KS 288. f. 5/865/1982.

[55]Head of Department Ferenc Szabó's report on his meeting with councillor Kokeiev of the Soviet embassy in Budapest: Soviet diplomat's briefing on evaluations related to China. Budapest, 31 January 1981. HNA XIX-J-1-j-Kína-57 001088/1981.

[56]Ambassador László Iván's cable. Beijing, 24 June 1983. HNA XIX-J-1-j-Kína-135 002652/6/1983.

allies. Disputes over significant differences of opinions surfaced between the CPSU represented by Rakhmanin and the East German and Hungarian parties. At the Sofia Interkit in May 1982, the East Germans refused to sign the final protocol of the meeting. In 1983, Rakhmanin stressed that 'the Soviet Union aims to frustrate cooperation between Beijing and imperialism, while the socialist community aims to counteract China's policy to divide socialist countries.' At the same time, the SED representative pointed out: 'By the decision to acknowledge Eastern European socialist countries as being socialist, the Chinese leadership intends to demonstrate interest in the experiences of these countries gained in building socialism.'[57]

The differences of opinion originated, among other things, in the evaluation of reforms. At the Prague Interkit in December 1983, Mikhail I. Sladkovsky, director of the Institute of Far Eastern Studies of the Soviet Academy of Sciences, 'gave a lengthy elaboration on the impossibility and harmful features of "Chinese type socialism", stating that socialism as a scientific doctrine was universal, and no Soviet, Yugoslav or Chinese models existed.'[58] Meanwhile, Zhu Rongji, who as vice-chairman of the State Economic Commission headed the first major Chinese economic delegation to the five Eastern European Soviet bloc countries in March-April 1984, indicated that 'China and Hungary both seek to build socialism according to their national characteristics.'[59] In August 1984, during Hungarian Deputy Prime Minister József Marjai's visit to Beijing – which took place four months ahead of Soviet Deputy Prime Minister Ivan Arkhipov's visit to the PRC – Chinese Premier Zhao Ziyang spoke approvingly about Hungarian reform experiences. Marjai's visit was closely reported in Chinese media. The *People's Daily*'s extensive coverage included Vice-Premier Li Peng's comment that 'China and Hungary share the overall goal of building socialism,' and Zhao Ziyang's note that 'we attach great importance to Hungary's achievements in socialist reconstruction and experience in economic reforms.[60,61] Zhao had a genuine interest in Hungarian reforms. During the visit of Hungarian economists, including János Kornai, probably the most influential East European economic theorist, the Chinese Prime Minister, who also headed the State Commission for Restructuring the Economic System, met and talked for two hours with the delegation.[62]

As by the mid-1980s both the USSR and the PRC showed the intention and will for the normalisation of relations, Eastern European countries had a relatively free hand in widening the scope of their relations with China. Only the development of inter-party and military-to-military relations were still out of question.[63] The summary of Sino-Hungarian relations prepared by the Hungarian MFA in August 1985 concluded:

---

[57]Head of HSWP CC International Department Géza Kótai's submission of the Protocol of the China-Consultation of representatives of CC International Departments of the Ten Fraternal Parties Held on 6–7 December 1983 in Prague. Budapest, 27 December 1983. HNA M-KS 288 f. 32. cs. 110/1983 ő.e. 384–389.

[58]Head of HSWP CC International Department Géza Kótai's report on the Consultations of the CC International Departments of the Fraternal Parties of Ten Socialist Countries. Budapest, 14 December 1983. HNA M-KS 288 f. 32. cs. 110/1983 ő.e. 631–638.

[59]Ministry of the Interior, III/II. Department: Deputy Head of Department Police Major General Dr. Miklós Rédei's report: Information on China. Budapest, 30 September 1985. HAHSS 1. 11. 4. S-II/2/85.

[60]'Li Peng zai yanqing Xiongyali buzhang huiyi fuzhuxi Maeryayi shi shuo: ZhongXiong liangguo jianshe shehuizhuyi zongmubiao shi yizhide' [Li Peng says at reception for Vice-Chairman of Hungarian Council of Ministers Marjai: China and Hungary share the overall goal of building socialism], *Renmin Ribao*, 21 August 1984.

[61]'Zhao Ziyang huijian Maeryayi shi xiwang tebie zhuyi fazhan ZhongXiong jingji jishu hezuo' [Zhao Ziyang meets Marjai and hopes to pay special attention to developing Sino-Hungarian economic and technological cooperation], *Renmin Ribao*, 25 August 1984.

[62]János Kornai and Zsuzsa Dániel, 'The Chinese Economic Reform – As seen by Hungarian Economists (Marginal Notes to our Travel Diary),' *Acta Oeconomica* 36, no. 3/4 (1986): 289–305.

[63]Head of Department Bálint Gál's report: 'Consultation in Moscow on China, Indochina, and Korea,' Budapest, December 1984. HNA XIX-J-1-j-SZU-144–006143–1984 (135. d.).

The development of bilateral relations is our common interest. Further development can be hindered only by the interests of our allies ... and possible negative foreign policy steps. We plan to further increase the level of relations. Its pace depends on the steps made by our allies.[64]

The second half of the 1980s saw a softening of tone from the Soviet side. Although the basic pattern of relations between China and Eastern European relations remained largely unchanged even as Soviet control over its satellites began to relax, by the mid-1980s Sino–East European relations gained importance for their own sake. With trade relations expanding and political normalisation underway, reference to a reform community became a common theme in both Beijing and in Budapest, both in terms of domestic and foreign policy. As party relations were re-established in 1986–7, the East Europeans welcomed China's return to the great family of socialist states and hoped that expanding economic relations would open up new market opportunities. Intending to strengthen China's socialist identity and legitimise the party's reform policies, the reform-minded Chinese leadership also attributed Eastern Europe an important role in Chinese domestic propaganda. Furthermore, in foreign policy Beijing wished to win the socialist states' sympathy for its reform course and acceptance for the new concept of 'socialism with Chinese characteristics.'

The timing of Hungarian leader János Kádár's visit was particularly important for the Chinese reform forces. The reform-minded leaders wanted to create the appropriate political climate to push forward political and economic reforms at the 13th CCP Congress, held between 25 October and 1 November.[65] With Hu Yaobang's removal from the post of party general secretary in early 1987, the struggle between conservatives and reformists within the leadership flared up again. A strong advocate for reform, Zhao Ziyang seemed to have succeeded temporarily and believed that it was important for the reformists to gain support from Eastern Europe as well. With the visit, the Hungarian Party provided unconditional support for the forthcoming decisions, the new policy line, the planned reform steps, and the new political leadership. Deng staged this visit as a demonstration in support of China's reform policies as well as its policy of opening up to the outside world, especially toward socialist states.[66] The Chinese media widely reported on Kádár's visit. *People's Daily* quoted Deng Xiaoping stressing that 'to reflect the superiority of socialism it is necessary to reform' and Zhao Ziyang reiterating that 'China is on the right path.'[67]

By 1987, when the practical aspects of the relationship had increasingly come to the fore, the situation seemed to change and Hungary seemed to lose its prioritised position in China. This was partly due to the fact that as certain elements of economic reforms had been introduced in other Eastern European socialist countries as well, reform was no longer a 'Hungarian specialty.'[68]

Paradoxically, even as the Chinese seemed to show great interest toward Hungarian reform experiences, and certain elements of Hungarian reforms served as an example to be emulated by China, we see a decrease in the overall volume of bilateral trade. In 1980,

---

[64]'The Present State of Sino-Hungarian Relations', Budapest, August 1985. HNA XIX-J-1-j-Kína-10 002023/9.

[65]'Chinese Evaluation of the HSWP General Secretary's Visit', HAHSS, 1.11.4, S-II/2/87, 229.

[66]'Meeting with the Chinese Embassy's Leading Diplomats', 30 October 1987, HAHSS, 1.11.4, S-II/2/87, 245.

[67]Cang Lide, 'Deng Xiaoping huijian Kadaer shi shuo: yao tixian shehuizhuyi youyuexing jiu yao gaige' [Deng Xiaoping meets Kádár and says: to reflect the superiority of socialism, it is necessary to reform], *Renmin Ribao*, 14 October 1987. Ailiyashi Beila (Éliás, Béla), 'Zhongguo zai zhengque daolu shang qianjin' [China is on the right path], *Renmin Ribao*, 29 October 1987.

[68]Chinese views on Hungarian Economic Reforms and Sino-Hungarian Trade Relations. N.D. (late 1987) HAHSS 1. 11. 4. S-II/2/87, 32–42.

China's overall foreign trade turnover grew by almost 30 percent, but the trade volume with socialist states did not follow the trend.[69] Sino-Hungarian trade reached its peak in 1979, followed by a decrease in the following two years.[70] Apart from Chinese political considerations, which obviously favoured Western imports, for most companies from the socialist countries trade with China became more difficult because of the growing competition with Japanese and Western firms. The Chinese made no secret of their basic principle that they would decide what to import from each country on the basis of quality, technical level, and price of products, and not political sympathies or antipathies.[71] In the case of Hungary the most important factor in the decrease of trade relations was that the Hungarians were not able to provide the quantities of goods laid down in the annual agreements, could not keep to deadlines, and were unable to match Chinese expectations in terms of quality. The Hungarians even attempted to play the 'improvement in political relations for growing trade' card, but the Chinese responded: 'To their utmost regret, this kind of link cannot be made at present.'[72]

Changes in Sino-Hungarian trade can also be taken as an indicator of how much relevance China really attributed to Hungarian reforms. Although the Hungarian experience could influence China's own reform of the economic management system, the Chinese experience with Hungarian trading partners could lead nowhere else but to disappointment. Problems with Hungarian agricultural machinery exports provide us with a telling example. Whereas Chinese authorities showed great interest in Hungarian reforms of agriculture and the establishment of agro-industrial complexes, Hungarian exports of agricultural machinery remained negligible.[73] In 1980, only two items of equipment were in – partial – use. In one of the two cases, the Hungarians solved the problems that had arisen during delivery and installation of a chicken farm by 'a series of dismissals, multiple travels of professionals, plan amendments and additional deliveries,' but in the case of a feed plant, one unit of the machinery could not be set into operation at all, as even the Hungarian experts were unable to determine the problem.[74]

In 1988, when in Beijing it was widely acknowledged that 'the domestic political practice followed in Hungary ... cannot serve as model for them,' the Chinese continued to 'pay close attention' to Hungarian reforms. Chinese diplomats in Budapest still claimed that 'the temperature of Sino-Hungarian relations is much higher than that of Sino-Soviet relations.'[75] As a Chinese diplomat in Moscow put it – in all probability referring to the first visit of Chinese economists to Hungary in 1979, 'China learned the reforms in Hungary many years ago. ... The Chinese do not forget that Hungarians were the first to offer their hands of friendship at times when Sino-Soviet relations were frozen.'[76]

---

[69]Nicholas R. Lardy, *Foreign Trade and Economic Reform in China, 1978–1990* (Cambridge: Cambridge University Press, 1992), 12.

[70]Hungarian MFA 4th Territorial Department: The State of Hungarian-Chinese exchange of goods. Budapest, 28 October 1982. HNA XIX-J-1-j Kína 78–57-006148/1982.

[71]Hungarian ambassador in Berlin Szalai's cypher telegram: On the transformation of Chinese economy. Berlin, 7 January 1980. HNA XIX-J-1-j Kína 78–50 00244/1981.

[72]Ambassador Róbert Ribánszki's cable: China's economic problems and the question of Hungarian-Chinese trade relations. Beijing, 9 March 1981. HNA XIX-J-1-j Kína 78–50 001931/1/1981.

[73]Ambassador Róbert Ribánszki's report (reporter: Dr. Zsuzsa Mészáros): A brief review of Chinese publications on Hungarian agriculture. Beijing, 22 March 1980. HNA XIX-J-1-j Kína 78–55 002712/1980.

[74]Ambassador Róbert Ribánszki's report (reporter: Dr. Zsuzsa Mészáros): On Chinese agriculture. In appendix: Hungarian agricultural machinery and equipment in China. Beijing, 13 November 1980. HNA XIX-J-1-j Kína 78–55 006671/1980.

[75]'Chinese and Japanese Diplomats on Foreign Political Issues,' 18 July 1988, HAHSS 1. 11. 4. S-II/2/88, 27–8.

[76]ibid.

Conclusion

Hungarian economist and political scientist Mária Csanádi, based on her Interactive Party-State model, which identifies the general system characteristics of party-states and thus puts them on common analytical grounds, argues that the Hungarian model was simply not applicable in China.[77] Nevertheless, despite controversies over the contents of political reform, politicians and political analysts in both countries looked at the commitment to reform as a binding force between Eastern Europe and China right until the spring of 1989. In February 1989, the Hungarian ambassador in Beijing wrote: 'Reference to Chinese political reform efforts can be used to form the general international environment for Hungarian political reforms, and it will be possible to maintain the idea of a general reform community in the future, too.'[78] Su Shaozhi came to a similar conclusion. A devoted advocate of reform, Su, in his article published in 1989 referring to the political changes within the HSWP in 1988, claimed: 'Hungary's reform has now entered upon a new stage, which gives encouragement to reformers of the other socialist countries in Eastern Europe, as well as to China.'[79]

In the 1980s, the social and economic reform processes in China resembled those in Eastern Europe, and, as a result, China and the European socialist states faced similar problems and dilemmas. Although both Hungarian and Chinese leaderships stressed the importance of taking into consideration the differences in circumstances and local characteristics, their goal was to build a socialist market economy. Both countries introduced market mechanisms to force production units to compete and boost growth in productivity, support managerial initiative and worker enthusiasm, and increase the standard of product quality in order to meet consumer demands. They also had to find solutions to fight inflation, unemployment, budget, and foreign trade deficit. Paradoxically, the same reform processes – which on both sides initially ran parallel, serving as a point of reference and contributing to the renormalisation of relations – had, by 1989, led to diametrically opposite political solutions. The former binding force turned into a source for difference and separation.

Acknowledgement

The author would like to thank OTKA (K 78484) and the Needham Research Institute Jing Brand Fellowship for their support of research into relations between the Soviet Bloc and China.

Disclosure statement

No potential conflict of interest was reported by the author.

---

[77]Mária Csanádi, *Self-Consuming Evolutions*.

[78]Ambassador Iván Németh (reporters: Sándor Mészáros and Sándor Kusai), 'The Evaluation of Hungarian Political Processes in China,' 21 February 1989, HNA XIX-J-1-j-Kína-1,2–0073/4–1989.

[79]Su Shaozhi, 'A Chinese View on the Reform of the Economic Mechanism in Hungary: A Comment,' in Peter Van Ness, *Market Reforms*, 210.

Index

agricultural/agriculture 4, 32, 45–9, 53, 62, 77, 80, 82, 85, 109, 122; cooperatives 40–2, 53, 111; delegation 49, 82–3; machinery 45–6, 54, 122; techniques 6, 81, 83
Albania 6, 70, 89–91, 94, 97–9, 101–6
alternative path, development 35–7
Avramov, Rumen 87

Beijing 3, 31–6, 38, 41–2, 45–52, 54, 56–63, 65–72, 90–1, 95–6, 100, 102–6, 108, 114, 116–23; leadership 108, 116
Berlin 49, 56, 59, 66, 70, 72, 101
Böröcz, József 5
Botevgradska Komuna 79, 84
Brisby, Liliana 78
Brown, James 78
Budapest 5, 11–13, 21–2, 28, 58–9, 61, 67–8, 70, 72, 109–11, 118–19, 121–2
Bulgaria 9, 22, 73–89, 101
Bulgaria mobilisation 80–1
Bulgarian Economic Leap 77, 80–1, 85, 89
Bulgarian leadership 6, 78–81, 83–6, 88

Chervenkov, Vălko 78
Chinese economists 110–11, 118, 122
Cold War 2, 6, 26–7, 57, 62, 90, 92, 94, 99, 104, 106, 108
cooperative members 44, 46, 53
Council for Mutual Economic Assistance (COMECON) 4, 85, 88–9
Csanádi, Mária 123
cultural exchange 30, 37, 60
cultural miscommunication 27
cultural revolution 59, 67, 69, 71, 104, 109, 111
culture 3, 5, 10, 12, 26, 29–34, 37–8, 48
cultured consumerism 29
Czechoslovak 6, 29–30, 34, 38, 40–2, 44, 46–7, 49–50, 53–4
Czechoslovak-Chinese relations 50, 53–4

Eastern bloc press 56, 71–2
Eastern Europe 2–6, 29, 58, 61–2, 70, 72, 91, 94, 96, 105, 107–8, 112, 114–16, 121, 123

East German China 56
East German leadership 62, 66–7, 71
East German press 65–6
East Germany 5, 28, 34, 59, 62, 69, 71–2, 97
economic cooperation 41, 60
Economic Leap campaign, Bulgaria 73–89
economic management 108–11, 114, 118; system 2, 109, 112, 114, 122
economic reforms 3, 105, 107–8, 111, 113, 115–16, 120–1
educative entertainment 8, 16, 23
Enlai, Zhou 60

global competitiveness 38
Gomulka, Wladyslaw 60
Great Friendship 28, 30
Great Leap Forward 35, 38, 48, 51, 59–61, 63, 67, 74, 76–80, 82, 84, 86, 88
Grupka Mijalowska 94–101
Guangyuan, Yu 113
Guangzhou 30–2, 35–6
Gypsy Dance 18

Habsburg absolutism 13
Havas, Ervin 16
heimat culture 31
high culture 5, 33, 36
Hungarian leadership 60–2, 64, 69
Hungarian reforms 108, 112, 120–2; experiences 108, 120–1
Hungary 5, 7–10, 12–14, 16–24, 29, 34, 58–61, 63–5, 69, 72, 107–11, 113–23

industrialisation 4, 40, 45, 63, 76–7, 79–80, 85–6, 88–9
International Monetary Fund 110
intra-bloc relations 2, 56, 59

Jersild, Austin 4

Kádár, János 121
Khrushchev, Nikita 25, 58
Krátká, Lenka 41

INDEX

Kremlinologists 57
Kremlinology 56–7

leftist factions 101
Lindner, Gerda 56, 72
Lüthi, Lorenz 27

Magyar 7, 12, 17–19
Mao 2, 61, 67–8, 70, 91–2, 96, 100–4, 113
market mechanisms 114–15, 123
Mijal, Kazimierz 6, 90–2, 101, 104–5
Mijal affair 102
Morning in the Camp 20–2, 24
Moscow 3, 5–6, 25–6, 29–30, 37–8, 40–1, 47–8,
   51–2, 58–65, 67–72, 79–80, 89, 91–2, 95–8,
   100–6, 117–19
Moscow Restaurant 32, 35, 38
Mukden 22
Münnich, Ferenc 60

national independence 18–19
Népszabadság 59–61, 63, 65–6, 68–9, 71
Népszava 22

open socialism 114

Palmowski, Jan 31
peaceful coexistence 3, 26, 36, 38, 48, 65, 116
Peking-Pankow axis 76
people's communes 6, 48, 50, 61–3, 67, 76, 79,
   83–5
physical labour 80
planting techniques 81
Poland 5–6, 22, 29, 34, 58–9, 63, 69, 71–2, 77,
   90–3, 95–106
polemical exchanges 27
Polish force 92
Politburo resolution 110, 117
political leadership 67, 88
political movements 58
Prămov, Ivan 82
private entrepreneurs 114
Průšek, Jaroslav 41

Qiaomu, Hu 114
Qingyun, Jian 37

Rábai, Miklós 19

Radchenko, Sergei 27
Rákóczi March 13
revisionism 36, 38, 49, 52, 99–100, 106

Second World War 41
Shanghai 30–1, 33, 38, 46
Shenyang performances 13, 22
Sino-Czechoslovak cooperation 40–54
Sino-Hungarian reform community 116–22
Sino-Hungarian relations 64, 107, 120, 122
Sino-Polish relations 60, 106
Sino-Soviet Alliance 5, 37
Sino-Soviet relations 25, 27–9, 32, 35, 37–8, 42,
   59–60, 62, 70–2, 76–7, 111, 117, 122
Sino-Soviet split 5–6, 27, 38, 41–2, 90–1, 94,
   103–4, 106, 109
socialism 22, 24, 28, 30–1, 33–5, 43, 62–3, 67–8,
   93–4, 99–101, 103, 106, 110, 113–14, 120–1
socialist bloc 28, 32, 34–5, 37, 57, 61, 68, 114;
   exhibits 28–9
socialist camp 2–5, 51, 74, 80–1, 89
socialist exhibits 25–38
socialist globalisation 3–4
socialist publics 31
socialist world 2–4, 6, 27, 29–30, 32, 34, 37–8,
   43, 115
soil cultivation 81
Soviet leadership 68–9, 71, 76, 78, 89, 94–5,
   106, 112
state socialism 24, 74, 106–7
state socialist press 56–7

Third Five-Year Plan 74, 78–9
Trybuna Ludu 59–60, 63–9, 71
twinning project 40–2, 53

unpaid labour 6, 73, 80–1

Vámos, Péter 3
village knowledge 36

Warsaw 5, 58–60, 64, 70, 72, 92–3, 95–7, 100,
   102, 104, 106
Werblan, Andrzej 94

Xiaoping, Deng 113

Zhivkov, Todor 78